Writing Baseball

THE SOUTHERN ILLINOIS UNIVERSITY PRESS SERIES

Series Editor's Note

In 1943, G. P. Putnam's Sons began a series of major league team histories with the publication of Frank Graham's history of the New York Yankees. From 1943 to 1954, Putnam published histories for fifteen of the sixteen major league teams. The Philadelphia Athletics ball club was the only one not included in the series, though Putnam did publish a biography of Connie Mack in 1945. Of the fifteen team histories, only one, the St. Louis Cardinals history, originally published in 1944, was expanded for a later edition.

Thirteen of the fifteen team histories in the Putnam series were contributed by sportswriters who were eventually honored by the Hall of Fame with the J. G. Taylor Spink Award "for meritorious contributions to baseball writing." Three Spink recipients actually wrote eleven of the team histories for the series. The famed New York columnist Frank Graham, after launching the series with the Yankees history, added team histories for the Brooklyn Dodgers and the New York Giants. Chicago sports editor and journalist Warren Brown, once dubbed the Mencken of the sports page, wrote both the Chicago Cubs and the White Sox team histories. Legendary Fred Lieb, who, at the time of his death in 1980 at the age of ninety-two, held the lowest numbered membership card in the Baseball Writers Association, contributed six team histories to the Putnam series. He also wrote the Connie Mack biography for Putnam.

For our reprints of the Putnam series, we add a foreword for each team history by one of today's most renowned baseball writers. The bibliography committee of the Society for American Baseball Research has also provided an index for each team history. Other than these additions and a few minor alterations, we have preserved the original state of the books, including any possible historical inaccuracies.

The Putnam team histories have been described as the "Cadillacs" of the team history genre. With their colorful prose and their delightful narratives of baseball history as the game moved into its postwar golden age, the Putnam books have also become among the most prized collectibles for baseball historians.

Richard Peterson

THE PITTSBURGH PIRATES

HONUS WAGNER

THE
PITTSBURGH
PIRATES

FREDERICK G. LIEB

With a New Foreword by Richard "Pete" Peterson

Southern Illinois University Press
Carbondale and Edwardsville

First published 1948 by G. P. Putnam's Sons
Copyright © 1948 Frederick G. Lieb
Writing Baseball series edition published 2003 by Southern Illinois
    University Press
Series editor's note copyright © 2001 and foreword copyright © 2003 by
    the Board of Trustees, Southern Illinois University
Printed in the United States of America
06 05 04 03   4 3 2 1

Library of Congress Cataloging-in-Publication Data

Lieb, Fred, b. 1888.
    The Pittsburgh Pirates / by Frederick G. Lieb ; with a new foreword
by Richard Peterson.— Writing Baseball series ed.
        p. cm. — (Writing baseball)
    Originally published: New York : G.P. Putnam's Sons, 1948.
    Includes index.
        1. Pittsburgh Pirates (Baseball team). I. Title. II. Series.
GV875.P5 L5 2003
796.357'64'0974886—dc21
ISBN 0-8093-2492-X (pbk. : alk. paper)   2002030602

Reprinted from the original 1948 edition published by G. P. Putnam's Sons.

Printed on recycled paper. ♻

The paper used in this publication meets the minimum requirements of
American National Standard for Information Sciences—Permanence of
Paper for Printed Library Materials, ANSI Z39.48-1992. ∞

CONTENTS

ILLUSTRATIONS

ix

FOREWORD

BARNEY DREYFUSS, perhaps the greatest owner never elected into the Baseball Hall of Fame, once boasted to Fred Lieb, "We are a first-division town, and I'm a first-division club owner." In Dreyfuss's thirty-two years as owner and president of the Pittsburgh Pirates, his ball clubs, with few exceptions, lived up to his boast. In 1900, Dreyfuss moved from Louisville to Pittsburgh after becoming president of the Pirate franchise and brought the best of Louisville's players with him, including future Hall of Famers Honus Wagner and Fred Clarke. From that time on, the Pirates, after struggling in their early years, developed into one of the most successful franchises in baseball history and, by the time of Dreyfuss's death in 1932, had established a long and storied winning tradition.

In the first decade of the twentieth century, the Pirates won four National League pennants, including three straight from 1901 to 1903. In 1903, after a Dreyfuss challenge to the newly formed American League, Pittsburgh played the Boston Red Sox, known as the Pilgrims at that time, in major league baseball's first World Series. Following an unexpected and disappointing loss to Boston, Pittsburgh went on to win its first World Series championship in 1909 against Ty Cobb's Detroit Tigers in the ball club's first year in Forbes Field, described in its day as a "modern palace."

After more than a decade of frustrating near misses and even a few second-division flops, the Pirates bounced back to win their fifth National League pennant in 1925. In one of the most dramatic World Series ever played, Pittsburgh became the first team in World Series history to overcome a three-to-one deficit in a best-of-seven series when it defeated the great Walter Johnson and the Washington Senators in a seventh and deciding game played in the rain and fog at Forbes Field. The Pirates won their sixth pennant in 1927, the last National League title in the Dreyfuss years, but they were swept in the World Series by the New York Yankees fabled Murderer's Row, led by Babe Ruth and Lou Gehrig.

Fred Lieb's team history of the Pittsburgh Pirates ranges from the ball club's earliest professional days in the late nineteenth century as the Pittsburgh Alleghenies to its spring training preparations for the 1948 season, but the core of this book is the Dreyfuss era. Considering that William Benswanger, Barney Dreyfuss's son-in-law, took over the presidency of the Pirates after his father-in-law's death and remained in that position until Dreyfuss's widow sold the franchise in 1946 to a syndicate headed by John Galbreath and Bing Crosby, Lieb's book is essentially the story of the Dreyfuss dynasty.

Of course, no one was better suited, professionally and personally, than Fred Lieb to write the story of Dreyfuss's Pittsburgh Pirates for the Putnam team history series. His career as a sportswriter began in 1909, the year the Pirates won their first World Series championship, when he wrote a series of biographies for *Baseball Magazine.* He became a full-time journalist in 1911 with the *New York Press* and continued writing about baseball until he passed away in 1980 at the age of ninety-two. At the time of his death, he had the lowest numbered membership card in the Baseball Writers Association. A great fan of the game, as well as a prolific writer, Lieb once estimated that he had seen over eight thousand major league games and had covered every World Series from 1911 to 1958. In 1972, he joined his contemporaries, Ring Lardner, Damon Runyon, and Grantland Rice, in the writer's wing of the Baseball Hall of Fame when he received the J. G. Taylor Spink Award "for meritorious contributions to baseball writing."

Lieb's incredible longevity as a journalist put him in a unique position among baseball writers and gave him a great advantage in writing his many biographies and histories. As Lieb reminds his readers in the preface to *The Pittsburgh Pirates,* he not only watched the games played by "the fabulous old Pirates," he knew many of them personally, including the great Honus Wagner. He also mentions his close friendship with Barney Dreyfuss and their mutual admiration—Dreyfuss for Lieb's honesty and Lieb for Dreyfuss's integrity. Lieb, who believed Dreyfuss stood for "what was best in the game," even had his own nickname for Dreyfuss, "'the first-division man.'"

When I was growing up in Pittsburgh in the late 1940s and the 1950s, Honus Wagner and Pie Traynor were local personalities, hardly the stuff of baseball heroes, at least to my youthful vision. I had Ralph Kiner, who appears in the last few chapters of Lieb's book, to fuel my hero-worshiping, but not much else. The Pirates of my youth were among the worst teams in baseball, right down there with the Chicago Cubs and the St. Louis Browns. But they were my team and much more real to me at the time than any of the great Pirate teams of the past.

I wish I had read Lieb's team history of the Pittsburgh Pirates when I was growing up—it was published in 1948, the same year my father took me to my first Pirate game. It may not have changed my love for those truly awful players and teams that I was to watch with hopeless hope in the 1950s, but Lieb's vivid prose and wonderful anecdotes would have brought to life Barney Dreyfuss's winning tradition and all those great players and teams that made it possible.

This reprint of Fred Lieb's *The Pittsburgh Pirates* is an invitation for baseball readers to enjoy Lieb's wonderful stories of the great Pirate teams of the first half of the twentieth century and the many Hall of Fame baseball players who became heroes in Pittsburgh uniforms or passed through Pittsburgh on their way to immortality. Lieb's book is rich with accounts of World Series triumphs and disappointments, of epic encounters on the playing field, like that between Wagner and Cobb, of mutinies in the clubhouse, of courageous comebacks, and of devastating defeats, including the infamous "homer in the gloaming."

Fred Lieb may have been a poor prophet when he predicted at the end of his team history of the Pirates that, going into the 1948 season, it wouldn't be long before Pittsburgh would be winning pennants again and playing in the World Series, but his book is delightful proof that, as historian and storyteller, Fred Lieb had few equals and that, among baseball's long-standing major league teams, there are few that can match the winning tradition of the Pittsburgh Pirates.

Richard "Pete" Peterson

July 2002

⊖

PREFACE

⊖

THE AUTHOR, a native-born Philadelphian, became Pirate conscious at a tender age. While in his early teens, he was pedaling his bicycle up north Broad Street—past the old Philadelphia club's Huntington Street grounds—when a baseball came sailing over the right-field wall and whizzed past his ears. "I'll bet Honus Wagner hit that ball," exclaimed a youthful companion riding alongside of him, as other kids, on foot, scrambled after the ball.

They looked up the box score of the Pirate-Phillies game in the *Philadelphia Inquirer* next morning, and there it was sure enough, an agate line which read: "Home run—Wagner."

Almost getting konked by Hans Wagner's home run was enough to make any youngster a Pirate addict. Furthermore, our Philadelphia National League teams were so poor in those days that we took a sort of vicarious pleasure in the high jinks of the Pirates as they slapped down the hated Giants and lesser National League teams, including our lowly Phillies. After all, a Pennsylvania boy had to root for a Pennsylvania team even though it played in the other corner of the state.

Later, as a New York sports writer, I had the pleasure of meeting the fabulous old Pirates—Fred Clarke, Hans Wagner, Tommie Leach, Kitty Bransfield, and George Gibson, and there never was any feeling of a letdown. They were just as exciting Buccaneers in their hotel rooms or in the lobby of a training hotel as when they thrilled a kid fan with their exploits on the ball field. Even today I still get a big kick out of exchanging pleasantries with old Honus, and hearing him tell droll tall tales of his heroics on the diamond.

The writer is also proud of his friendship with the legendary Pirate club president, the late Barney Dreyfuss, and frequently enjoyed the confidences of this great baseball leader and pioneer. Dreyfuss once said, "I like your writings because I can tell from them that you like baseball." I, in turn, liked Dreyfuss because he always stood for what was best in the game that I liked.

My nickname for him was "the first-division man." Barney liked it, took a justifiable pride in it, and never tried to hide a contempt for a chronic second-division club owner. While he was proud of having given Pittsburgh six championship teams, he was even prouder of his first-division record. "I can't always win, but I can give Pittsburgh first-division ball," he used to say. In his thirty-three years as boss man of the Pirates he finished in the lower crust only six times.

Up to the seasons of 1946 and 1947, when the Pirates sloughed around in the seventh and eighth notches, the old first-division tradition held up amazingly. Barney's son-in-law, Bill Benswanger, was another first-division man. Despite the lowly finishes of '46 and '47, the Pirates' first-division record in this century still is the best of any team in major-league baseball. Beginning with 1900, the year Barney Dreyfuss took over in Pittsburgh, the club has been in the second division only eleven times. During that period the Giants and Cubs, with the next best records among National League clubs, finished among the lower four on thirteen and fourteen occasions, respectively. The Yankees have had only eleven second-division clubs in the American League, but they didn't come into the loop until 1903.

What's more, the men who took over the Pittsburgh club from the Dreyfuss estate late in the season of 1945—Frank McKinney, John Gailbreath, Tom Johnson, and Bing Crosby—aren't second-division people. They were tremendously impressed with the almost unbelievable crowd of 1,283,611 fans that supported their 1947 seventh-placer. They can't—and won't—let down that faithful following. Why, if necessary, Bing Crosby will sing them back into the first division!

It has been fun to write the story of the Pittsburgh Pirates. There have been few clubs with as colorful and eventful a background. Over the years, the ball club wrote its own story—vivid baseball drama of the highest order. All the author needed to do was to write down the deeds of valor of these Pirate warriors and piece them together.

There were the interesting pre-Dreyfuss days of Captain Kerr, Ned Hanlon, and Connie Mack; the tense controversy that ended with the young immigrant club owner, Dreyfuss, buying out his early partners; the story of how Barney thwarted Ban Johnson's raiders during the American League war; the record of early three-time winners, including Fred Clarke's 1902 club, which beat the second-place Brooklyns by twenty-seven and a half games; the perennial hunt for a first baseman after the trading of Kitty Bransfield; the feuds between the Pirates, Giants, and Cubs; Dreyfuss' battles with John McGraw; the batting championships of Wagner, Beaumont, Paul Waner, Arky Vaughan, and Debs Garms; Babe Adams' dramatic World Series victories of 1909—the year Dreyfuss built his new baseball temple; the wholesale base thefts by Max Carey, the divinity student; the days of Charley Grimm, Rabbit Maranville, and the "Banjo Boys" of 1921–24; the turbulent spirit, Burleigh Grimes; the Pirate mutiny on the high seas; the Kiki Cuyler insurrection; the near pennants of 1932 and 1938 during the Benswanger regime; the players' union and near strike of 1946; the sale of the club to the present owners; the $125,000 gamble on Hank Greenberg in 1947; and Ralph Kiner's home-run thunder.

This book wouldn't have been possible without the kind and valuable assistance of the men who made Pittsburgh baseball history, and those who wrote it. I wish to extend my appreciation to Fred Clarke, Hans Wagner, and Tommy Leach of the old Pirates, Max Carey and Kiki Cuyler of the latter Pittsburgh champions, Ed Barrow, the former Yankee president, who developed Wagner in Paterson and had Fred Clarke on his newspaper-carrier team in Des Moines; also William E. Benswanger, Dreyfuss' presidential successor, who helped immeasurably with the later chapters.

When I first conceived the idea for the book, a cherished friend during the greater part of my sports-writing career, the late Havey Boyle of the *Pittsburgh Post-Gazette*, helped with material on early Pirate and Pittsburgh baseball history. Havey, a beautiful soul, passed from this life much too soon—on March 18, 1947.

Two men who were especially helpful were Charles "Chilly" Doyle, who as *Pittsburgh Sun-Telegraph* baseball writer has floated on the clouds and descended to the depths with the Pirates in the last three decades, and that expert on Pirate lore and legend, James L. "Jimmy" Long, director of the Pirates' publicity department.

Further acknowledgments are made to another old traveler of the Pirate trails, Ed Balinger of the *Pittsburgh Post-Gazette;* Lester Biderman of the *Pittsburgh Press;* Harry Keck of the *Sun-Telegraph;* Vince Johnson of the *Post-Gazette;* A. K. "Rosey" Rowswell, the Pirates' "voice of the air waves"; also to J. G. Taylor Spink, publisher of *The Sporting News,* for the use of valuable clippings and back files of his bible of baseball.

FREDERICK G. LIEB

THE PITTSBURGH PIRATES

I. BASEBALL SEED IS PLANTED EARLY

As FAR BACK as the post-Civil War period, Pittsburgh and the surrounding country has been a hotbed of baseball enthusiasm. Pittsburghers not only play the game wholeheartedly, but they root for their favorites with equal gusto. A little baseball was played in Father Pitt's bailiwick prior to the tragic fratricidal strife of the early sixties, but it was the young men who returned from the Union armies who really started swinging bats and driving baseballs through Pittsburgh's then soot-laden atmosphere.

One of the returned soldiers was the beloved Al Pratt, who at eighteen pitched for Pittsburgh's Enterprise club in 1866. Pratt was one of the early Pittsburgh baseball pioneers; he lived in the western Pennsylvania metropolis until his nineties, became a dyed-in-the-wool Pirate fan, and was affectionately known to several generations of rooters as Uncle Al Pratt.

About the time that Al was pitching for the strong amateur Enterprise team, other outstanding Pittsburgh nines of the sixties were the Olympics and Xanthas. They had quite a three-cornered rivalry, and most of their games were played at old Union Park, in what now is known as the Northside, and which then was the City of Allegheny. In fact, a good part of Pittsburgh's early baseball history was written in Allegheny.

One of the early days of grief for Pittsburgh rooters came in the summer of 1869, when the Olympics, who had bowled over most everything around Pittsburgh, journeyed down the river to Cincinnati to take on the famous original Cincinnati Reds, baseball's first out-and-out professional team. It wasn't that the Olympics were defeated that hurt; everybody expected that, but in the language of "Schnozz" Durante, the score was "downright humiliatin' "—a little matter of 54 to 2. It was Cincinnati's forty-third consecutive victory, in a string that stretched to seventy-nine before it was checked by the Atlantics of Brooklyn in 1870.

Pittsburgh went along with strong, independent clubs until 1876, when the city also decided to have a "hired team." It was the centennial year, in which the National League was born in New York, February 2, 1876. The Steel City, which had sprouted during the war, when it supplied Lincoln's armies with munitions, wasn't big enough yet to be considered for a major-league franchise, as the National League's western members were Chicago, St. Louis, Cincinnati, and Louisville. However, it is interesting to note that twenty days after the league was launched, Pittsburgh's first professional team, the Alleghenies, was organized on Washington's Birthday. The club was awarded a franchise in what then was known as the International Association, the first minor league. The Alleghenies played their first game at Union Park, with its little 2,500 capacity stand, on April 15, 1876, when the Alleghenies downed the Xanthas, 7 to 3.

In 1877, James Galvin, later one of the early Pittsburgh club's twirling aces, joined the Allegheny club, and started a brilliant pitching career. A game of that year that brought a proud gleam in Jimmy's eyes until the day of his death was a 1-to-0 victory, won from Tommy Bond of the National League's Boston Red Stockings, on May 2, 1877. Galvin not only outpitched the able Bond, but provided the game's only score with an eighth-inning home run.

Ball clubs, other than those in the National League, had little protection over their players when a club owner in a rival league felt in a mood for a raid. All of the Allegheny players left the club for other pastures after 1877; the Alleghenies then engaged a team of inferior athletes and joined a reorganized International League in 1878. It was a dismal spring for early Pittsburgh and Allegheny enthusiasts; the club disbanded June 8, after playing twenty-six games, of which it won only three. The home-town fans were saved much of this torture; all but three games were played on the road.

For a spell, that woeful 1878 spring left a sour taste in the mouth, and for three years Pittsburgh remained out of league ball. The town's baseball activity centered around strong independent teams, especially the East Liberty Stars, who played their games on a large field on Collins Avenue, the East End Gymns, and a strong county team. The city also boasted one of the most formidable colored teams in the country, the Keystones.

2

In 1882 Pittsburgh made its first appearance in a major league, when the Allegheny club became a charter member of the original American Association, an early rival to the National League. In fact, the new league was largely the brain child of H. D. "Denny" McKnight of Pittsburgh, and Justice Thorner of Cincinnati.

The genesis of the new league was a strong exhibition tour made by the Athletics of Philadelphia, an independent member of the so-called League Alliance, in 1881. The Athletics, a charter member of the National League in 1876, dropped out after one season; St. Louis called it quits after two indifferent campaigns, and Cincinnati surrendered its N.L. franchise after the season of 1880.

The Athletics, with one of the best clubs in the country, played to especially good crowds in Pittsburgh, St. Louis, Cincinnati, and Louisville, far better crowds than were then drawn in most National League games.

It gave the whiskered Denny McKnight his big idea. In talking to the Cincinnatian Thorner, he said: "Why don't we start a big league of our own? We've got the population and the interest. We're the most baseball-minded section of the country. Let's build around the Athletics in the East, and we've got the territory in this part of the country."

Thorner was interested, so was the management of the Athletics, and in 1882 a second major league, the American Association, was launched with six charter members, the Alleghenies, the Athletics of Philadelphia, the Eclipse club of Louisville, the St. Louis Browns, Cincinnati, and Baltimore. Not only was Denny McKnight the president of the Allegheny club, but as a reward for pioneering the new circuit, he was elected the loop's first president. The Alleghenies finished that season on an even keel; they were fourth, with a percentage of .500, winning thirty-nine games and losing thirty-nine.

Uncle Al Pratt, whose pitching sparked the independent years after the Civil War, was the first manager of the Allegheny Association team. Since his early exploits with the Enterprise team, he had won national recognition as the ace pitcher for the Forest Citys, of Cleveland. Pratt lasted as manager until mid-season of 1883, when he resigned and was succeeded by Denny Mack. (Denny's real name was Dennis McGee.) Mack started the 1884 season, but soon gave way to Bob Ferguson. But, in a bad year, Bob turned the job over to Horace Phillips, August 18, 1884, and the latter carried on into Pittsburgh's early National League period.

The American Association expanded to an eight-club league in 1883, taking in the Metropolitans, of New York, and Columbus, Ohio. On the road, the western Pennsylvania outfit began to appear in the league standings as Pittsburg, spelled without the final h, but at home the club retained its nickname of Alleghenies. It was a drab season, as the Alleghenies finished seventh, with a dismal percentage of .300, while in an internal explosion Denny McKnight was deposed as the Pittsburgh-Allegheny president, though he retained the presidency of the league. E. C. Converse was named to head the erratic ball club.

In 1884, in its third year, the old American Association went whole hog and boosted its membership to twelve clubs. The enlarged league brought no relief to the harrassed Pittsburgh fans; the Alleghenies plunged deeper into the second division, limping home eleventh, with an ignoble percentage of .277.

Pittsburgh fans and newspapers began to yowl. "We've had enough of that kind of baseball and don't intend to stand for any more of it," was one of the plaints. "If that's major-league baseball, we don't want it. Pittsburgh and Allegheny fans are long-suffering, but there is a limit, and we are fed up with the ball that is being foisted on us."

The Pittsburgh promoters didn't need this anvil chorus to prod them into action. They were fully cognizant of the distressing situation. As from the earliest days, neither Pittsburgh owners nor fans could ever reconcile themselves to second-division ball. Opportunity knocked when the Columbus club, one of the strongest in the league, was lopped off, as the American Association was again reduced to eight clubs after the season of 1884.

Converse told Phillips, his manager: "Horace, I hear Columbus is dropping out of the league. Jump on a train for Columbus, and see what you can do about grabbing off some of their players."

Horace reached into the Columbus grab bag with both hands and came back with practically the entire Columbus outfit: Pitchers Ed Morris and Frank Mountain; Catchers Fred Carroll and Rudolph Kemmler; Infielders James "Jocko" Fields, Charles "Pop" Smith, Billy Kuehne, and John Richmond; and Outfielders Tom Brown and Fred Mann. Ed Morris made his home in Pittsburgh, and like Uncle Al Pratt, for many years was one of Pittsburgh's most beloved baseball figures. He died in 1937 at the age of seventy-eight, just as the Pirates were preparing their golden-jubilee celebration.

Practically the entire seventh-place club of 1884 was junked, as the only players salvaged were George "Doggy" Miller, a catcher, and Left Fielder Charley Eden. The 1885 club was further strengthened by the return of Pitcher Jimmy Gavin, who had pitched for Buffalo in 1884, and the acquisition of another pitcher, Hank O'Day, from the Toledo club. O'Day then was a carefree Chicago Irishman with a good fast ball; Hank later became the crusty but highly efficient National League umpire. O'Day remained in Pittsburgh only one season, moving on to Washington in 1886.

The injection of the Columbus players and other new blood paid prompt dividends. The club advanced to third place in 1885, and in 1886 was the runner-up to Von der Ahe's and Comiskey's strong St. Louis Browns, the club that vanquished Anson's famous Chicago White Stockings in the 1886 World Series. In the 1886 American Association race, St. Louis won 93 games and lost 46, while Pittsburgh-Allegheny fans drew a lot of pleasure over Phillips' second-placers, who won 80 games and lost 57, for a percentage of .584.

The author is indebted to Ray L. Kennedy, director of the present-day Pirates' farm system, for the loan of his uncle's scrapbook, giving box scores and accounts of all the games played by the Alleghenies in 1886. Some of the heads were classics, such as: THE BOYS GOT THERE. . . . In spite of a Biased Umpire the Alleghenies Secure Another Game. And among the notes we read such gems as:

The ladies were out in force yesterday, about 200 being present....
Morris wants to keep cool. Don't let the wicked coacher bother you,
Ed.... The word, "Welcome," worked artistically in whitewash, just
in front of the pitcher's box, was one of the features yesterday.... The
crush at the gates yesterday was simply immense, several persons being
literally carried through the entrance against their will. They did not
kick, however.

One of Pittsburgh's most vociferous rooters at that time was a
long skinny kid with an elastic larynx named Al Lang. He lived
a few blocks from the old Monongahela House in Pittsburgh,
where clubs playing the Alleghenies used to be quartered. Lang
was nuts on baseball, and almost from the time he could walk,
old-time Association ball players permitted him to ride on top
of the horse-drawn vehicle that conveyed them to and from the
ball park.

"I simply will not have you loitering around that hotel and
with those rough baseball men," Ma Lang remonstrated. "The
first thing you know you'll grow up a loafer—just like the rest
of them."

Mrs. Lang raved and stormed, but Al just couldn't get baseball
out of his blood, even when later he drove a Pittsburgh laundry
wagon and mixed up his deliveries, dreaming of a Pittsburgh
pennant. Today he is known to all baseball as Florida's beloved
"Sunshine Ambassador" to the big leagues—Albert Fielding Lang.
An ex-Mayor of St. Petersburg, Florida, he has induced most of
the big-league clubs to train in his adopted state in the past
three decades, and in 1946 St. Petersburg dedicated Florida's
finest ball park, Al Lang Stadium, as a monument to the ebullient
former Pittsburgher while he still was alive and in good voice.

⊖

II. PITTSBURGH IS ADMITTED TO
OLD NATIONAL

⊖

EVEN THOUGH THE St. Louis Browns surprised the baseball world in the fall of 1886 by pinning the shoulders of the famous Chicago White Stockings to the turf, the National League was regarded by most fans as the real "big league." Unquestionably it was the baseball aristocrat of the eighties. The American Association was largely a two-bit league, stressing twenty-five-cent admissions, while the National League was a fifty-cent circuit. If a player played in the National League, he was a somebody; if a city had a franchise in the National, it was on the Bigtime.

The American Association also had a rather loose agreement among the various clubs, whereby a club had the right to resign from the league. Shortly after the close of the 1886 season, the Pittsburgh club heard rumors that the National League was ready to ditch Kansas City, after one year's trial. The Missouri cattle town was too far west, and such teams as Boston, New York, Philadelphia, and Washington ate up what little gate receipts they received in Kansas City by making the long trek to western Missouri. Even before the league's official meeting in December, it was common knowledge over the baseball grapevine that "K. C. was out."

That gave William A. Nimick, by this time president of the Pittsburgh club, his fruitful idea. Why not make a bid for the Kansas City franchise, and get into the National League? It was a rash thought, which would antagonize Nimick's American Association associates, but baseball was still in a pioneering era, when big-league clubs were not two-million-dollar propositions. A club owner had to think and act fast.

Shortly before the National League's annual meeting in New York, the Pittsburgh club threw the old Association into consternation by tendering its resignation. Nimick promptly applied to the National League for admission, and the old league voted to take in the Alleghenies. And Pittsburgh has been a National League stronghold ever since. At the same meeting in which Pittsburgh was taken in, Indianapolis was also awarded the St. Louis franchise. Unable to buck the strong Browns, St. Louis withdrew from the National League a second time, after playing second fiddle to Von der Ahe's pennant winners of 1885 and 1886.

Another reason why Pittsburgh moved into the National League without any qualm was the deal that the American Association handed its first president, the Pittsburgher Denny McKnight. In the fall of 1885, the Metropolitans (the American Association club in New York) sold two of their crack players, Pitcher Tim Keefe and Shortstop "Dude" Esterbrook to the New York National League team, the Giants. As the result of these sales, the angry Association club owners expelled the Mets from the loop.

However, on the eve of the sale of the players, Owner John B. Day and his manager, Jim Mutrie, sold the Mets to Erasmus Wiman of Staten Island. Denny McKnight decided the sale was fictitious, fined Mutrie $500 for so-called "treachery," and admitted Washington to the league to take the place of the Metropolitans. Wiman procured an injunction against the Association, which later was made permanent. It checked Nimick in his attempted transfer of the club to Washington, and the Mets played the 1886 season on Staten Island. But the upshot of the matter was that the American Association declined to back up McKnight. He was deposed as president in 1886, when Wheeler C. Wilsoff was elected president-secretary-treasurer.

With the American Association giving Denny the run-around, and showing no loyalty to the man who was the organizer of the league, the Pittsburgh club felt it was absolved of all loyalty to the Association. And, unless it is Brooklyn, which shifted from the American Association to the National League three years later, there is no city in the Ford Frick belt that is more rabidly pro-National League today than Pittsburgh.

2

It is possible the National League also threw some inducements to the Pittsburgh owners to throw their lot with the older circuit. While Horace Phillips took over practically his entire runner-up American Association club of 1886, the new Pittsburgh Nationals were permitted to acquire three high-grade players, Pitcher Jim McCormick and Outfielder Abner Dalrymple, of the White Stockings pennant winners, and First Baseman Alexander McKinnon, of the disbanded St. Louis club.

The release of McCormick and Dalrymple was quite a blow to Chicago fans. During the course of the 1886 race, McCormick compiled a winning streak of sixteen straight. That's still one of the big streaks in the record book. However, there were rumors at the time that Al Spalding, the Chicago owner, and Cap Anson, his manager, were keenly disappointed at the showing of the White Stockings in the 1886 World Series with the Browns, and soured on some of their athletes.

"What can you do in the National League with your boys?" President William Nimick asked Phillips, his manager.

"We were second in the Association, and we ought to do as well, maybe better, in the National League," replied Horace. "Those three new players are going to help us, and I know McCormick will pitch his heart out against Chicago. There are a few boys on the club who don't like to behave, but I can handle them. I'll be tough if I have to be."

The American Association team had played its early games at Exposition Park, but after using this field in 1882 and 1883, the Allegheny-Pittsburgh club moved back to Recreation Park, the former Union Park, in 1884. And it was at Recreation Park that the Pittsburgh club played its first National League game, April 30, 1887.

This early ball yard was located on the Fort Wayne railroad tracks, in what now is the North Side of Pittsburgh, and was touched by Allegheny, Pennsylvania, and Grant Avenues, and North Avenue West. The outfield bordered on the railroad tracks. At the turn of the century, Recreation Park, which had been used for football by Western University of Pennsylvania (now the University of Pittsburgh), was turned into a wooden saucer for motor-paced bicycle riding. It was called the Colosseum, and the manager of the track was Tim Hurst, the picturesque ebul-

lient umpire, and at one time Von der Ahe's manager of the
St. Louis Browns. Bike racing in Pittsburgh and Tim's Colosseum
were no howling success, and then for one season the old park
was used for football by the old Pittsburgh Professionals. One
of the members of the team was a great kicking fullback from
Bucknell, Christy Mathewson, the famous pitcher of the New
York Giants.

When the Pittsburgh club opened its first National League
season back in 1887, it thrilled its 4,000 admirers with a 6-to-2
victory over the Chicago champions. And in their second game
a few days later, the Alleghenies whipped the Detroits, the
ultimate 1887 winners, by an 8-to-3 score. James Galvin pitched
and won both games, and Jimmy didn't win from pushovers, defeating big John Clarkson of the White Stockings and Charley
"Lady" Baldwin of the Detroits, two of the great pitchers of the
eighties.

Those two early spring victories had Pittsburgh fans doing
handsprings. "I guess this National League isn't going to be so
tough," they exclaimed. "Horace hasn't the Browns to beat this
year; he ought to win in this league."

However, the club failed to follow up its fine start, and Phillips
couldn't make good his prediction that his boys would do as well
in the National League as in the 1886 Association. His club
limped home a mediocre sixth with fifty-four victories and sixty-
eight defeats. The only clubs under Phillips' Alleghenies at the
finish were Washington and Indianapolis.

Yet, Horace had an alibi, as tragedy struck his club in midseason and hit him in a spot that was to prove a vexing jinx for
many Pittsburgh managers who followed him. McKinnon, the
former St. Louis player, was one of the best first basemen in
the game; he did a bang-up job and soon was the most popular
player on the squad. Aleck hit hard and timely, fielded well, and
was as punctual as a Kiwanian striving for an attendance prize.
He never missed a game until the afternoon July 4 game in
Philadelphia. He had played the morning game but told Manager
Phillips he just couldn't make it for the afternoon performance.
Horace grumbled, but let Aleck sit it out.

Phillips expected his first baseman back next day. In that era
ball players paid little attention to their diet, and often ate
gluttonously between holiday morning and afternoon games.
Sometimes their beer, clams, and strawberry shortcake didn't

mix. But this was no upset stomach after a Fourth of July celebration. McKinnon was even sicker next day, and left for his
home in Boston. His teammates never saw him alive again. He
died in Boston, July 24, shocking not only Pittsburgh fandom,
but sports fans all over the country.

That left Phillips with a big hole at first base. Many subsequent Pittsburgh managers were to find themselves in a similar
predicament. When McKinnon first became ill, Horace tried
Cliff Carroll, an outfielder, and Billy Kuehne, utility infielder, at
first base, but after Aleck's death, he moved Sam Barkley, his
starting second baseman, to first. Art Whitney looked after third
base, and "Pop" Smith guarded shortstop.

The 1887 Alleghenies opened with Abner Dalrymple in left,
Tom Brown in center, and Jack Coleman in right. However,
Dalrymple also became ill in June, and repeatedly was out of
the line-up. "Now we know why Anse let Abner go," yelled the
fans. Ed Beecher was picked up in midseason from the disbanded
Hartford club. Then Tom Brown couldn't hit the size of his hat,
and in August he was released to Indianapolis. After that,
Beecher or an idle catcher took care of the third outfield assignment. As for Cliff Carroll, he was one of that "good hit, no field"
kind of flychaser.

Three pitchers did practically all the work. They were the two
Jims—Galvin and McCormick, and Ed Morris. Galvin was the
work horse of the staff, pitching forty-eight games, while McCormick and Morris each worked thirty-six. A fourth pitcher, Billy
Bishop, hurled only three games. Doggy Miller and Fred Carroll
did most of the catching, while a third catcher, James "Jocko"
Fields, came from the Buffalo club in May. Jocko frequently was
pressed into outfield service. It was a tough year for pitchers, and
a great one for hitters. It took four strikes for a pitcher to whiff
a batter, and bases on balls were scored as base hits. This bit of
foolishness was repealed after one season.

3

The 1888 Pittsburgh club suffered exactly as many defeats as
the 1887 team—sixty-eight—but it won twelve more victories than
the first Pittsburgh National Leaguers. Even though the Alleghenies finished with a fairly respectable percentage of .492,
through a trick in the percentages they were again sixth.

The club started the season with only two experienced pitchers, Galvin and Morris, as Jim McCormick, the sixteen-straight winner from Chicago, announced at the end of the 1887 season that he would retire from baseball and open a café in Paterson, his New Jersey home town. Neither the Pittsburgh club nor the Pirate fans gave much attention to the pitcher's statement. "Just trying to get more money out of Bill Nimick for next season," said the fans. Whether McCormick tried to use his retirement threat as a club for bigger money never exactly was known. Many thought if Nimick had raised the ante sufficiently, Jim would have forgotten all about his Jersey business. However, McCormick went through with it and never again was seen on a big-league diamond. He was the first outstanding player to retire while still at the peak of his game.

Big-league clubs then carried only three starting pitchers, and the gap in the staff wasn't filled until June 28, when Phillips signed Harry Staley, of the St. Louis Whites, a team which unsuccessfully tried to buck the Browns and quickly disbanded. Horace also procured another valuable player from the Whites, Jake Beckley, the mustached first baseman, who quickly became a fixture on the early Pittsburgh club. In an earlier effort to fill his first-base hole, Horace had procured Pitcher Al Maul from the Phillies. Maul was a pretty good hitter, but after weeks of experimentation, Al was still a pitcher trying to play first base. Unfortunately Beckley was injured in September, and Coleman, the outfielder, finished the season in Pittsburgh's jinxed first-base position, with Maul out in right field. Dalrymple played his last game with the club, September 8.

Fred Dunlap, one of the game's best second basemen, was procured from Detroit in 1888, and the fleet-footed Billy Sunday followed McCormick and Dalrymple from the old Chicago champions. Sunday played center field, and though he was a brilliant fly hawk and streak of lightning on the bases, Billy was a lightweight at bat. Even in those days the fans used to remark: "Billy is fast enough, but he can't steal first base." Sunday had already become interested in religion. A deeply religious ball player was a distinct novelty in that stage of the game. Most of the men were two-fisted drinkers, who led gay night lives and gambled out of all proportion to their earning power. The language of the bench and clubhouse wasn't exactly training for a seminary.

Some of Sunday's fellow players thought Billy was a bit queer, but most of them respected him and his views—also his speed.

The famous Detroits, 1887 World's Champions, were bothered with season-long injuries in 1888, and slipped from first place to fifth. Fred Stearns, the owner, first sold his stars for $45,000, a lot of money for ball players on the hoof in that period, and then the league transferred the franchise to Cleveland. Pittsburgh fared well when Stearns unloaded his talent, as Bill Nimick purchased the club's crack center fielder and captain, Ned Hanlon—one half of the old "Big Four"—Third Baseman "Deacon Jim" White and Shortstop Jack Rowe, and a secondary pitcher, Pete Conway. However, both White and Rowe held out for a share of the purchase money, and they refused to join the Alleghenies until July 8, 1889, after their old Detroit teammate Hanlon became acting manager.

The fuss and excitement of trying to sign White and Rowe, and the stress of managing the club proved too much for Phillips. The owners were demanding and wanted to know why Horace wasn't getting more out of the team. The fans were highly critical. "When do we get that winner?" they asked, with unfeigned irritation. "Why must Pittsburgh always be in the second division? Is there a law to that effect—or something?"

Something in poor Horace snapped. He started acting oddly, and began harboring strange delusions in his conversations with Nimick and the players. Nimick sent for Hanlon, the new team captain, Dunlap, and Sunday. "Have you noticed anything wrong with Phillips?" asked the club president.

"Well, he just don't seem able to concentrate," said Ned. "He'll say one thing today and he'll tell you something entirely different tomorrow. And he'll go up in the air and ask why something was done without consulting him, when it was Horace who ordered it."

"I don't like it," said Nimick. "Horace isn't a well man, and I am afraid it is even more serious than that."

On July 31, Nimick gave Phillips a two weeks' leave of absence, so that he might pull himself together. Then came a confusing three weeks in which most everyone but the bat boy led the club. On August 9, Billy Sunday was named manager, but it didn't last long. Then on the sixteenth we read that Fred Dunlap wanted to resign the captaincy, having taken it only a few days before. Phillips returned for a few days, but on the twenty-

fourth Nimick finally made Hanlon the manager. Shortly thereafter, Phillips suffered a complete nervous breakdown. He subsequently lost his mental faculties, was placed in a sanitarium, never
recovered, and died some years later.

Ned Hanlon, captain of the team, really was a "natural" as
Phillips' managerial successor. As captain of the Tigers, Hanlon
was largely responsible for that team's outstanding success in
1887. "Wattie" Watkins had taken the bows as Detroit manager,
but it was Ned who had called the moves on the diamond.

Hanlon was a Connecticut Irishman, coming from Montville,
Connecticut, and was destined to become one of the managerial
geniuses of baseball, winning three National League pennants
with the fabulous Baltimore Orioles, and two in Brooklyn. As a
player, he was much on the Billy Sunday type. Ned couldn't hit
as most of the other stalwarts on the early Detroits, Sam
Thompson, Dan Brouthers, Hardy Richardson, and Jim White,
but he was a wizard in center field. Few could approach him
when it came to pulling down long flies, or darting in for the
short ones behind the infield. He was death to Texas Leaguers.
Hanlon was aggressive, crafty, a fighter on the field, and had little
difficulty winning the respect of the other players. They recognized him to be a born leader. Even then, he put on some of the
inside strategy that later made him famous in Baltimore, when
he had John McGraw, Willie Keeler, and Hughie Jennings to
execute the plays.

Between the mental patient, Phillips, and the fiery Hanlon,
the 1889 Pittsburghs came home in fifth place, one position
higher than in 1887 and 1888. They were up in position but
down in percentage, winding up with .462, 30 points under their
1888 finish.

The club met with considerable success on its home diamond
in Allegheny, but for some reason the Steel City players were
pushovers whenever they crossed the Alleghenies and moved
East. All three of their eastern trips were debacles. The Giants
were the 1889 champions; Boston and Philadelphia had strong
first-division teams, but there was no sense in the manner the tail-
end Washingtons feasted on the Pittsburghers.

All season the club won only five games in the East and lost
twenty-nine. On their first swing along the Atlantic seaboard, the
Alleghenies won four games and lost ten. But that was good in
comparison with what followed. On the second eastern trip they

dropped the entire eleven games. Is it any wonder that Horace Phillips blew his top? On the third eastern swing in late summer they won one and lost nine. "How can a club that often looks so good at home be so lousy on the road?" wailed home-town rooters.

4

The Pirates encountered labor troubles in 1946, when the Players' Guild almost pulled a strike on Bill Benswanger, then the kindly Buccaneer president, and his colorful manager, Frankie Frisch. But those latter-day troubles were like a light rash compared to the fever that swept the Pittsburgh club in 1890.

The ball players of the National League formed a union, known as the Brotherhood, in 1887, and by 1890 they felt they should put the pressure on their employers for a bigger share of baseball's profits than their meager salaries. The players procured promoters, desirous of getting in on the "soft money," to back a third circuit known as the Players League, and new clubs were placed in Pittsburgh, New York, Brooklyn, Boston, Philadelphia, Chicago, Cleveland, and Buffalo.

Practically all of the better players of the National League and the major American Association jumped over to the new league, and in Pittsburgh almost the entire club played leapfrog. All jumped with the exception of Billy Sunday and a mediocre pitcher, Bill Sowders. Billy, by this time, really had religion and probably felt his duty was to stay with his old club. Both Doggy Miller and Fred Dunlap at first listened to the lures of the new league and then flopped back to the National League club.

Manager-outfielder Ned Hanlon was one of the first jumpers, and with him went Pitchers Jim Galvin, Ed Morris, Harry Staley, and Al Maul; Catchers Fred Carroll and Jocko Fields; Infielders Jake Beckley, Bill Kuehne, Jim White, and Jack Rowe. All jumped to the Pittsburgh Brotherhood team, with the exception of Rowe and White, who went to Buffalo. A Chicago jumper to the Pittsburgh Brotherhood club was the six-foot, six-inch pitching giant from Charleroi, Pa., John Kinley Tener. A bank clerk during the off season, Tener was treasurer of the Brotherhood; he later became Governor of Pennsylvania and president of the National League.

What happened to the Pittsburgh National League club that

season shouldn't happen to three skunks and a weasel. Nimick held on during the troublesome year as president, but an energetic, never-say-die chap, J. Palmer O'Neil, ran the club, and how he managed to survive the season and play out the full schedule is still one of the game's mysteries. Guy Hecker, once a crack pitcher with Louisville, was engaged as manager. Guy collected one of the oddest assortments of old men, kids, farm boys, and trolley leaguers that ever masqueraded as a major-league ball club. Exactly 50 players wore the Pittsburgh uniform at some time or other that season, playing anywhere from one game to 138. Doggy Miller, the man who hopped back, had the distinction of being the 138-game player.

The 1890 Pittsburghs burrowed their way so deeply into the league cellar that they penetrated the very bowels of the earth. In diving into this bottomless pit, the Alleghenies won only 23 games and lost 113, for the pitiably low percentage of .169. Among the dusty old records was a losing streak of 23 straight, which ran from August 12 to September 2, inclusive. Three of these games were lost in Brooklyn in one day, on Labor Day, September 1. The Dodgers, winning the pennant in their first season in the National League, smacked down Hecker's team once in the morning game of the holiday, and made it stick by bowling over the hapless Alleghenies twice in the afternoon double-header.

While the 1890 Pittsburgh Nationals continued to play at Recreation Park, the Brotherhood team pitched its rival camp at Exposition Park. As Hanlon had by far the better team, the Brotherhood got whatever patronage there was, and in one National League game the gate fell to a low of seventeen paid admissions. In an effort to get a little money back, league games were shifted to some of the smaller cities in Ohio, West Virginia, and western Pennsylvania.

Actually the Pittsburghs of the Brotherhood war year lost 114 games, rather than the 113 which appear in the league's records. By solemn action, the league tossed out a game that Pittsburgh lost to Cleveland at Canton, Ohio, September 18, by a score of 11 to 1. This was ruled to be an exhibition. Yet the league directors, in their wisdom, termed a Pittsburgh game in Wheeling, West Virginia, on September 23, a championship contest. In that one, the Giants slapped down Guy Hecker's misfits by the more respectable score of 7 to 5.

National League Service Bureau

BARNEY DREYFUSS

Pittsburgh Sun-Telegraph   *Pittsburgh Pirates Publicity Department*

FRED CLARKE   TOMMY LEACH

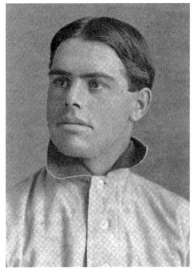

Pittsburgh Pirates Publicity Department

GEORGE GIBSON

J. Palmer O'Neil was the miracle man who kept the Pittsburgh craft afloat during these perilous times. He should have been the man to found the Optimist Club. No matter how long the losing streak, or how humiliating the defeat, O'Neil never lost his serenity, sense of humor, or affable disposition. He always could remark: "Well, anyway, it was a nice day."

Like a magician pulling rabbits out of a hat, Palmer produced dollars to meet hotel and railroad bills, and to pay his boys and old men their skimp salaries. What's more, he traveled in first-class style and stopped at the best hostelries, which then accepted ball clubs. As for himself, O'Neil couldn't have looked more prosperous if he had conducted a bankers' special. His clothes came from the best tailors; he dressed immaculately, and he smoked nothing cheaper than twenty-five-cent cigars.

III. PITTSBURGH CLUB IS "PIRATICAL"

ONE DISASTROUS year finished the Players League. Many of the athletes lost the savings of their entire career in the unhappy venture. But the baseball war broke the victors, as well as the vanquished. John B. Day, the Giant owner, never retrieved his fortune; the famous Chicago club was wrecked for a decade, and the Pittsburgh club had a tough time getting back on its wabbly feet.

Yet out of these troubled times, the Pittsburgh club acquired its nickname, "The Pirates," one of the most famous sobriquets in baseball, which has stuck to the club for nearly six decades. Prior to 1891, the club had had no more intimate nickname than the geographical term of Alleghenies.

The victors in the baseball war, the National League and American Association, exacted no penalties from the jumping players, but ordered their return to the clubs from which they had jumped in 1889. The Athletics of Philadelphia had two of these leaping athletes, Louis Bierbauer, a second baseman, and Harry Stovey, a base-stealing outfielder. With the Quaker City having both a National League and Brotherhood team in 1890, the Athletics failed to put a team in the field that season, but after the peace the American Association claimed all the players who had jumped from those early A's. However, through some oversight, perhaps the mistake of an office clerk, the names of Bierbauer and Stovey did not appear on the American Association's printed reserve list for 1891.

The Pittsburgh and Boston National League clubs took advantage of this oversight. The western Pennsylvania club signed Bierbauer, and the Bostons induced Stovey to ink a Beantown contract. The Association immediately set up a howl, said the names of the two players failed to appear on their list through an error, and asked for their return. J. Palmer O'Neil, who had been elected to the Pittsburgh presidency as a successor to Nimick as a reward for keeping the club afloat in 1890, failed to budge from his stand. "The American Association did not reserve Bierbauer, so he was a free agent, and we were free to sign him," Palmer insisted.

The two major leagues then agreed to submit the matter to a board of arbitration, and in arguing their case the American Association spokesman said: "The action of the Pittsburgh club in signing Bierbauer was piratical." Somehow, no one around the Pittsburgh club seemed ashamed, and it wasn't long before the piratical Pittsburgh club became known as the Pirates.

Even though the board of arbitration upheld the action of the National League clubs, and awarded Bierbauer and Stovey to the Pittsburgh and Boston clubs, respectively, the American Association took its reverse in poor grace. They withdrew from the so-called "National Agreement," and instead of fighting the Players League in 1890, the two major leagues fought each other in 1891.

Of Pittsburgh's 1889 jumpers only seven returned: Pitchers Galvin, Staley, and Maul, Catchers Carroll and Fields, First Baseman Beckley, and Center Fielder Hanlon. Though Ned had contributed much to the wrecking of the Pirates the year before, he was re-engaged as manager, as Palmer said: "We'll just forget the Players League ever happened." However, of the returned jumping septet, only Galvin, Maul, and Beckley played with the Pirates for the entire 1891 season.

Among the new players that year was the tall Brookfield, Mass., catcher, Connie Mack, who had jumped from the Washington club to the Buffalo Players League team. Connie was one of the players who lost even his proverbial shirt in the Brotherhood venture. Other new acquisitions were Roger "Pete" Browning, the former Louisville slugger, and "Silver" Flint, who had been a great pitcher with the St. Louis Browns, but both Pete and Silver were then well past their prime.

The collapse of the Brotherhood brought no surcease to Pittsburgh's tail-end blues. The 1891 club won 32 more games and lost 33 less than the woeful misfits of 1890, but when the official statistician turned over the league standing to the printer, Pittsburgh still rested at the bottom. The Pirates had a fairly respectable percentage of .407 and didn't hit bottom until the very last day of the season.

Hanlon's failure to get the club out of its tail-end rut brought about new managerial repercussions. The Pirate ownership had no appreciation of the managerial genius who was in, their employ, and went after a big name. They thought they found him in Bill McGunnigle, who had a most unique record in 1889 and 1890, winning successive championships for Brooklyn, the first in the American Association and the second in the National League. There was some trouble about Bill's terms with Brooklyn in 1891, so he took over the Providence team of the old Eastern League. The Providence club tossed in the sponge in late July. Feeling a man who could win two pennants in two major leagues in successive seasons might be the miracle man for the Pirates, O'Neil fired Hanlon and engaged McGunnigle, August 1. Hanlon went on to Baltimore, where he soon became the National League's outstanding manager; as for McGunnigle, he quickly fell back to obscurity.

With the end of the Players League, the Pirates moved back to Exposition Park, briefly used in the early eighties and by the Brotherhood team in 1890. Even though the Allegheny River frequently backed into the outfield after spring floods, much interesting Pirate history was written on this field. It was located on the river, near the old covered bridge that crossed the Allegheny between the old Exposition buildings on the Pittsburgh side and what was the lower part of Allegheny. It is down toward what is known as the point, where the Allegheny and Monongahela Rivers converge to form the Ohio. River Avenue, Cremo Street, and South Avenue all touched the park.

Every time there was a sudden rise in the rivers, the waters of the Allegheny backed up through a sewer into Exposition Park, and the park became better suited for ducks and canoeing than for baseball. A good-sized lake would form in center field and eventually take in second base. Flood gates were put in the sewers, but they worked only under certain conditions. The custom of the Pittsburgh club annually opening away from home dates back to the nineties and first decade of this century, when high water on the Allegheny and Monongahela made it advisable to keep the Pirates on the road for the first week of the season.

The ball park got its name, Exposition Park, from the fact that whenever circuses and other big tent shows came to Pittsburgh, they camped in that locality, and sons of Pitt knew it as the Exposition Grounds. After the Pirates pulled out in 1909, the park was later used by Pittsburgh's clubs in the independent United States and Federal Leagues. On the site of the old historic park there is now a plant for a carloading and distributing company, with part of the grounds still used for carnivals and smaller tent shows.

2

After guerrilla warfare between the National League and American Association all through the season of 1891, the two leagues decided not to bump heads any longer. They merged into a twelve-club circuit, which for some years thereafter was known as the National League and Association. It tended to make the circuit a stronger league, as all of the nation's larger cities were now included, and it also employed all of the country's top-ranking players. The St. Louis Browns, Louisville Colonels, Baltimore Orioles, and Washington Senators of the Association were all admitted to the merged league, with the players of the four disbanded clubs placed on the open market.

The formation of the new twelve-club league also saw a new deal for the Pirates. The entire club was reorganized, with Captain William W. Kerr, who was the big man in Arbuckle Coffee, the principal backer, and Phil Auten of Chicago a close associate. Some other Pittsburgh capital was interested, and William C. Temple, a famous Pittsburgh sportsman, was elected president. Temple was an enthusiastic promoter of All-Star baseball and football events in the Pittsburgh area. With the early World Series between the pennant winners of the National League and American Association discontinued, Temple introduced the famous Temple Cup series to take its place. It was a postseason series between the champion and second-place clubs, played under World Series conditions. Temple offered a beautiful cup as a trophy, which first was contested for in 1894. It now is in the Winter Park, Florida, home of A. W. Mason, William Temple's son-in-law.

McGunnigle was let out after the drab finish in 1891, and Al C. Buckenberger was named Pirate manager. Al was a diligent and conscientious worker and succeeded in putting together quite a team. William "Adonis" Terry, Phil "Red" Ehret, and Charley Esper were added to the pitching staff; Tommy Burns, Chicago's great third baseman, gave the entire infield a lift, and a whole raft of new outfielders were brought in: Joe Kelly, Elmer Smith, Pat Donovan, Jake Stenzel, an old Association star, and George Van Haltren, a Californian.

Kelly was a big fish who was permitted to get away. He was released to Baltimore in midseason, and under Hanlon's able direction became one of the batting lights of the great Orioles. Elmer Smith came from Allegheny; he had been a left-handed pitcher with Cincinnati and Kansas City, but his arm went bad in 1891, and he turned to outfielding. Elmer became a hard and timely hitter and was an early intimate of Catcher Connie Mack. Elmer long was one of the favorite baseball characters around Pittsburgh, and died there, November 5, 1945, at the age of 77.

Everything considered, Pittsburgh's first season in the twelve-club league, in 1892, was fairly satisfactory. The club finished sixth, but in the enlarged loop this meant the bottom rung of the first division. The Pirates won 7 more games than they lost, 80 wins and 73 defeats for a .523 percentage. It was the first time since the 1886 American Association runner-up that a Pittsburgh club finished on the right side of the .500 mark.

Even so, there were managerial squabbles. Like Finnegan, Buckenberger was in ag'n, out ag'n, and then in ag'n. Though Temple was president, Captain Kerr was the man behind the throne. He was a likable chap, but from the start a good second guesser.

"Something's got to be done to get more out of this ball club," Kerr told Temple. "I don't think Al is getting all he can out of the men. Tommy Burns was a smart player in Chicago, and should have learned something in all the years he played for Anson. Why not make him the manager?"

Captain Kerr had only to suggest, and it was done. What's more, he didn't demote Buckenberger, but kicked him upstairs. Tommy Burns was moved into the manager's seat, and "Buck" promoted to acting president. But by July 29, Burns was ousted, and Buckenberger was restored to command. Tommy had been one of Anson's hell raisers in Chicago, a roguish fellow who liked to play pranks on Cap and his teammates. Nature never had intended him for a managerial role.

The long string bean of a catcher, Connie Mack, thought he had a good season in 1892. He caught 86 games and hit .257, which wasn't bad for Connie. And he could hand out soft salve and lots of taffy behind the plate. Connie didn't go in for rough, abusive, or vulgar language, but he would flatter an opposing player, or do anything to engage him in conversation.

"You've had a great day, Anse," he would tell the manager-captain of the Chicagos. "How can a man of your age still hit so well?"

While Anson was trying to think up the right kind of a reply, Connie would signal for Galvin, Ehret, or Baldwin to throw in a fast one. People said Mack wasn't baseball's best catcher, but he was one of the brainiest. He could tip bats, and was so sorry and profuse with his apologies that he almost convinced the batsman it was accidental.

Mack was all set to ask for a raise, when at the end of the season, he, along with eleven others of the leading Pirate players, was summoned to Captain Kerr's office. The Captain had a tough message for his players and didn't try to soften the blow.

"Boys, you know what the league has been up against," he said bluntly. "You fellows did your part to wreck us during the Brotherhood fight, and most of the clubs still are in debt. Merging with the American Association hasn't ended our troubles. Well, from now on the league has decided that the top salary for any player will be $2,400. All of you fellows can sign now at that figure. But if you hold off until next spring, it will be only $2,100."

Mack later admitted he and the other Pirates signed the proffered contracts with heavy hearts. "I was sorely put out," said Connie. "I felt the game that I had made my life's work was moving backward instead of going forward. I've always thought that 1892 action by the National League, limiting even the biggest stars to $2,400, made the success of the American League possible nine years later."

The winter after Kerr handed down his salary ultimatum, one of Mack's discouraged, disgruntled Pirate teammates wrote to Connie that he thought he would quit the game. Mack wrote back: "My only fear is that the game may quit."

3

Pittsburgh had been in the National League six seasons, but it wasn't until 1893 that Pirate fans really enjoyed the experience. In Pittsburgh's nineteenth-century baseball, the 1893 campaign marked the high tide of Pirate fortunes. The Pirates didn't win the pennant, but they did the next best thing, finishing second to a strong Boston club. Frank Selee's Red Stockings wound up with 86 victories and 44 defeats and a percentage of .662. The Pirates, in the fight until the last few days of the race, won 81 games and lost 48 for a .628 rating. That meant that at the finish ten other clubs trailed the Pittsburghers. It was the winter after this eventful season that Temple got his idea for the Temple Cup series, but alas, the Pirates were never to get into this competition.

It was a Buckenberger year; Al not only served as manager, but Kerr also permitted him to act as the figurehead president. Al did a swell job of rebuilding, and important acquisitions on the 1893 Pirates were: Pitchers Frank Killen, a left-hander, and Addison Gumbert; Catcher Joe Sugden, and Infielders Pebbly Jack Glasscock and Jack Lyons.

Pebbly Jack, a native of Wheeling, W. Va., was one of the great shortstops of his day, a Marty Marion of the nineties. He was acquired from the St. Louis Browns, but was thirty-five years old, and had passed his peak. Killen was a real pitching jewel, a left-hander with sinews of steel and the heart of a lion. His 35 victories of that 1893 season have never been equaled by a left-hander. Frank won 35 and lost 12 for the magnificent percentage of .745. Pitchers weren't pampered in those days, but Killen was a special horse for work, often pitching three times a week. Frank later ran a hotel and tavern in Pittsburgh, and was found dead in a streetcar, October 3, 1939, the victim of heart disease.

The play of the underdog 1893 Pirates not only had all Pittsburgh baseball-crazy, but fired the imagination of the entire country. Outside of New England, the nation's fans were almost unanimous in rooting for Buckenberger's fighting charges. It was a wild and hectic season, with almost everything happening. The club started off its early spring campaign most inauspiciously, and failed to win a single game in April. Fans feared the worst and held their noses when they discussed the ball club. "Is that the Pirates we are smelling?" they asked.

But they were soon smelling a different aroma, as April showers brought May flowers. May was a delirious month, with Pirate defeats few and far between. By May 4, they vacated the cellar; on May 8, they left the second division for good, and by the last day of the month they scrambled into first place. There was a soft spot in early July, when the Buckenbergers skidded back to fifth, but late in the month Pittsburgh was running third, with only Boston and the Phillies ahead of them.

The Beaneaters started to pull away in August, and for a while it looked as though second place would be a battle to the wire between the two Pennsylvania clubs, Pittsburgh and Philadelphia. But, the Phillies faltered on the stretch, and had to be content with fourth. Pittsburgh couldn't catch Boston, but the Pirates had no competition for the "place" position, winding up seven and a half games ahead of the third-place Clevelands.

The 1893 second-placers lined up with Frank Killen, Red Ehret, Bill "Adonis" Terry, Ad Gumbert, Mark Baldwin, Henry Gastright, Tom Colcolough, pitchers; Connie Mack, Joe Sugden, George Miller, catchers; Jake Beckley, first base; Lou Bierbauer, second base; Jack Glasscock, shortstop; Denny Lyons, third base; Elmer Smith, left field; George Van Haltren, center field; Patsy Donovan, right field. Jake Stenzel, Frank Shugart, Jim Gray, and Sam Gillen helped out in emergencies.

The Pirates were the fence busters of the year, hitting .319 as a team, against only .272 for the champion Bostons. Stenzel was the league's nominal leader with .409 for 51 games. Elmer Smith hit .366; Van Halren, .350; Donovan, .331; and Beckley, .324. In addition to Killen's masterful hurling, the other regular pitchers did pretty well: Terry, 15-6; Gumbert, 11-7; Ehret, 17-18. But it wasn't quite good enough!

Connie Mack remembers that season of 1893 for more reasons than that it was a second-place year for Pittsburgh. He met with a severe injury, which ended his career as a first-string catcher. The accident was suffered in a game with the Boston champs, and Mack was trying to break up a double steal.

Bobbie Lowe was on first base and Herman Long, the great shortstop, on third, when Bob lit out for second base. Mack threw the ball down to his second baseman, Bierbauer, and then Long, a big fellow and hard slider, set sail for the plate. Bierbauer's return throw to Mack was hurried and a bit on the inside. Connie half kneeled to cover the plate, and as Long slid home, Dutch ripped open the tall catcher's left leg from the knee to the ankle. Connie was carried off the field, not only with a torn leg, but also a fractured ankle. He was out for practically the remainder of the season; Long didn't escape either, as Herman was incapacitated for three weeks.

"I always figured that accident shortened my playing career by about five years," Mack related to the author. "Shin guards such as Roger Bresnahan later introduced to baseball would have saved me. After the accident I was much slower on the bases, and when I tried to stoop behind the plate, it would catch me in the calf, where I had been spiked."

Prior to Connie's spiking, it looked as though he were in for his best season, as he was hitting .325 for 36 games, far above his usual gait.

"Some of the boys later told me my injury beat them out of the 1893 pennant, but I don't know whether I was that good—or important," modestly reminisced old Connie.

IV. CONNIE MACK IS PIRATE SKIPPER

FOLLOWING PITTSBURGH'S great second-place fight in 1893, big things were expected of the team of 1894. The excited fans would settle for nothing less than a pennant, and yelled: "This year we'll beat out Boston." Captain Kerr was sure he finally had a winner; in fact, he took over the presidency from Buckenberger. As Pittsburgh gossip had it: "The Captain wants to have the glory that goes with being president of the champions."

However, it was another one of those disappointing seasons for Pittsburgh fans. The Pirate pitching staff fizzled early, perhaps missing Mack's regular catching (he took part in 63 games), while the entire club fell off sharply at bat. Boston eventually was dethroned after three straight winners, but it was the former door-mat Baltimore Orioles who beat out Selee's Beaneaters, making the remarkable leap from eighth in 1893 to first, under Ned Hanlon, the Pirate discard, with Joe Kelly providing much of the batting power. As for the Pirates, they soon became enmeshed in the second division, and wound up in seventh place with a .500 percentage. The club lost 17 more games than did the 1893 runner-up.

Like Sam Breadon, former owner of the present-day Cardinals, Captain Kerr wasn't one to string along with a loser. And the coffee man was prone to blame his difficulties on his manager.

As early as midseason, he sent for Connie Mack, his catcher. "I don't like the way this club is being run, Connie," the owner told the gaunt backstop. "I've been watching your work for some time. You're a smart ball player, and I think you have the makings of a manager. What do you think about it? How would you like to run the team?"

Mack, a fair shooter and loyal to his chief, immediately started thinking of Buckenberger, and made excuses for the manager. "It isn't Al's fault that we're not higher," said Connie. "Buckenberger is a good manager, but we've had a lot of bad breaks. My own accident of last season is one of them. I'm not the catcher I used to be."

"That's all true," shot back Kerr. "But, tell me why a club that ran second to Boston is now down in the second division. Something is wrong; our pitchers aren't pitching, and our hitters aren't hitting. I think Buckenberger has lost control of the team. And, Mack, I think you're the man to run it."

Connie spoke up pluckily. "I'd be afraid to manage a club for you, Captain Kerr," he said. "You're always second guessing the manager. That doesn't help any."

"Oh, that's how the boys feel, is it?" snapped Kerr. "Well, I'll string along with Al for a while longer, but if things don't improve I've simply got to make a change."

Things didn't improve, but grew worse. On September 1, Kerr summoned Mack again. "Connie, I want you to take over the ball club," he said. "And there is no use in you turning it down because of loyalty to Al. I've definitely decided to make a change, and Buckenberger is out. So it's either you, or someone else."

In the six weeks since Kerr broached Mack with the first offer, the catcher had done a lot of thinking. He knew his days as a big-league player were running short. And by this time he was a widower, with three growing children, including Roy and Earl, now officials in the Philadelphia Athletics. They were kids with good appetites, and needed plenty of shoes. Connie had to give some thought to his family and his future.

With still a rather heavy heart, Mack accepted. "I'm sorry for Al, but if that's what you want, I'll do the best I can for you."

Mack took over, September 3, 1894, and approximately fifty years later, all Pennsylvania, from Lieutenant Governor Bell down, celebrated Connie's managerial jubilee at Shibe Park, Philadelphia. And it was fitting that Mack's debut as head man in Allegheny should be properly celebrated. The new skipper's first day in command was an augury of the brilliant managerial career that followed. Connie's Pirates overwhelmed Mack's old alma mater, the Washington club, by the substantial score of 22 to 1.

A few years before, Harry M. Stevens, who was to be the sports world's number-one caterer, with his legend, "From the Hudson to the Rio Grande," came from Columbus, Ohio to take charge of Pittsburgh's score-card sales and other concessions. Harry was an English-born puddler from Niles, Ohio. He later won fame and fortune at the Polo Grounds, New York, as the man who made America hot-dog conscious, and who parlayed a bag of peanuts into millions. His able sons, Frank, Hal, and Joe, now continue the business started when the elder Stevens personally hawked score cards at Exposition Park.

Associated with Stevens in his Pittsburgh venture was a strong-fisted, black-haired, beetle-browed chap from the Middle West, who had been a circulation manager in his home town of Des Moines and a young advertising man in Chicago. He, too, was to go high in baseball. The name was Edward Grant Barrow. He managed Paterson, Toronto, Detroit, and the Red Sox, and served as president of several minor leagues. As business manager and later president of the Yankees, he was largely responsible for fourteen American League pennants and ten World Championships that were won by that powerful team.

Stevens and Barrow had not only the baseball concessions at Exposition Park, but also sold programs in the Pittsburgh theaters. With Al Buckenberger, the deposed Pirate manager, Stevens and Barrow acquired the Wheeling franchise of the newly organized Inter-State League in 1895. Barrow joined the club as secretary, but when the manager quit after a month, Ed took over the reins and had his club in first place when the league disbanded in mid-July. Charlie Powers, sports editor of the *Pittsburgh Leader*, was then president of the Iron and Oil League, and he told Barrow to put his Wheeling club into that circuit, where Edward won another pennant. From there he followed Stevens east. By an odd coincidence, Barrow had an early association with two young players who were to become Pirate immortals—Honus Wagner and Fred Clarke.

2

Connie Mack still looks at his first complete season as Pittsburgh manager as "the season of might-have-beens." He almost

became baseball's miracle man that year and still thinks that if
Frank Killen, his left-handed pitching ace, hadn't been injured
in midseason, he would have won Pittsburgh's first major-league
pennant in 1895. That would have made him such a big figure
in Pittsburgh that it is possible he never would have left, and
western Pennsylvania, rather than the southeastern corner of the
state, would have seen Mack's managerial genius in fruition.

The 1895 Pirates trained at Hot Springs, Ark.; the club encountered a good warm spring, and Mack brought a well-condi-
tioned club back to Allegheny. His most important player
acquisitions were three pitchers: Emerson "Pink" Hawley, Billy
Hart, and Jack Foreman, all right-handers. During the season,
Mack also brought up a little left-hander, Gussie Gannon, from
Erie. He became the father of a well-known, sports-loving priest
of the Pittsburgh district, Father James Gannon, and uncle of
Bishop Mark Gannon of the Diocese of Erie. Connie employed
another new pitcher, James Gardner, who was signed by Kerr
to an unusual contract. Gardner was an opulent law student,
who agreed to pitch only in Pittsburgh's home games. He turned
in a good job, too, winning eight games out of ten.

Montford "Monte" Cross, who later became Mack's shortstop
on his Athletic champions of 1902 and 1905, came the previous
year, while in 1895, Connie tried out a batch of new infielders:
Frank Genins, Billy Clingman, Billy Niles, Bill "Chauncey" Stuart,
and Jack Corcoran. All worked their way into the line-up at
sundry times, with Genins winning fame as Mack's Jack-of-all-
trades. Mack took part in only fourteen games and engaged Tom
Kinslow, an irresponsible chap from Washington, D. C., to help
out his catching department.

The Pirates were hotter than a Guatemalan stew for the first
half of the season; they bobbed in and out of first place and for
weeks at a time led the long twelve-club procession. And Pittsburgh fans expected their team to stay up there. When the Pirates
slipped back as low as third on June 2, we read in the Pittsburgh
letter to Sporting News "that the mighty have fallen," and "that
class of fickle fans known as 'knockers' are making life miserable
for Con Mack and loyal supporters."

But despite injuries, the club bounced back into the lead
July 19, slipped to second for the remainder of the month, and
led for the last time on August 9. After that came the denoue-
ment, and in the latter half of August and September Mack's

team fell through the league standing like a drunken paper hanger falling off a ladder. From their vantage point in early August, the team plummeted to a dismal seventh, with 71 victories, 61 defeats, and a percentage of .536. Connie was heartbroken when the season was over, and Kerr almost blue with vexation.

The Pirates suffered their big blow on June 11, when Frank Killen, the ace southpaw, was severely spiked in Baltimore. At the time the Pirates and Hanlon's Orioles were battling desperately for possession of first place. Frank's injury was much like Mack's casualty of the previous season. While the pitcher was covering the plate, he had his left leg badly spiked, and remained in a Baltimore hospital for forty-nine days. When Killen rejoined the Pirates in late summer, he wasn't in shape to do much pitching. He won only seven games that season, and lost six.

"When I say that Killen won thirty-five games for the club in our big season in 1893, and again won thirty-one games in 1896, my last season in Pittsburgh, you may get some idea of what his injury meant to me," said Mack. Up to the time of Killen's injury, Mack employed Killen, Hawley, and Hart as his leading trio. In his effort to keep in the race in July and early August, he literally worked "Pink" Hawley until his knuckles were red, calling on him almost every other day. "Pink" was credited with 29 victories against 21 defeats. Hawley finally cracked from overwork, and when he did, the entire team crashed with him.

Mack also had difficulty in keeping his players out of brothels and grog shops. There were a number of gay blades on the Pirates team; fun then came first with them, and their ball playing was secondary. Managers had to take much more from ball players in the gay nineties than they do today, and some critics said Connie was too easygoing, and that his players took advantage of him. Two of the worst culprits were Pitcher Jack Foreman and Catcher Kinslow.

Connie was especially wrought at Kinslow and once smacked down hard at the erring catcher. While the Pirates were playing in Baltimore, Kinslow asked permission to run over to his home town, Washington. He was to report back the following day, when the Pirates had moved on to Washington. At the time the team was generally crippled, and Mack's catching staff had been reduced to Bill Merritt. When the club arrived in the capital, there was no Kinslow. Mack eventually learned of his whereabouts and sent word that it would cost Kinslow three times his daily salary for every day he stayed away. That brought him back, but Mack released Kinslow the following winter.

Even though Mack had played in the National League since 1887, it is interesting that few fans, including those in Pittsburgh, knew that his actual name was Cornelius McGillicuddy, until a rather amusing incident in that same 1895 season. In fact, Mack said he had never seen his real name in print until he took his Pirates to New York, and O. P. Caylor, former sports editor of the *New York Herald,* ran a streamer across his sports page: MCGILLICUDDY AND HIS PIRATES IN TOWN TODAY.

"I was curious to know how Caylor came to know my real name," recalled Mack, "so I looked him up and asked him where he had heard it. Caylor used to own a paper in Carthage, Missouri, and sold it to a cousin of mine by the name of Eugene Roach. After the sale, Gene learned that Caylor was a sports writer, and remarked he had a relative who was a big leaguer. Caylor naturally was interested and asked his name. Gene told him: 'Why, McGillicuddy of the Pirates.'

"Caylor replied: 'I don't know any player on the Pirates by that name.'

"Gene then said: 'Oh, he's on the Pirates all right; he's the manager.' Then Caylor understood I was McGillicuddy."

Oddly enough, the Giants seemed to think it was funny, and during the game, they yelled, "Mister McGillicuddy" and "Cornelius McGillicuddy" at the lean Corsair skipper.

It naturally got back to Pittsburgh, and when Mack returned to Exposition Park shortly afterward, the grandstand also seemed to think it amusing, and the fans took up a cry: "McGillicuddy! Hey, McGillicuddy!"

After the game, a crowd of boys, such as always gathers around ball parks, followed Connie from the clubhouse entrance to his boarding house, calling out to pedestrians: "Look! Look! There goes Mr. McGillicuddy."

And while Mr. McGillicuddy was one of the finest sportmen who ever made baseball his profession, he wasn't above some inside baseball tricks, if he thought it would benefit the Pirates. There used to be an icebox in the Pittsburgh club's offices, and Connie conceived the idea of stuffing boxes of baseballs into the icebox, and "freezing" them overnight. The practice supposedly "froze" the life out of baseballs.

The next trick was to finesse the iced balls into the game while opponents were at bat, and to work back the natural baseballs when the Pirates came up for their batting turn. Connie had various ways of sneaking in the frappéd baseballs. A boy was usually stationed on the grandstand roof, whose job was to retrieve foul balls. In those days umpires weren't so fussy, and balls that had been fouled into or over the stands were put back into play. When the Giants, Beaneaters, or Chicagos were at bat, Connie had the kid on the roof drop down an iced ball. Later, when it was to Mack's advantage, the boy let fall an untreated pellet.

George Moreland, the former Pittsburgh statistician, once told me about Connie Mack's icebox trick. The author asked Connie whether the tale was true or exaggerated. A twinkle came into his keen blue eyes, and he said with a smile: "We used to have to resort to a lot of tricks to win ball games, and maybe that was one of them."

There is no manager in baseball who has been as good a friend of the umpires as Connie Mack. Even when baseball was still a rough and rowdy game, his players knew just how far they could go in protesting an umpire's decision. It has been said: "Connie Mack never was put out of a game in over sixty years of baseball," but that isn't literally true. The late Hank O'Day, a Pittsburgh American Association pitcher in 1885, gave Connie the old heave-ho in 1895 and almost called in the entire Allegheny Police Department to remove the skinny catcher-manager from the park.

It still was in the single umpire days, and the poor fellows needed three pairs of eyes to see everything that happened on the ball field. Hank called out Patsy Donovan on a play at second base at Exposition Park, which Connie still says wasn't even close. "If ever a man was safe in baseball, it was Patsy that afternoon," Mack insists.

Connie was furious, and his saintly tongue must have slipped a few cogs, because O'Day barked: "Mack, you're through for the day and fined $100." But Mack refused to budge, and continued berating Hank.

Finally O'Day called a policeman, and said: "I want you to put that man off the field."

When the copper tried to put a hand on Connie, Mack shook him off, and asked: "Did you see me do anything wrong?" "No, I didn't, Mr. Mack," replied the policeman. "Well, then, you have no right to put me off the field." That had the cop stumped, and he called the sergeant.

By that time Connie decided the matter had gone far enough, and before the sergeant called up City Hall for instructions, Mack removed himself to the clubhouse.

There was another brush with an umpire during his Pittsburgh days, which still gives Connie a good laugh. He calls it the funniest thing he has ever seen on a ball field. It took place in a Pirate-Cincinnati game; Tim Hurst was the umpire, and old Arlie Latham the involuntary fun maker.

Mack was catching and tagged out Latham at the plate on a close play. Hurst ruled that Arlie was out. Latham yelled something at Tim and then threw his cap to the ground. Hurst kicked the cap in the direction of first base. Latham picked up the cap and slammed it into the ground again. Tim gave it another kick. They continued playing the game until Hurst had kicked the cap all the way down the foul line to the right-field fence.

3

Mack's last season as manager of the Pirates in 1896 wasn't a happy one. With Killen again ready to take his regular turn on the mound, it was hoped that the club would forget its September collapse and revert to its fine play of the early part of the 1895 season. Killen came back and won 31 games, but the remainder of the staff bogged down. Despite his bad leg, Mack tried to steady his pitchers by going in back of the plate again, and caught 71 games. But his 1896 entry proved a fifty-fifty club, which won one day, lost the next, and never got far from the .500 mark. The team finished in sixth place, with 66 victories and 63 defeats. Some trades hadn't worked out well, and there was more trouble in enforcing discipline. Several key players got out of hand.

An early chill developed between Mack and his boss, Captain Kerr, and other Pirate stockholders. It was the old Buckenberger story over again, and the manager was held responsible for the team's shortcomings. They would ask Mack why this and that hadn't been done, and his answers weren't too tactful.

After Connie had lost a heartbreaking game on the road, he

received a wire from Kerr, asking why he hadn't lifted a pitcher. Mack shot back a wire: "I told you so." He was reminding Kerr of his promise not to second guess him.

The plucky, if tactless, telegram was the beginning of the end. In mid-September, Kerr called Mack to his office and advised him he had decided on another managerial change, and that Connie's contract as skipper would not be renewed for 1897.

"You can stay with us as catcher and coach, if you wish," added Kerr.

"No, thank you," said Mack. "I guess it'll be better if I pull out entirely."

Mack resigned September 21, to take effect at the close of the season. Connie moved to Milwaukee in Ban Johnson's Western League, taking over as manager and part owner. The Milwaukee post paved the way to Mack's big opportunity in Philadelphia, when Ban Johnson expanded his Western loop into the flourishing American League of today.

After Mack had won a string of pennants in Philadelphia, Kerr met him at a World Series, in which the Athletics was one of the contending teams. After shaking hands, Kerr remarked: "Connie, do you know what was my biggest blunder during the time I owned the Pirates? It was letting you go as manager in 1896."

After Kerr served notice on Mack that his managerial contract would not be renewed, the Captain made a September trade with the Giants: First Baseman Jake Beckley, for the young New York first sacker, Harry Davis, a young Philadelphian from Girard College. Mack didn't know of the deal until he saw Jake pack up his belongings in the Pirate clubhouse.

"I didn't make the deal for Davis but I had to take all the abuse for it," recalled Mack. "Jake Beckley was about the most popular player in Pittsburgh; he was a powerful hitter and had a strong, loyal following. I still recall persons hollering at me from Pittsburgh windows: 'Why did you trade Jake Beckley?'"

The deal had an interesting sequel for Mack. Davis didn't stay long in Pittsburgh; in fact, at one time he tired of the game and went to work as a clerk for the Pennsylvania Railroad in Philadelphia. When Mack first put an American League club in Philadelphia in 1901, his early first baseman, Charley Carr, quickly won disfavor with Philadelphia fans. Mack lured Davis out of his railroad office, and Harry became his first baseman on four championship teams and on four occasions won the home-run crown of the American League.

In addition to Harry Davis, other players added to the 1896 Pirates were: Infielder Tom Delahanty, one of the five Delahantys to reach the majors; Shortstop Fred Ely; Dick Padden, later a crack American League second baseman; and Pitcher Charley Hastings.

4

When Captain Kerr picked a successor for Connie Mack he again reached into the playing ranks and turned the key to the helmsman's cabin over to Patsy Donovan, the club's hard-hitting right fielder. Like Mack, Patsy was a New England Irishman, hailing from Lawrence, Mass. Donovan was a keen-witted aggressive player, who knew a lot of baseball. He later had a wealth of managerial experience and handled the Cardinals, Senators, and Red Sox. It was during his stay in Boston that Joe Wood rose to stardom, and the Red Sox assembled what since has been termed baseball's greatest outfield: Duffy Lewis, Tris Speaker, and Harry Hooper.

Donovan tried to manage the Pirates according to Captain Kerr's directions, but he had even less success than the strong-willed Mack. The Corsairs picked up Catcher Tom Leahy to replace Mack, came up with a rattling good left-handed pitcher in Jesse Tannehill, and added several infielders: Jimmy Donnelly, John Rothfuss, and Jesse Hofmeister. Walter "Steve" Brodie, the hard-hitting outfielder, was procured in a deal with the Orioles. Steve could clout the ball, but was slow of foot and not too nimble above the ears. The 1897 Pirates limped home in eighth place, and Patsy was out as manager.

This time Kerr decided to fire himself as president, as well as Donovan as skipper. He appointed William H. "Wattie" Watkins, an experienced baseball man, to come in as president-manager of the 1898 team. Wattie had been manager of the famous Detroit World's Champions of 1887, when Ned Hanlon was his playing captain. As a player, Watkins narrowly escaped death when hit by a pitched ball, and his hair had turned from black to white the night of the accident. He later became Justice of the Peace at Marysville, Michigan.

"They say I do too much interfering with my managers," Captain Kerr told Watkins. "You've had a lot of experience running ball clubs. I want you to take over the entire works. Make trades; get new players; sign 'em to their contracts. You'll be president in the front office as well as manager on the field."

"I couldn't want a fairer arrangement than that," said Watkins. "If I don't deliver, the responsibility will be mine."

"That's right, and that's how I want it," said Kerr.

However, the all-Watkins year didn't pan out either; the National League increased the number of games on its schedule, but at the finish Pittsburgh was again in eighth place in the twelve-club league, with 72 victories, 76 defeats, and a percentage of .486. That season the battery of Bill Hoffer and Frank Bowerman was obtained from the Baltimore Orioles, which famous club was breaking up, and another pitching newcomer who was to write considerable Pirate history was a young schoolteacher from Goshen, Ohio—Sam Leever. The stalwart Samuel was an acquisition from the Richmond club of the old Atlantic League.

After one year's experimentation, Kerr decided that the dual role of president-manager for Watkins hadn't worked out to his satisfaction. What's more, when he owned a ball club he found it difficult to sit back and not offer advice—and criticism. By 1899, the last year of the twelve-club National League, the energetic Kerr was back in the president's chair, and Watkins didn't even last out the season as manager.

The team got off to a wretched start, and by May 16 the Pirates had won only eight games out of twenty-seven. Perhaps Captain Kerr was justified in taking severe measures. Anyway, without consulting Watkins he ordered the team's captaincy taken away from Shortstop Fred Ely and given to Pat Donovan, the former manager. At the time the captain was still an important factor on the ball field. Huffed at this switch in team captains without his knowledge or consent, Watkins resigned as manager four days after the move. Kerr quickly accepted the resignation, though Watkins remained for a spell in the business office, and returned Donovan to the management. The New Englander did a pretty good job, too, for after the woeful spring start, Donovan inspired the club sufficiently to lift it above the .500 mark. The 1899 Pirates gained one position, winding up seventh, with 79 victories and 73 defeats.

When the season was over, a disgruntled fan yelled: "How long! How long must we endure second-division baseball? Everybody wins pennants but Pittsburgh."

Yet, better days were coming. Two players who were acquired in 1899 were to give Pittsburgh fans many a thrill with top-ranking performances: Jack Chesbro, the famous spitball pitcher, and Clarence "Ginger" Beaumont, the slam-banging, fast-running outfielder. Chesbro, known as Happy Jack, was a big-chested man from North Adams, Mass., who could do things with a baseball. Like Sam Leever, Chesbro used the Richmond Atlantic League club as a springboard to the National League.

Beaumont was the stuff of which batting champions are made. In those days, Clarence was a terrible handle to hang on a ball player; he much preferred his nickname of Ginger. Ginger was a former Beloit College star, and Kerr purchased him from Connie Mack's Milwaukee club. Beaumont gave early indications of his prowess with a phenomenal day at Exposition Park, July 22, 1899, when he made six hits and scored six runs in a game against the Phillies. Surprisingly enough, all of the hits were singles of the infield variety, a fine tribute to Ginger's speed. What's more, Beaumont, a left-handed batter, garnered all six hits off Wiley Piatt, a left-handed pitcher.

V. BARNEY DREYFUSS ENTERS THE SCENE

AFTER OPERATING eight seasons as a twelve-club league, the National League again voted to cut down to an eight-team circuit in 1900. Andy Freedman, a Tamany politician in New York, who owned the Giants, had long sponsored a move in the old league "to cut off the deadwood."

His campaign met with eventual success when the National League club owners voted to lop off Louisville and Cleveland in the West and Washington and Baltimore in the East. No piece of legislation passed in baseball ever had more far-reaching effects than this reduction to the present eight National League cities. It made possible the expansion of the American League to the east, as Ban Johnson took up vacated territory in Cleveland, Washington, and Baltimore, brought about the destructive war between the two present big leagues, and was responsible for the golden era in Pittsburgh baseball.

The owner of the Louisville club was a little energetic man of 125 pounds, a 34-year-old German-Jewish immigrant, who was already finding America the land of opportunity. Until his death, in 1932, he spoke with a pronounced German accent, but he was destined to become the power behind Pittsburgh baseball, and one of the game's most successful, able, and forward-looking club owners.

The National League learned early that Barney Dreyfuss was a battler. In the nineties only four major-league clubs played Sunday baseball: Chicago, St. Louis, Louisville, and Cincinnati.

41

Louisville, with one of the smallest populations in the loop, depended largely on its Sunday gate, so some of Dreyfuss' fellow club owners decided to give little Barney the works.

In an early attempt to cut off some of the alleged deadwood, the bigwigs of the National League decided on a schedule that gave Louisville no Sunday games. Fortunately for Barney, Joe Vila, the former enterprising sports writer of the old *New York Morning Sun,* pulled one of his spectacular scoops. While A. H. Soden, president of the Boston club and chairman of the schedule committee, was having a few beers at the old Fifth Avenue Hotel in New York, the enterprising Joe lifted the draft of the schedule from Soden's coat and copied it down while standing in a telephone booth. Vila printed the schedule in full the next morning.

After reading Vila's scoop, Dreyfuss yelled bloody murder during the following day's meeting. His English wasn't good at that early day and his pronunciation even worse, but he raised so much hell at the meeting that Soden's schedule was scrapped and a new one drawn up giving Dreyfuss his full quota of Sunday games.

It looked as though the winter of 1899-1900 would be a tough one for Dreyfuss. His Louisville ball park burned down in the fall. Then he learned from his alert secretary, Harry C. Pulliam, later president of the National League, of the contemplated move to cut down to eight clubs and leave Louisville out in the cold.

"What'll I do?" Barney asked Harry.

"Get hold of some money; get hold of lots of it, and get it in a hurry," advised Pulliam. "Then be ready for anything that may happen. And I'd try to cultivate the friendship of Jim Hart in Chicago, John T. Brush in Cincinnati, and Frank Robison in St. Louis. They like you, and they're for you."

"I can get the money, all right," said Barney.

In the meantime, Dreyfuss had been tipped off by two good publisher friends in Pittsburgh that Captain Kerr and Philip A. Auten, his associate, were tired of losing money on the Pirates and were ready to get out.

Early in 1900 John T. Brush, then the Cincinnati club owner, called up Dreyfuss and asked him whether he could meet him at French Lick, Ind. "It's a business matter of considerable importance, and I think it may mean a lot to you," said Brush. And it was no understatement!

When Barney arrived at the Hoosier resort, Brush quickly

talked turkey. "W. H. Watkins [the former Pirate manager] has put up $5,000 on an option to buy the Pittsburgh club," he said. "I was backing Watkins, but for reasons of my own I find I will be unable to go through with the deal. You know what's going to happen in the league. How would you like to pick up the option and stay in the National League?"

"Well, I would have to go back to Louisville and talk to some people and see whether they would go along with me," said Dreyfuss.

His Louisville friends said they would stand behind him, so early on the following Monday morning Barney, accompanied by Watkins, appeared in Kerr's Pittsburgh office. Kerr at first insisted that the option had expired and that Watkins had forfeited his $5,000.

Dreyfuss eventually convinced the Captain that wouldn't be fair, and Kerr asked: "Do you want to take up the option?"

"Well, the reason I'm here is that I'm interested in getting into Pittsburgh baseball," said the Louisville club owner.

Before Barney left he had made an agreement with Kerr that Dreyfuss would get a half interest in the Pittsburgh club providing he would bring the best Louisville players with him. As the league had not yet dropped Louisville officially, the transaction was made in the form of a trade, with Pittsburgh giving up $25,000 and five players, Jack Chesbro, George Fox, John O'Brien, Arthur Madison, and William Gould, for 14 Louisville players, the pick of the Colonels, topped by the fighting manager-left fielder, Fred Clarke, and the great all-round player, Hans Wagner. Others were: Second Baseman Claude Ritchey; Third Baseman Tommy Leach; Catchers Charley Zimmer and Cliff Latimer; Pitchers Charles "Deacon" Phillippe, Pat Flaherty, George Edward "Rube" Waddell, Walter Woods, and Elton Cunningham; and a few lesser athletes, Mike Kelly, later for many years the owner of the Minneapolis club, Tom Massitt, and C. Doyle.

After the National League streamlined itself to eight clubs, Jack Chesbro returned to Pittsburgh, and another pair of Colonels, Fred Ketcham and Louis Deal, joined the exodus to the Pirates.

The Pittsburgh club had a reorganization, and at a stockholders' meeting, Dreyfuss was named president; Phil Auten, vice-president; W. W. Kerr, treasurer; Harry C. Pulliam, secretary, and Fred Clarke, manager.

2

Dreyfuss, the new Pirate president, was born in Freiberg, Baden, February 23, 1865, was educated in his native Germany, and was early employed as a bank clerk in Karlsruhe. Disliking the idea of compulsory military training, young Barney emigrated to the United States when he was seventeen years old. Landing at old Castle Garden at New York's Battery, the young fellow's destination was Paducah, Kentucky, Irvin Cobb's old home town, where Barney had relatives. He had just about enough money to get to his Kentucky destination, but in his German schoolbooks he had read much about Niagara Falls and had been fascinated by pictures of the great cascade. To him, America and Niagara Falls were almost synonymous, so by carefully budgeting his meal money and sitting up several nights in day coaches, he went from New York to Paducah by way of Buffalo and Niagara Falls and saw the great natural wonder he had dreamed about.

Through Paducah relatives, Barney obtained his first American job with the Bernheim distillery. What's more, he really started at the bottom—cleaning whisky barrels for six dollars a week. But Dreyfuss was intelligent, smart at figures, and soon was advanced to an office position in the organization. Eventually he climbed to the head bookkeeper's stool.

If it hadn't been for failing health when Barney was in his late teens, he might never have become interested in baseball. He worked nine hours on his high stool, and then was up until midnight studying English and taking courses to make himself more proficient. He never had robust health and soon suffered from headaches, poor digestion, and a general rundown condition.

A Paducah doctor gave him some sage advice. "You're working too hard, Barney, and not getting any recreation or fun out of life. If you want to live a while in this country, you've got to stop working and cramming all the time. Get into some outdoor activity. Did you ever play baseball?"

"No," said Barney; "I don't know anything about it."

"Well, it's time you learned."

Dreyfuss took the hint and soon was captivated by the red-blooded American national game. He was in the country only a little over a year when he organized a semipro ball club in Paducah, and even played a little second base on it. When the club went to Memphis for a game, Paducah won by a score of 22 to 2. Discussing the contest later, Barney, who had an uncanny memory for names, faces, places, and details, remarked: "The score was bigger than the gate receipts, so I fed it to the squirrels in the public square in Memphis." The late George B. Dovey, a former president of the Boston Braves, was a member of Barney's Paducah team.

Though Dreyfuss left Germany so he wouldn't have to goose-step with the former Kaiser's minions, Barney was no pacifist and got some more sunshine, fresh air, and exercise serving with Bullitt's Light Artillery, later absorbed into the Kentucky National Guard. In later years, when Barney was in a particularly good humor, he would take a faded picture out of his desk drawer, showing a determined, mustachioed artilleryman, looking ready to conquer the world. "We marched at Cleveland's inauguration," he would say not unproudly.

Barney was also an early Kentucky colonel, other than being president-owner of the Louisville Colonels. "While I was running the Louisville club there were just two Republicans in Kentucky," Dreyfuss would reminisce. "By some magic or other, one of them managed to get himself elected governor of the state. As I was the other one, he made me a colonel, but I never did get a uniform out of it."

3

When the Bernheim distillery interests moved to Louisville in 1888, Dreyfuss, who by this time was credit man, went along. Louisville then had a team in the old American Association, along with Pittsburgh, the old St. Louis Browns, and early Athletics. It was called a "beer and whisky league," as most of its backers were brewery or distillery people. While the principal Louisville owners were Dr. Stuckey and George Ruckstool, there was whisky money behind the club, and Barney acquired a small block of stock shortly after his arrival in Louisville. He just liked to mess around with baseball.

By 1890, Dreyfuss was elected treasurer of the club. Shortly after Louisville was admitted into the twelve-club National League, Harry Pulliam was elected president of the Colonels, and Barney served under him as secretary-treasurer. When Barney obtained control of the club, he and Pulliam exchanged places, Dreyfuss moving up to the executive position.

The inside operations of a big-league club had an early fascination for him, and by nature he was a man who had little toleration for a team that wasn't a winner. His club need not necessarily be a champion, but if it stayed in the race and finished well in the first division, he was pleased, if not completely satisfied.

In his latter years his proudest boast was the many years of first-division baseball that he gave to Pittsburgh, his adopted city. "We are a first-division town, and I'm a first-division club owner," he once told the author. "I just couldn't—I wouldn't—stand for a second-division team." In the thirty-two years that he served as president of the Pirates, his clubs finished in the second division only six times, including his last two years on earth. Dreyfuss actually looked at the second division as something akin to a disgrace. If you finished there, you were a failure.

Admitting that four clubs had to finish in the lower four, he merely shrugged his shoulders, and said: "Well, it's not for me." He had a great pride in his own ability and accomplishments. He believed firmly in Barney Dreyfuss. "Smartness pays off in baseball as well as in any other activity, and I think I'm a pretty smart fellow," he once confessed. "America is, and always has been, a land of opportunity, and if I had put the same time, energy, brains, money into another business, I would have succeeded just as well, and perhaps made more money. But baseball is my business."

He drank little and never touched tobacco. Once he remarked quite philosophically: "When I wanted to smoke, I couldn't afford it. When I could afford it, I didn't want to smoke."

He wasn't too easy to get along with, and at times could be severe, dominating, critical, and stubborn. Many ball players felt he was a hard man to deal with. Yet he befriended many of the men who had worked for him. He had his periodical feuds and brushes with Pittsburgh sports writers. He was also a relentless fighter. In debates in the National League council halls, his fellow club owners often accused him of being arbitrary, unreasonable, and obstinate. "Barney, you're like a bulldog," Charley Ebbets, former Brooklyn president, once told him. "You get hold of something, and you never let go." When Dreyfuss lost the great George Sisler through the adverse vote of chairman Garry Herrmann, of the old National Commission, Barney started a one-man fight to unseat Herrmann from his Commission job. Herrmann was also president of the Cincinnati Reds, and he and

Barney were close, early associates in the league. But that counted for naught when Barney went on the warpath; after a four-year campaign, Dreyfuss had his revenge when Herrmann was ousted from his Commission chairmanship.

Pittsburgh wasn't always in agreement with Barney's moves on the Pirates. There were even times when the town was incensed at the little man from Freiberg. But Barney took his own counsel and if he made mistakes, well, he made them, and they were on his own head. He offered no excuses.

Yet when the former Paducah bookkeeper closed his earthly books, his contribution to baseball was large. He was one of the game's greatest and most far-seeing club owners. If, when in a moment of anger or peeve, he occasionally did a small thing, his vision was wide and his heart and keen mind were always on the side of better baseball. He said baseball was his business, so it was his business to keep the game and his club prosperous. Instinctively he recognized that clean baseball—a game above the slightest breath of suspicion—was the only baseball that paid.

VI. THE MIGHTY HONUS

BARNEY DREYFUSS had no first-division clubs during his sojourn in Louisville. He had to call on all of his native shrewdness to get by, but even though his 1899 Louisville club finished ninth, two positions behind Pittsburgh, he was in the process of building a strong first-division club when the National League voted to streamline down to eight clubs.

Major-league outfits had no full-time paid scouts in the nineties, and Dreyfuss, the Louisville owner, would have had little money for a scouting staff even if the system had then been in vogue. But from the first, Barney always believed he knew ball players and could pick them. From the time he began signing the Louisville club's checks, he kept his so-called "dope book." Barney learned to do his own scouting through the columns of the baseball weeklies, the *Sporting News* and *Sporting Life,* Spalding's and Reach's *Guides,* and the sports pages of the daily newspapers. Whenever he read that a minor-league batter was having a succession of good days, or a pitcher was racking up a string of victories, the player's name went into the dope book. If the price on the player wasn't too high, and anything over $1,000 was almost prohibitive, there was a good chance he would land on Dreyfuss' Colonels. And considering the ninth-place finish of the 1899 Colonels, Barney brought a surprisingly good crop of players to Pittsburgh from his Louisville club, including two of the immortals of baseball history, John Peter (Honus) Wagner and Frederick Clifford Clarke. Without them Pittsburgh's great baseball success in the first decade of this century would not have been possible.

Wagner is not only the greatest all-time Pirate and the foremost National League ball player, but many persons consider him the number-one ball player of all time. In that group is that doughty former American Leaguer, Ed Barrow, former manager of the Tigers and Red Sox and the man who had Babe Ruth in both Boston and New York.

Only recently Barrow revealed to the author that but for a matter of $100 the Pittsburgh club would have had Wagner three years before the Louisville-Pittsburgh merger of 1900. We'll come to that a little later. After Barrow broke away from the Pittsburgh district in 1896, to accept the management of the Paterson, N.J., club, he recruited his players largely from western Pennsylvania. He knew several of Honus' older brothers, including Al, a railroad engineer, whom Barrow always claims could have been as good a player as Hans.

Barrow received a tip that Hans, after a little early minor leaguing, was a free agent, and that any go-getting young manager who had the enterprise to take a trip to Hans' home town of Mansfield (now Carnegie), Pa., could sign young Wagner for the asking. In fact, Al Wagner told Barrow: "You don't want me, you want to sign my brother, John. He's the real ball player of the family." Al directed Barrow to Mansfield.

"Arriving in Mansfield, I asked some fellows loitering around the station where I might find Hans Wagner," related Barrow. "They told me if I'd walk down the railroad track for a mile or so, I'd likely run into him. One of them agreed to accompany me as a guide. It was in the early spring, and there was still some snow around. In some places I had to wade through puddles left by the spring thaw. We walked up the tracks about two miles and came upon a group of boys and young men. A husky, but clumsy-looking chap was throwing pieces of coal against the side of a freight car. I knew at once he was the player I was looking for, and I signed him then and there to a Paterson contract for a little over $100 a month."

Wagner, himself, confirms the story that Ed Barrow signed him on the railroad tracks. "Only Ed doesn't tell it all," said Honus. "He left out the best part. When we saw him come, we all ran like hell, and he had to chase us before he could get me. We thought he and his partner were a couple of railroad bulls who were trying to arrest us for throwing rocks at company property."

"Shortly after I signed Wagner, Captain Kerr, of the Pittsburgh club, sent for me and wanted to buy Honus' contract," continued Barrow. "I refused, but I told the Captain I would give him first chance at the Dutchman, if he developed. Wagner had a good season with Paterson in 1896, and a better one in 1897. By that time I had become president of the Atlantic League, but I still retained my interest in the Paterson club.

"In midseason of 1897, Harry Pulliam, who was secretary of the Colonels for Dreyfuss, offered me $2,000 for Wagner's release. In accordance with my verbal agreement with Captain Kerr, I immediately wired him of Pulliam's offer. He wired back that he would match the $2,000 Louisville offer and buy Wagner. In the meantime, Pulliam asked for a little more time. He called up Barney Dreyfuss in Louisville, and Barney authorized Harry to boost the bid by $100. I then advised Captain Kerr of the new offer. I never heard from Kerr again and don't know to this day whether he received my second wire or felt that I was playing one club against the other, which I wasn't. I really wanted to play fair with him and give him every opportunity to get this great prospect. However, not hearing from the Captain, I let Wagner go to Dreyfuss and Pulliam for $2,100.

"Yet, there seems a certain justice that Wagner should have spent his greatest years in Pittsburgh, because he was headed for the Pirates almost from the time I first signed him."

2

Wagner was born in what was formerly Mansfield, Pa., on February 24, 1874. Oddly enough, the great player's birthday was only a day later than that of the man for whom he worked during his entire major-league career, Barney Dreyfuss. The elder Wagners were born in Germany, and the family's name for John Peter was "Hans" or "Johannes," German terms for John. Hence the Honus, the name by which Wagner was known to millions of fans. Later on, as his infield wizardry made him his league's outstanding ball player, writers and the fans also referred to him as "The Flying Dutchman." To such intimates as Fred Clarke, Tommy Leach, and Kitty Bransfield, he was usually just plain "Dutch."

Honus went to work at the early age of twelve in the coal mines and industrial plants of western Pennsylvania, but he was happy only in the great outdoors. All five of the Wagner brothers played baseball, and used to have a Wagner Brothers ball club.

"That's how I could play all positions," Hans later confessed. "On our family team you had to know how to play everywhere, as we always were shifting."

In naming Wagner as his candidate for baseball's greatest all-time player, Barrow stressed the Dutchman's versatility. "He became baseball's greatest shortstop, because he eventually helped his club most in that position. But had Honus remained at third base, first base, or the outfield, he could have been just as great in those positions."

The late John J. McGraw, of the Giants, who also had Honus first on his all-time player list, also stressed Wagner's ability to play anywhere. Tommy Leach lists Wagner first also; for many years he was Wagner's distinguished fellow player in Louisville and Pittsburgh. "I saw Wagner play every position but pitcher and catcher, and it would have made no difference where Honus finally settled," said Tommy. "He was just a standout, towering over any other player of the past or present."

The Wagner brothers also had a family basketball quintet and for twenty years Honus played professional basketball during the winters, much to the distress of Barney Dreyfuss. He used to report for baseball in the spring, his hulking body covered with "wire burns," the result of rubbing his huge frame against the wires of the early basketball cages. Dreyfuss had a great dread his star would suffer a cracked knee, or other lasting injury.

"Barney used to fret about my basketball playing," recalls Hans. "I would tell him ball players, especially a big fellow like me, needed a lot of winter exercise to keep from getting soft. But he was always afraid I'd damage a knee. He kicked so much that I asked him to come out some night and see me play. Basketball was just a sport for me, and I got a lot of fun out of it. After Barney came to see me, he still objected, but not so strongly, and let me play." But, eventually, late in Wagner's career, Dreyfuss won his point.

While Ed Barrow signed Wagner for Paterson, Honus' big-league springboard in 1896, the hefty Dutchman had collected a few hundred dollars for playing ball before that. He played semipro ball around Carnegie and hooked up briefly with

Mansfield, Ohio, of the Ohio State League. There John Peter did everything but catch, and frequently took his turn on the mound. However, his first real baseball employer was the late George Moreland, well-known Pittsburgh baseball figure, first as a club owner-manager of teams in the western Pennsylvania-Ohio steel, coal, and oil belt, and later as one of the country's foremost baseball statisticians.

Moreland had Al Wagner on his Steubenville club of the Tri-State League in 1895, and things weren't going well. Al suggested to George that he engage his kid brother, Hans, to help out.

"What does he play?" asked George.

"You can play him anywhere," shot back Al.

"Oh, he's that kind of a player," said Moreland, unimpressed. "A Jack-of-all-trades and a master of none. I've seen that kind of ball player before."

"But, you haven't seen Hans," Al insisted.

Steubenville wasn't too far from Mansfield, Pa., so Moreland told Al he could send for his younger brother. The next morning, when Moreland came down for breakfast, there was Hans in the hotel lobby, his uniform wrapped up in a newspaper parcel. He hadn't even waited for a passenger train but came by hopping a freight.

Moreland put Hans in left field that day, saying "because I had to put nine men in the field." Hans had no shoes and played in his stocking feet, but the pitchers on the other side couldn't get him out. He also played shortstop for Moreland at Steubenville and hit .402 in 44 games. Wagner also played 20 games that season for Adrian in the Michigan State League, and after the Steubenville club blew, his last 65 contests for Warren, Pa., in the Iron-Oil League. A teammate on the Warren team was Claude Ritchey, of Emlentown, Pa., who later was to play second base alongside Honus for many years, on the Pirates. The Flying Dutchman played in three leagues in 1895, and then, in the 21 seasons from 1897 to 1917, in only one—the venerable old National.

3

Wagner, perhaps the greatest of right-handed hitters, was eight times National League batting champion, the last time when he was 37 years of age, in 1911. He put almost as many records in the National League book as did Ty Cobb in the American, though that amazing little Giant, Mel Ott, knocked out a number of Wagner records in recent years. Even so, Honus has many of the most important ones left: playing in the most National League games, 2,785; was the most times at bat, 10,427; cracked out the most hits, 3,430; for the most total bases, 4,888, as he led the old league in singles, 2,426, doubles, 651, and triples, 252. His lifetime batting average through 21 National League seasons was .329. And as evidence that he whacked the stars as freely as the bushers, he hit the great Christy Mathewson for .324 in the 327 times he faced him, and .356 in 135 times at bat against Brooklyn's immortal southpaw, Nap Rucker.

Wagner never knew what it was to finish under .300 in his minor- or major-league career until he was 40 years old. Hitting, with him, was a gift and his great proficiency was due to his patience and faithful practice. Yet hitting with him was sheer fun, whether in a league game or in batting practice. He was never happier than when he had a bat in his hand.

It wasn't often that the Pennsylvania Dutchman fell into a batting slump. When one gripped him it was usually of brief duration, and Honus had his cure. "When I'd stop hitting, I'd look down at my feet and see what was wrong," he said. "I'd shift my feet a bit, and then the hits would start coming again."

There are numerous good anecdotes about pitchers trying to find Wagner's weakness. John McGraw, who as Giant manager tried for years to find something that John Peter couldn't hit, told a number of them. And there was no man who had a greater admiration for the Dutchman than McGraw.

A brash young pitcher who had just joined the Giants had been called to the mound in the late innings in a game against the Pirates. Wagner was coming up, and as the kid left the bench he inquired of McGraw, "What shall I pitch to him?"

"Just pitch—and then duck," advised McGraw.

Another McGraw story was of a pitcher named "Crazy" Schmidt, who was briefly with Baltimore in the old twelve-club National League. Wagner at the time was still with Louisville. Having none too good a memory, but wishing to succeed in the majors, Schmidt kept a notebook in which he wrote down the weaknesses of National League batsmen.

As Wagner came to the plate, Schmidt pulled the book from his hip pocket and began thumbing the pages. McGraw, the

Oriole third baseman, walked over to the pitcher's box and asked: "Well, have you found the Dutchman's weakness?"

Schmidt put a fat thumb on one of the pages and replied: "It says here, give him a base on balls."

Wagner never hit .400 in the majors; his high was .381 in 1900, when he won his first National League batting crown. While Wagner frequently led his league in doubles and triples, he was never much of a home-run hitter. During his entire career he batted against the old dead ball, and against the trick deliveries permitted prior to 1920. Only twice did he hit as many as ten home runs. Yet there were times when he'd get his near-200-pound chassis behind a swing and really smack that old mushy pellet. Poll Perritt, former Giant pitcher, used to tell of a homer that the mighty John hit against his delivery: "I threw Wagner a fast ball and was still in my follow-through, with my arm extended in front of me, when the ball came back at me like a rifle bullet. I couldn't have ducked if I tried, but fortunately the ball sailed under my arm and then began to rise, and cleared the center-field fence."

After his retirement from active play, Honus expressed the wish that he might have played long enough to get a crack at the Jack-rabbit ball that came in with the Babe Ruth home-run era. "I used to do pretty well," said John, "but I'd like to have had a few cracks at that lively ball. Even so, I don't think I would have had too many home runs. I wasn't that kind of a hitter. I didn't lift a ball the way Babe Ruth did, but was more of a line-drive hitter."

4

Wagner was a bulging, squat giant, with a wide, thick chest, and legs so bowed one could have rolled a barrel through them. Weighing around 190 pounds, he had big awkward-looking feet, and great gangling gorilla-like arms. The arms hung loosely hinged from his wide shoulders and from the ends dangled great hams of hands.

Looking at the man, one got the idea that he possessed great strength but that he was clumsy and awkward. Yet Hans could have taken on his famous fellow star, the graceful Nap Lajoie, in a foot race, and beaten him by yards in a 100-yard-dash, or a sprint around the bases. He moved with the speed of a large bear, and it was something to see those bowlegs move around the bases, a treat present-day fans can only imagine. One had to see it to appreciate Wagner. He led his league in stolen bases almost as often as in hitting, stealing 720 bases, with a high of 61 in 1907, when the big fellow was 34 years old. Only the deer-limbed Ty Cobb, Eddie Collins, and Pittsburgh's own Max Carey excelled Honus in wholesale base larcenies in the last half century.

He wasn't as ruthless a base runner as Ty Cobb and he never deliberately injured a fellow player. But like players of his day, he kept his spikes filed to a razor's edge, and when he was under way, it took a hardy infielder to block his path. Powerful as a gorilla and hard as nails from his winter basketball and summer baseball, when he got into motion he generated the momentum of a runaway locomotive on a downgrade.

Honus was spiked frequently but rarely took time out for an injury. That would have been being a sissy. From 1898, his first complete National League season, to 1916, his last regular season, he fell under the record of 123 games only once, playing 113 in 1914. But as late as 1915, when he was in his nineteenth season in the National League, at the age of 41, he played in every one of his team's 156 games.

After playing all outfield positions, third base, and first base in his seasons in Louisville and early years in Pittsburgh, Wagner finally settled at shortstop in the latter part of the 1902 season, and he then played there for the better part of sixteen seasons. Of all positions, shortstop was the one in which he could use his uncanny skill to the best advantage. With those long arms and great baskets of hands, he seemed to draw balls to him like a magnet. It made no difference whether they were on the ground, or in the air, in back of third base, the outfield grass, or over second base, Honus was there. They still tell a story in Pittsburgh how Wagner slipped in the river mud in old Exposition Park, and while sitting on the ground threw out his man at first base.

Honus recalls some of his early difficulties with rough boys in the league. "I had been in the league only a short while, when we were playing Baltimore," he reminisced. "They used to call them the rowdy Orioles, and they weren't fooling. I hit a long ball deep into the outfield and should have made an easy home run out of it, but when I got to first base, Jack Doyle gave me the hip and Heinie Reitz almost killed me when I rounded second. Hughie Jennings tripped me at short, and when I got to third John

McGraw was waiting for me with a shotgun. I did well to get a triple out of it.

"After the game, Fred Clarke, our manager, said to me: 'What the hell kind of a way is that to play baseball? Letting everybody kick you around! If you can't do any better than that, you won't be with us when we leave Baltimore the day after tomorrow.'

"So the next day I hit a ball down to McGraw, and it was a close play at first. But if Doyle had any idea of giving me the works again, I beat him to it. I banged into him with my shoulder and knocked him into right field. McGraw's throw sailed into the outfield and finally bounded into a stand, and it worked the same as a home run. After I scored and returned to the bench, Fred Clarke smiled his approval: 'That's the way to play the game, Dutch,' he said. 'Make 'em respect you.'

"Around the same time, with a man on base, Fred says: 'Lay one down.'

"Well, I see a fat pitch coming up and I think it's too good to pass up. I line it over the fence for a home run. As I round third, I see Clarke coming out from the bench, and he meets me at the plate as I score. I think he is going to congratulate me, but he bawls me out: 'Hey, you Dutchman, didn't I tell you to bunt? We obey orders on this club, and that hit over the fence will cost you twenty-five dollars.'

"But I said: 'What d'you mean bunt? I don't know what a bunt is. I've been around for only a week.'

"I talked him out of the fine, and about a week later I came up with runners on base. Clarke said: 'Bunt another one for me, Dutch.' Then he gives me the wink, and I know he means for me to give it the business."

5

As a player John Wagner was modest and shy, almost to a fault. As a present-day Pirate coach, he is a more loquacious fellow than when he was the National League's top star. Honus didn't like swell hotels, or restaurants where they served a lot of fancy food. He wanted a place where he could get his teeth into a good steak without a lot of trimmings, corned beef and cabbage, and such dishes as Mama Wagner used to cook in Mansfield.

After Wagner had won six batting championships, the National League wanted to honor John Peter at its annual meeting in

New York in 1909, but had a difficult time inducing Honus to come east for the meeting. "I'm a hitter, not a speaker," he protested. While he was at the very apex of his career, a New York newspaper sent one of its ace sports writers to see Wagner and get an interview. It was a hot, sultry summer night, and Honus had his bath tub filled with ice and beer bottles. "Help yourself," said the Flying Dutchman, but he was freer with his beer than his conversation.

He said that in his early days in the league ball players weren't much for conversation, on his own club as well as others. "Why, I was three years in the league before ball players began speaking to me, and then not too nice, either," he reminisced.

"I remember when I was playing third base for Louisville, we had a game with the Giants. Jot Gore, one of the New York outfielders, belted his second home run of the game. As he was passing third, I said to him, 'Nice hit.' He looked around at me and yelled back, 'Go to—.'

"However, I always considered Barney Dreyfuss my pal. I could talk to him, and frequently he would come to me and discuss young players, asking: 'How do you like that young pitcher?' or 'Do you think our new outfielder has it?' "

Present-day top-ranking players make fortunes in their by-products. Babe Ruth made as much money on the side as he collected in his princely big-league salaries. Bobbie Feller doesn't overlook a bet in capitalizing on his fame as a pitcher, and after he lost his big baseball pay during four wartime years, no one can blame him. Yet Wagner seemed to think it was below his dignity to capitalize on his fame as a ball player.

At a time when vaudeville was in its heyday, and Wagner was champion batsman of the National League, and Ty Cobb and Nap Lajoie the great batting rivals of the American, a theatrical manager tried to build up a postseason act featuring Honus, Ty, and Nap. He made the two American Leaguers flattering offers, provided they could get Wagner. When they wrote to Wagner, he replied, "Not interested," even though it would have meant nearly $1,000 a week for him.

Lajoie then called on Honus and pointed out it would be easy money, picked up with little effort. All they were asking of Wagner was to appear on the stage, say a few words, take three swings, and wallop a phony ball into the wings. "It's no use, Nap," he replied. "I'm a ball player, not an actor."

Likewise he turned down an offer to pose as manager of the men's furnishing department of a Pittsburgh department store during the off season. Honus could have made his own hours, as long as he showed up once a day. But again the answer was a polite but positive No.

Nor would he endorse cigarettes or tobacco. A tobacco company once asked John Gruber, for many years the Pirates' official scorer, whether he could get Wagner's permission to use his picture in connection with some cards inside the package. They offered Gruber ten dollars if he could get Wagner's signature.

Wagner sent Gruber a note: "Dear John: I don't want my picture in cigarettes, but I don't want you to lose the ten dollars, so I am sending you a check for that sum."

Gruber framed the check, and it hung in his den until the day he died.

Wagner remained a bachelor until near the end of his playing career, December 30, 1916, when he married Miss Bessie B. Smith, who has been a fine companion in his latter years. Since returning to the Pirates as a coach, he has lost much of his shyness as a player, and is more of a mixer. He now goes to baseball dinners and has lost his fear of the dais. In fact, he has won new fame as a storyteller and likes to entertain young Pittsburgh players with his tall tales. And John has told them some lollapaloosas.

There is the story of Wagner's minor-league days, when the batter hit a terrific drive over the center-field fence. The center fielder backed helplessly to the boards and sorrowfully saw the ball sail out of the yard. But it seems a railroad train was passing at the time, and the ball dropped into the engine's smokestack. Just around that time, the engineer (maybe it was Honus' brother, Al) gave his locomotive a little more steam. With the first puff of smoke, the ball was coughed up again. The locomotive puffed and huffed, and pretty soon it coughed the ball right back into the baseball orchard, where the outfielder caught it for as pretty a put-out as anyone had ever seen. What's more Honus insists it actually happened.

Even that isn't the craziest thing that Wagner says he saw happen. His version of this battiest incident follows: "I hit a drive to left field, and the left fielder jumped up the screen to get the ball. The ball struck about two inches above his outstretched glove, and bounded back on the field. I looked up as I reached second, thinking the hit was good for a double, but I see that outfielder still on the screen as though he is nailed there. He's cussin' and shoutin' and trying to shake himself loose. Well, before anyone else can recover the ball, I've stretched it into a home run. You wanna know what happened to that outfielder? When he jumped up for the ball, his belt caught on a wire, and there he stayed until someone pried him loose."

When Zack Taylor, the former catcher, joined the Pirates as coach in 1947, Honus, without cracking a smile, said: "It's easy to get to the park nowadays, ain't it? Back in the days when we played in Allegheny, I used to ride to our old Exposition Park on horseback. One day that darn horse wouldn't get on the ferry boat, so I rode him right into the river and made him swim across, with me on top of him."

Then he regaled Zack with a tale of his first automobile: "It was so high I could look into everybody's second-story windows as I drove by. And it had five hundred pounds of tools in it. And whenever we bounced over a trolley track, the tools rattled more'n the car."

Arthur Daley, the *New York Times*' able sports columnist, quotes a Pirate rookie as saying: "Mr. Wagner, I don't think I can believe your stories."

"That may be so, sonny," replied Hans, "but I never told you anything that you can't repeat to your mother."

VII. FRED THE FEARLESS

THREE YEARS BEFORE Barney Dreyfuss bought Honus Wagner for the Louisville club, he acquired a player who was as vital to the success of later-day Pittsburgh teams as the mighty Honus —Fred Clarke, the team's Hall of Fame left fielder and dynamic playing manager.

It is almost uncanny how many great players were influenced by Ed Barrow in the former Yankee president's eventful career. As a young man in his early twenties, Barrow was circulation manager of the *Des Moines Leader,* and one of the kids who had a paper route was an untiring lad named Fred Clarke.

"I've an amusing recollection of the time I worked for Ed Barrow," recalled the seventy-three-year-old present-day rancher and oil man. "We were all waiting in an alley for our papers, when another kid and I got into a fight. I pushed him through a window. It cost thirty-five cents, and though that seemed an awful lot of money at the time, Ed made me pay every penny of it."

To create interest among his seventeen route boys, Barrow got up a team called the Stars, and entered it into the Des Moines City League.

"Fred Clarke played one of the outfield positions and from the start displayed a real knack for hitting the ball," said Barrow. "My brother, George, caught for the Stars. I managed, and also tried to pitch, and played first base. Around 1892 Fred and George Barrow decided they were good enough for a try at pro ball, and landed in the old Nebraska State League. Fred made it, but my brother soon returned home and obtained what he thought would prove a steadier job."

Fred himself said he landed his first baseball berth through the want column of the *Sporting News*. "I got the job through the ad I inserted, offering my services as a player," he said. "The Hastings, Nebraska, club answered my advertisement and offered me forty dollars a month.

"They put me in the outfield, and I was lucky to catch half of the drives they hit out to me. I found pro ball a little tougher than when I played with Ed Barrow's carrier team in Des Moines. I still wonder how a manager, even in a league deep down in the sticks, could put up with such a terrible outfielder. An old-timer told me I could improve my fielding with practice, so I went out to the ball field at 8 o'clock in the morning and practiced until game time in the afternoon. And eventually I reached a point where I could catch fly balls pretty well.

"My early experience in Hastings proved one of my most unpleasant in baseball. The league blew up in July, and when it did, I had overdrawn my small pay by seven dollars. The manager told me if I would give him my personal note for fifteen dollars, he would give me a ticket home to Des Moines. But as soon as I put my signature on the note, he told me I could go to the hot spot. Was I sore? Probably the sorest young pup in all Nebraska. In my long career in baseball, that is the only obligation I ever owed. And I'll continue to owe it as long as I live."

By this time Fred had professional baseball in his blood and wanted more of it. He started the 1893 season with St. Joseph, Mo., a team which played under the co-operative system, but in midseason Clarke received an offer from John McCloskey, then managing Montgomery, Alabama, in the Southern League. Afterward Clarke and Honest John were rival managers in the National League.

Clarke was to see another league collapse from under his feet in his second year as a pro. "When I landed in Montgomery, I received $100 in advance, on arrival, and put $50 in the bank to be sure I would have a ticket home in an emergency," related Fred. "While we were playing in New Orleans, yellow fever broke out in Montgomery. We started back but were forced off the train at Mobile, where armed men prevented anyone from going to Montgomery. We played ten days in Mobile, when we finally were permitted to board a train for Montgomery. However, it was not permitted to go into the station. A horse-drawn bus met us about ten miles outside of town, and finally got us into the plague-stricken city. We got back on a Monday, only to receive more bad news. The league had folded up because of the yellow fever scare, and the bank in which I had deposited my $50 closed on the preceding Saturday. But by the next Saturday, the St. Joe club wired me transportation, and I was able to finish the season with that club."

It was around this time that baseball almost lost Fred Clarke. The Cherokee strip was opened September 16, 1893, and Fred, later the intrepid base runner, was on hand early to make the run into the strip. However, other horses were faster than the young ball player's steed, and he didn't get there "fustest, with the mostest men." "I know now I was lucky I didn't get a claim," Fred says today. "If I had, it would have been necessary for me to remain in Oklahoma and prove the claim, and I would have missed the big opportunity which professional baseball gave me, and my rich experiences and contacts with the old Louisville Colonels and the Pirates."

The Southern League was reorganized in 1894, and this time McCloskey had the Savannah club, and he asked Clarke to go with him to the Georgia cotton port. Barney Dreyfuss' notebook showed that Fred was hitting .311 for 54 games, when the league again ran into midseason difficulties. Barney had some business in Memphis, and there came across his old friend, the unhappy John McCloskey. John unburdened his tale of woe. His team had experienced a terrible trip, and he was in such financial straits that he was at his wit's end to find a way of getting the squad back to Savannah.

"I'll try to help you, Mac," said the sympathetic Dreyfuss. "You have a young outfielder named Clarke, who looks like he might develop into a good ball player. Now I'll pay the fare for your entire ball team from here to Savannah, if you are willing to turn this boy over to me." Honest John snatched the offer, and Dreyfuss bought the railroad tickets for a sum slightly under $200. Clarke thus became the property of the National League Colonels.

When Dreyfuss acquired Clarke it was with the stipulation that the young outfielder was to receive a $100 bonus, provided he reported within five days. Fred saw to it that he was in Louisville well before the five days were up.

Arriving in the Louisville club's apology for a clubhouse, Fred was handed one of Barney Dreyfuss' Colonel uniforms, which fitted him like an oversized Mother Hubbard. Fred put it on, and then asked the Louisville manager, Bill Barnie, for his $100. Barnie wrote out a check, but the Savannah recruit said he had found paper and promises as good as worthless on three different teams and now he was determined to have greenbacks or nothing. "But Mr. Dreyfuss' name is on the check," said Barnie.

"All the same I want it in money that I can feel," persisted Fred.

Barnie grumbled but eventually dug up enough small bills to make up the $100; Fred still didn't trust those Colonels, so he pinned the bills in the pants' pocket of his uniform.

Fred Clarke was only twenty-one when he played his first National League game, June 30, 1894. Louisville was playing the Phillies, a strong club, with an especially powerful array of hitters—Ed Delahanty, Sam Thompson, Lave Cross, and Billy Hamilton. Nap Lajoie hadn't yet joined the club, but there was dynamite in the bats of Arthur Irwin's warriors. In those days a rookie was received on a ball club with the same degree of enthusiasm as though he had reported with smallpox. Fred had brought along a small bat from Savannah.

Gus Weyhing, one of Philadelphia's better pitchers, was warming up, and older Colonels taunted Clarke with such scornful remarks as: "What are you going to do with that peashooter?" "Gus'll knock that little bat right out of your hands."

However, before the game was over, Clarke had won the respect of even those hard-boiled gladiators of the nineties. Few big-league stars ever broke in with such gusto. In five times up the youth from Des Moines banged out five hits, including a triple. When the game was over, Fred carried his little bat into the clubhouse, threw it to the floor with a resounding crash, and then called out for all to hear: "You don't need a big bat to hit those bushers."

The Louisville players were largely older men and most of them were drinkers. The kid from Des Moines felt he had to do as they did in order to be "one of the boys."

"It was still a time when young ball players were supposed to be seen—not heard," recalled Fred. "I would sit and drink and would never say a word until it became my turn to order another round of drinks. But I realized I was going badly, and not helping myself.

"Barney Dreyfuss recognized it, too, and he called me into his office. He didn't lecture me, merely said: 'Fred, you know if a man goes into any kind of a business and neglects it, it will surely go to the dogs.' Then without saying another word, he left me.

"I couldn't get it out of my mind and I lay awake thinking about it most of the following night. Then at last I got his full meaning. I went to see him the next day, and said: 'From now on, Mr. Dreyfuss, it will be business.' And from that day on I never again neglected business, whether it was baseball or any later activity. I do not think any employer ever gave a young player better counsel."

From the start, Fred Clarke was a fearless, intrepid, inspired player. He played ball much as did Ty Cobb some years later. A league race was a miniature war, and each ball game a battle. Fred played his baseball hard, and to win. With his native intuition Barney Dreyfuss recognized that Clarke was a player out of the ordinary, a natural-born leader. By the time Ed Barrow's former route boy was only twenty-four, Dreyfuss promoted him to the management of the Colonels.

Yet Fred wasn't exactly a boy manager. He had come up the hard way, and at twenty-four he was already a mature fighting man. Perhaps nothing tells better the story of Fred Clarke and how he reacted to leadership and authority than the fact that in 1897, his first managerial year, he had the highest batting average of his career—.406.

2

When Clarke took over the merged Louisville and Pittsburgh clubs in the spring of 1900, he naturally favored his former Colonel athletes. The players retained from the 1899 Pittsburgh club were: Pitchers Jack Chesbro, Jesse Tannehill, and Sam Leever; Catcher Pop Shriver; Infielders Fred Ely, Frank Dillon, and Jimmy Williams, and Outfielders Ginger Beaumont, Tom McCreery, and Tom O'Brien, the latter recalled from New York.

Barney peddled off some of the Pirate players he took over for the best prices they would bring in the streamlined eight-club league. Outfielder Jack McCarthy brought the best figure, $2,000, when he was sold to Chicago, and Frank Robison, Cardinal owner, paid $1,000 for Patsy Donovan, the former Pirate manager–right fielder. Catcher Frank Bowerman was sold to the Giants and soon became Christy Mathewson's battery mate. Ban Johnson's Western League had just changed its name to the American League and had placed clubs in Chicago and Cleveland. The new loop was still a high-class minor league, but it was strengthening and shopped at Barney's bargain basement; Connie Mack bought Pitcher Frank Sparks and Second Baseman Heinie Reitz, the former Oriole, for his Milwaukee club; Cleveland took Pitcher Bill Hoffer, and Kansas City invested $750 in Pitcher George Gray.

Even so, at the start of the 1900 training season Clarke was left with twenty-six players, far more than a big-league club could afford at that time. Lou Deal, Fred Ketcham, Elton Cunningham, Mike Kelly, Tom Massitt, and Doyle, Louisville acquisitions, gradually were sifted out, and by May, Dillon, a Pirate holdover, was sold to the American League club in Detroit. Cunningham, a pony pitcher known as "Cunny," was hawked to Chicago and later became an umpire. He left with considerable ill feeling and for years held a grudge against Dreyfuss for not keeping him on the merged club. During the 1900 season, Catcher Jack O'Connor, hard-boiled St. Louisan, was acquired from the Cardinals. Jack and Pat Tebeau, St. Louis' first baseman-manager, were both products of the Mound City's tough Goose Hill district, and when Robison fired Pat as manager, he also had to get rid of O'Connor. The burly catcher became Jack Chesbro's favorite receiver.

Yet the backbone of the new Pirates was the Louisville acquisitions. In addition to the two standouts, Wagner and Clarke, the most interesting figures were: Claude Ritchey, the second baseman who had played with Honus five years before, in Warren; Tommy Leach, pint-sized third baseman; Deacon Charley Phillippe, lionhearted right-hander, and Rube Waddell, who was to become the game's greatest southpaw.

Leach, known as Tommy the Wee and still interested in baseball in Haines City, Florida, had hit .289 for Louisville in 106 games in 1899, but Clarke couldn't find an immediate spot for him in his remodeled Pirate line-up. Tommy, a five-foot, six-and-a-half-inch, 150-pound runt from French Creek, N. Y., was another of Barney's big bargains. In 1898 Leach had played for the late John Farrell at Auburn, New York, then in the old New York State League. Tommy hit .325 and was a nimble acrobat around third base. Farrell induced Andy Freedman, the Giant owner, to take Leach on a two weeks' trial. Freedman returned Thomas with a note to Farrell: "Take your boy back before he gets hurt. We don't play midgets on the Giants."

However, Tommy's .325 Auburn average was entered in Barney's dope book, and after New York returned the runt, Dreyfuss picked him up for $650.

If the Louisville players sent no reception committees to greet Fred Clarke and Hans Wagner, they were even less considerate of little Tommy. Whatever honors that came to Leach in later years were won against almost insurmountable obstacles.

"When I broke into the National League it was a case of fight your way in—and I mean fight," said Tommy. "We had to furnish our own bats, as well as gloves and shoes, and the only batting practice a rookie could get was to squeeze it in somewhere between morning practice and the afternoon game. And then you almost had to bribe somebody to pitch to you.

"It was a thrill when Clarke said to me, 'I want you to play third base today.' I had the bat that I brought from Auburn, and I was lucky enough to get two hits. The next day I came to the park early and thought maybe I would be permitted to take batting practice with the regulars. Instead I found my bat had been sawed into three pieces and lay in the bottom of my locker. I never found out who did it, which probably was just as well. I wasn't big, but I believe I would have crowned him with Wagner's hefty bat."

A smile still plays around Tommy's weather-beaten face, as he recalls his early difficulty in getting into National League parks. No one would believe he was a player. "When I first came into the league, we still dressed in our hotels and made the trip to the ball park in a bus," recalled Tommy. "New York was the exception; they already had a dressing room for the visiting players, and when we played the Giants we used to get into uniform right up there at the Polo Grounds.

"As most players were fairly good-sized fellows, I used to wait for some of the older Pirates and go into the park with them. However, one day the other men got in ahead of me, and I boldly approached the player's gate with my uniform roll tucked under my arm. The man stopped me and asked: 'Whose uniform are you carrying?'

"I told him it was my own. That annoyed him and he said: 'Just for being a fresh kid, I won't let you in, and you can stay there until the owner of the uniform comes out for it.'

"I tried to get him to send someone to the clubhouse to identify me, but he merely laughed. He still thought I was trying some trick to get in without paying. I must have been out there nearly an hour, when one of the New York players who came along late, passed through the gate. I told him my troubles, and the gateman finally let me in, though he still wouldn't believe I was a ball player.

"When I finally got into the park, Fred Clarke asked: 'Where the devil have you been? I ought to fine you for being late.' I'll tell you I never tried to go through that New York gate alone after that."

Both the cities of Louisville and Pittsburgh saw Rube Waddell, when that impish son of nature was only a few years out of his father's farm near Butler, Pa. Clarke saw Waddell's possibilities, but it took Connie Mack, the early Pirate manager, to bring out Rube's great ability in Philadelphia. By nature Connie Mack had more patience to deal with a character such as Rube than the energetic, hot-tempered Clarke.

Oddly enough, it was while Connie was still manager of the Pirates that he first knew of Rube. Waddell was then twenty and had already piled up a mess of sensational strike-outs around Butler. Rube had written Mack in his large, boyish handwriting that he was just the pitcher to lift the Pirates out of the rut.

Connie recalls mounting the stairs to see Captain Kerr, and in place of his usual taciturn face, the Pirate boss was grinning from ear to ear. "Did you notice a big fellow on your way up?" he asked Mack.

"Yes," replied Connie, "I passed him on the stairs."

"Well, he was Rube Waddell's father," laughed Kerr. "He told me to pay no attention to his boy, because Rube is screwy. The father told me he knew that to be a fact because he was screwy himself."

Pittsburgh then passed up Waddell, but Rube continued his parade of strike-out victims. In 1897 he had a great season with a strong, independent club at Franklin, Pa. Dreyfuss, still in

Louisville, heard of his feats, entered Rube's name in his dope book, and had Clarke offer him a contract.

"I won't sign unless I get twenty-five dollars a game," Rube wired.

Clarke wired back: "We'll give you $500 for the rest of the season." Rube's eyes popped at all of that money, and he readily accepted.

He reported to the Louisville club in Washington at 2 A.M. The drowsy clerk told him Fred Clarke didn't wish to be disturbed, but Rube demanded to know the manager's room number. Locating the room, he pounded on Clarke's door, calling out: "It's Waddell, reporting."

"Go away and introduce yourself to the other players," said Clarke.

Rube was back in an hour and a half. "I did what you told me, Fred," he said. "I waked them all up except the man in Room 128. You better find out what's wrong with him—maybe he's dead." (Room 128 was occupied by Dummy Hoy, the Colonels' deaf-mute outfielder.)

Rube pitched a few late-season games for Louisville in 1897, but Clarke got fed up with his peccadilloes and sent him to Detroit in 1898. After Rube was fined there on Clarke's order, the left-hander jumped the club, to hang up a new succession of strike-outs in Ontario. By 1899 he was hitting his real stride and had a record of twenty-six games won and eight lost for Columbus and Grand Rapids of the Western (later American) League. Recalled by Dreyfuss late in the season, he won seven out of nine games for the Colonels. As a consequence, he was considered quite an asset at the time of the 1900 Louisville-Pittsburgh merger.

VIII. NEW COMBINATION QUICKLY CLICKS

WHEN CLARKE finally got his 1900 line-up straightened out, the batting order he handed to the umpires was: Beaumont, center fielder; Clarke, left field; Williams, third base; Wagner, right field; Cooley, first base; Ritchey, second base; O'Connor, Shriver, and Zimmer, catchers; Ely, shortstop, and the pitcher. Later in the season Wagner moved in to third base, with McCreery in right field, while Tom O'Brien saw service in the outfield and first base. Wee Tommy Leach took part in only 45 games, mostly at third base, and the big boys almost had the little guy down, as Tommy hit only .215. It looked as though Andy Freedman might be right.

It was a joyous season for Pittsburgh fans, the most enjoyable they had had up to that time. It didn't take long for Barney and Clarke to click in Exposition Park, and they broke into Pittsburgh with a strong second-place club, a bright augury of what was to come. It was first division from the very start, and at the end of May the Pirates ran fourth to Philadelphia, Brooklyn, and St. Louis with a satisfactory .556. By June 30, Brooklyn had moved up to the front, and the Pirates had ousted the Cardinals from third place. At the end of July the Freebooters still ran third, but in August, Clarke's aggressive team moved ahead of Philadelphia into the runner-up spot and held it for the balance of the season. The Pirates had the league's best monthly performances in August and September, 13-10 and 18-9, respectively. At the finish the champion Brooklyns, led by Ned Hanlon, the old Pirate, had 82 victories and 54 defeats. Fighting the Dodgers to the last ditch, the second-place Pirates came across the wire with 79 wins and 60 reverses.

Clarke had superb pitching, with Tannehill, the left-hander, showing the way with 20 victories and 7 defeats. Deacon Phillippe had an 18-15 record, and both Sam Leever and Jack Chesbro hung up the same performance—15-13. Rube Waddell broke even in 20 games, and Dreyfuss' action in yanking back Rube from Mack's Milwaukee club cost Connie the 1900 American League pennant. It was the time Connie actually outsmarted himself; it almost broke his heart.

Rube became embroiled in trouble with Clarke early in the season and jumped the Pirates to hitch up with an independent team at Punxsutawney, Pa., where 20 strikeout games soon were a commonplace. Mack had a good team in Milwaukee but needed another starting pitcher. Tom Loftus, an old baseball character, tipped off Mack to Waddell's doings in Punxsutawney and remarked: "He's just the pitcher to give your club the pennant."

Mack knew that under baseball law Waddell was Pittsburgh's property, so his first step was to call on Dreyfuss and ask permission to dicker with Rube.

"Fred can't do anything with Rube; if you can manage him, you're welcome to Waddell," said Barney.

Connie next snared Rube out of Punxsutawney, though he had to get Waddell's watch out of hock, settle his restaurant, bar, and haberdashery bills, and pay express charges for a dog sent to Rube C.O.D.

Rube was an immediate success in Milwaukee, and his strong pitching soon had the Brewers fighting for the pennant with Comiskey's White Sox. Mack probably could have kept the Rube for the season if he hadn't overdone it. Milwaukee and the White Sox met in an important double-header, and Waddell won the first game in seventeen innings, and helped win his own game with a triple. When Rube struck out the last batsman, he was so elated that he turned handsprings all the way from the pitcher's box to the bench.

Comiskey had suggested that in view of the long first game, the second be limited to five innings. That gave Mack an idea. If Rube still felt so frisky after those seventeen innings, why not send him after the second game? Rube was a great fisherman, and while in Milwaukee one of his favorite spots was Pewaukee

Lake in Wisconsin. "Rube, how would you like to go to Pewaukee for a few days instead of going to Kansas City?" asked Mack. "Pitch the second game and win it for us, and you can have a few days off, and can rejoin us in Indianapolis."

"Give me that ball," said Rube. He pitched the second five-inning game. But that's where Mack blundered. The Associated Press gave little attention to the American League at that time, but when Waddell won two games in one day, including a seventeen-inning effort, they made quite a story of it. It was even featured in Pittsburgh, where Barney read it in his morning newspaper. By this time the Pirates had moved into second place and were daily hacking away at Brooklyn's lead.

"Hey, we need that Waddell ourselves," Barney said to Harry Pulliam. "He's not helping us win pennants by pitching doubleheaders for Connie Mack. Wire Mack that we need Waddell ourselves, and have Rube report to Fred Clarke in Boston."

Mack would rather have given up his eyeteeth than lose Waddell, but he knew the big left-hander was Dreyfuss' baseball property, and Barney was within his rights in recalling him. Sorrowfully he wired Rube at Pewaukee to report to the Pirates in the East.

Waddell wired back: "I won't report to the Pirates, and I won't pitch for Fred Clarke. I'll see you in Indianapolis."

Sure enough, when the Brewers reached Indianapolis, there was Rube awaiting them. Mack didn't encourage Waddell in his revolt, but when Dreyfuss wired to Connie, "Why doesn't Waddell report?" Mack wired back, "Come and get him."

Chief Zimmer, the Pirate catcher, was injured, and Dreyfuss sent him to Indianapolis to bring Rube back. Making little progress in his negotiations with Waddell, the Chief appealed to Mack. "What'll I do? Can't you help me?" he asked Connie.

"Try buying him a suit of clothes, some neckties, and fishing tackle. Maybe then you can win your way into his good graces," said Mack.

Zimmer took the advice and eventually delivered the hefty pitcher to Fred Clarke.

2

Not only were Pirate fans thrilled over the fact that Pittsburgh came home second for the second time in its National League experience, but the town also got a big boot out of having its first batting champion. It was long before the time of the most valuable player awards, and the batting crown was still the highest prize that could go to a player. And the crown was won by that doughty Dutchman from Mansfield, Hans Wagner.

Honus was then in his fourth season in the league, and his 1900 winning average of .381 was his major-league high. He had a season-long battle with Elmer Flick, of the Phillies, who five years later was to win the American League's batting title. While Wagner's eventual lead over Flick in the official averages was .381 to .374, in the early October, unofficial averages the two men were much closer, and they appeared tied on the last day of the season.

"Winning my first batting title in 1900 was my greatest thrill in baseball," recalled Honus. "The league race had been decided but there was a lot of interest in the batting championship, and it apparently hinged on what Elmer and I did on the last day. The fellows in the press box had figured we were tied and they had reports on Flick's game in Philadelphia, while I was fighting for the title at Exposition Park.

"I hit in my first time at bat, and we heard Flick did the same. He came up for his second time and was retired. So was I. We both hit in our third times up and still apparently were deadlocked. In our fourth times up we both went out. The Phillies were in a rally when Flick came up for his fifth and last try, but we got word Elmer didn't connect. But in my fifth time I cracked out a double, and they told me I had the championship by two points. It was the biggest bang of my life. But when the official averages came out, I had a seven-point margin on Flick."

Wagner was the only .300 hitter on Dreyfuss' first Pittsburgh club. Claude Ritchey, Honus' former associate in Warren, was the Pirates' second-best batter, with .295. Ginger Beaumont was next with .283, and Clarke right behind him with .281.

In addition to leading the National League at bat, Honus also showed the way in triples. For years thereafter, the Pirates were destined to be the triples leaders of their loop, winning the three-bagger crown eighteen times, as Wagner, Fred Clarke, Chief Wilson, Max Carey, Harry Hinchman, Billy Southworth, Pie Traynor, Kiki Cuyler, both of the Waners—Paul and Lloyd— Adam Comoroskey, Arky Vaughan, and Johnny Barrett each won the honor on at least one occasion.

Barney Dreyfuss' 1900 pay roll was $36,000, and no player drew over $2,400. Shortly after he took over, the young president told Fred Clarke: "I've $30,000 of my own money tied up in this thing." A quarter of a century later, when Clarke had some Oklahoma oil millionaires ready to buy the club, Barney put a $3,000,000 price on his baseball holdings.

Many years later, Barney boasted proudly: "We made $60,000 in that great second-place fight in 1900, and it was my Louisville boys who did it."

3

Dreyfuss always was a plugger for clean baseball, and frequently he had admonished the fiery Clarke: "I want a hustling, aggressive ball club, Fred, but I don't want rowdies and umpire fighters."

In a 1900 Sunday game in Chicago, Clarke twice broke up double plays, which Second Baseman Clarence Childs was trying to make. "You do that again," said Childs, who was also called Cupid, "and I'll sock you right in the nose."

"It was my 'misfortune' to have to do it again," reminisced Fred, "and Childs took a good punch at me. Naturally I hit back, and soon we were mixed up in a pretty good fight. Chicago used to be a great place to stage a fight of this kind, because the players would run in and grab you and hold you down. You would be yelling: 'Turn me loose, so I can get at him,' when you knew darned well you didn't want to be turned loose.

"Anyway, both the Chicago and Pittsburgh papers made much of it, and it just happened that we were to play the Cubs the very next day at Exposition Park. The papers all said that on our return to Pittsburgh, Childs and I would finish the fight.

"We had no sooner got off the train, when I received word that Barney wanted me to come to the office immediately. He didn't mince words but greeted me with: 'Fred, I'm tired of your rowdy tactics, and if you don't cut them out, I'll have to get rid of you.'

"I said: 'Mr. Dreyfuss, how many Monday games have we played at home this year?' He pulled out his little book in which he kept the score of games and attendances, and after thumbing through the pages replied: 'Seven. Why do you ask?'

"My comment was: 'Well, add up the crowds for the seven games, and figure out our average Monday attendance.'

"He said: 'The average is 2,200.'

"I didn't say another word, but left the office. We had a good game, before a fine Monday crowd, and beat the Cubs soundly. I was back in the office next morning, and Barney greeted me with a smile and said: 'That was a fine game yesterday.'

"Then I said: 'Yes, and a nice crowd. What was your official count?'

"He replied: '7,200.'

"I grabbed him playfully by the arm, and said: 'Barney, those rowdy tactics are just going to ruin you.' In all my long association with him thereafter, he never again criticized my aggressiveness, or my so-called 'rowdy tactics.' "

Chagrined over the loss of a tough game that season, which was in a measure due to bad baseball on the part of several Pirates, Barney came charging into the clubhouse and began bawling out the culprits. Clarke, as angry as Dreyfuss over the loss of the important game, yelled at his boss: "Get out of here, and stay out."

"What do you mean! I can't come into my own clubhouse?" Barney demanded. "Yes, that's right," Clarke repeated. "Any time you want to criticize and find fault, you call me into the office. I'll take the criticism for the team. As for the players who don't stay on their toes, they'll hear plenty from me." And, with only one or two exceptions, Dreyfuss strictly obeyed Clarke's orders to stay out of the Pirates' dressing room.

There was another occasion, however, when Barney found fault with Fred in an after-the-game post-mortem, and the manager really flared up. "We had a lot of arguments," said Clarke, "and this time I really was hot. Barney found fault with everything in general, and before we finished I had called him almost everything in the book.

"That night I got to thinking that that was no way to talk to one's boss and felt badly over the manner in which I had lost my temper. I was rather penitent next morning when I called at the office, and said: 'Barney, I am sorry for the way I acted yesterday and want to apologize.'

"He looked me over for a few moments and then said: 'Fred, I wouldn't give a darn for a fellow who always agrees with me.' "

4

With the club now well in the black, there was repeated friction during the season between the two interests, one led by Dreyfuss, the other by Captain Kerr. By nature Barney was assertive, if not domineering, and Kerr wasn't one who could play second fiddle. Yet Barney felt the new success of the Pirates was largely his doing. The club at the time had 500 shares of stock, with a par of $100 a share. An individual share was priced at $600.

The fight at first centered on secretary Harry Pulliam, who was Dreyfuss' man on the club. "Everyone felt, after our 1900 finish, we would win the 1901 pennant," related Barney in later years. "I could feel that the former owners were intent on freezing out Harry Pulliam and myself from the organization. For some reason or other, they didn't like Harry [he no doubt was too loyal to Dreyfuss] and wanted to fire him. I, on the other hand, was determined he should stay. The showdown supposedly was to come at a stockholders' meeting in December.

"We were a New Jersey corporation, and proceeded to Jersey City for our annual meeting. In the face of my opposition, the Kerr faction decided to abandon their plans at the first meeting. They merely elected directors and put off the election of officers. But I knew they were merely biding their time.

"The freeze-out of Pulliam and me was slated for a second meeting in January, in which the most important business was the election of officers. Pulliam attended the meeting feeling blue and low and had his resignation all written out. I got hold of it, tore it up, and told him to sit around and see what would happen.

"I had obtained a shrewd lawyer to attend the meeting, Pennsylvania State Senator William Edwards, and a brother of former United States Senator Edwards. My attorney was looking for any place where our opponents had left themselves vulnerable, and suddenly he had it. He had taken note of the fact that the same men who had elected themselves directors at the stockholders' meeting also acted as tellers of the meeting. Under New Jersey law, a teller is disqualified from holding office in a corporation.

"After the meeting began, Captain Kerr started to nominate a slate of officers. I told him he couldn't even be a director, as he had disqualified himself by acting as a teller at the previous meeting. I had given Senator Edwards one share of stock, and he supported me with a powerful argument.

"Then I had myself elected president and Pulliam secretary. Kerr was furious and went into court and tried to stop me with an injunction. However, Chancellor Pitney, who later became a United States Supreme Court Justice, sustained me."

The meeting between the rival factions grew more strained. A representative of Kerr approached Barney, and asked: "Mr. Dreyfuss, what do you want to do, sell, or buy out the Kerr-Auten interests?"

"Sell nothing," Barney fairly shouted. "I'm buying."

Asked what he would pay for the Kerr stock, he named a pretty stiff price. A few days later, Colonel O. B. Hershman, a newspaper-publisher friend of both parties, called on Barney, and said: "Captain Kerr has been to see me; he will sell." And so Barney Dreyfuss, at the age of thirty-five, was owner of the Pirates.

IX. WAR AND PENNANT COME TO PITTSBURGH

WHILE DREYFUSS was having his private war inside the Pittsburgh club, more serious war clouds were hovering in the baseball skies, in the winter of 1900-1901. Ban Johnson, the young energetic president of the old Western League, now terming itself the American League, with such enterprising lieutenants as Charley Comiskey, Connie Mack, Charley Somers, Clark Griffith, and Jim McAleer, had served notice on the National League that they had tossed aside their old minor-league swaddling clothes and would sell their product to the fans as a full major. The American not only took up vacated National League territory in Cleveland, Detroit, Baltimore, and Washington, but placed rival clubs in Chicago, Philadelphia, and Boston.

Having just swung a deal for almost 100-per-cent ownership of the Pirates, which severely taxed his resources, Barney had everything to gain if peace continued in baseball, and everything to lose if the game embarked on a disastrous "no-holds-barred" baseball war. Dreyfuss at first counseled, "Maybe we better see what Johnson and those American League fellows want," but his National League associates were not of a mind to make any concessions to doughty Ban and his cohorts.

"If they want to butt their heads against a stone wall, let 'em do it and go broke. If they want to fight, we'll give it to them," said such firebrands as Andy Freedman of New York and John T. Brush of Cincinnati.

Johnson's raiders struck quickly, and struck hard. The National

League still had at that time the $2,400 salary limit that had distressed Connie Mack in 1893. Many of the top stars of the National League quickly snatched the higher offers: the great Napoleon Lajoie and Pitchers Bill Bernhard and Chick Frazer of the Phillies; Jimmy Collins, the wonder third baseman, Buck Freeman, Chick Stahl, and "Parson" Lewis of Boston; Cy Young, Lou Criger, John McGraw, and Wilbert Robinson of St. Louis; Clark Griffith, Jimmy Callahan, Roger Bresnahan, and Sandow Mertes of Chicago; Fielder Jones and Lave Cross of Brooklyn; Sam Crawford and Topsy Hartsel of Cincinnati.

Pittsburgh at first lost only two players, Infielder Jimmy Williams, who hopped to John McGraw's Baltimore American League club, and Catcher Harry Smith, who had been drafted from Milwaukee but went to Mack's Philadelphia club before he ever signed a Pirate contract. Dreyfuss was especially burned up over the manner in which he lost Williams. The third baseman lived in Denver, and Barney sent him transportation money to go to Hot Springs, the club's training camp. McGraw actually took Williams off the train on which Jimmy was traveling, on Barney's transportation money, and signed him to a Baltimore contract. "I not only lose Williams but I pay half of his fare east, for that McGraw to steal him," wailed Dreyfuss.

Though the Pirates eventually lost some outstanding players before the dove of peace again descended over the baseball world, Dreyfuss was singularly fortunate in holding his athletes, not only top-ranking stars, but run-of-the-mine players. There were several reasons, and perhaps the most outstanding one was the loyalty of the team's top luminaries, Manager Fred Clarke and Hans Wagner. In no time Clarke had built a remarkable morale within the club. Dreyfuss also met American League offers and was severe when he found American League agents among his players. Pirates who jumped were labeled with the rather harsh word of "traitor." Shortstop Fred Ely was summarily dismissed when it was learned he was serving as an American League representative, and later Barney fired Catcher Jack O'Connor after the Goose Hill man took over for Ely and spread American League propaganda in the Pirate camp.

Johnson and his lieutenants trained their biggest guns on Wagner, Clarke, Leach, Chesbro, and Phillippe. Having signed Nap Lajoie, Wagner's great fellow star, Johnson was especially anxious to hook the Flying Dutchman. In 1901 Ban tried a personal raid and arranged to meet some of the Pirates in one of the upper floors of the Hotel Lincoln, now called the Hotel Mayfair, at 423 Penn Avenue. He attended the meeting with some local agents and gave the players a talk on the benefits of affiliating with the American League. But Barney Dreyfuss and Harry Pulliam were tipped off to what was happening and rushed to the Lincoln to break up the meeting. When Johnson heard the irate Pirate officials were on the way up, he beat a hasty retreat from Barney's wrath. Ban made his getaway in a freight elevator in the rear of the hotel, hiding behind a collection of garbage cans.

On another occasion two of Johnson's lieutenants did contact Wagner in Carnegie. The offer they brought from Ban was considerably in excess of what Barney paid the Dutchman. Barney again heard of it, and was panic-stricken. Failing to reach Honus by phone, he hitched his team and drove madly to Carnegie. He couldn't find Wagner, but John Robb, who frequently handled Hans' business, told Barney he could find him in the Elks Club. As Dreyfuss burst in, he found his star performer nonchalantly playing pool. Honus readily admitted the American Leaguers had been to see him.

"I'll pay you anything you want," said Barney excitedly, pulling out a contract.

"I can't sign tonight," said Wagner.

"Why not?" demanded Barney.

"Because I promised certain people I wouldn't sign tonight, and wouldn't sign with anyone until noon tomorrow."

Promptly at twelve o'clock noon the following day, Wagner walked into Barney's office, and said: "I'll sign that contract now, Mr. Dreyfuss." He signed for less than the American League offer.

Late in the baseball war Wagner was driving behind his high-stepper across the bridge leading into Carnegie, in a blinding snowstorm. He was returning from a one-mile stretch on which the gay blades of Carnegie held sleighing races. In the glare of a gas lamp, he caught sight of a familiar figure making its way across the bridge. It was Clark Griffith, the manager of the Chicago White Sox. Impishly Wagner drove his horse almost on top of Griff, and forced him into a snowbank. Griffith later called at Wagner's home and offered him the playing managership of the new club that the American League was planning to put in

New York. But Broadway had no allure for Honus; he turned it down.

2

A baseball pennant finally came to Pittsburgh in that first year of the baseball war, 1901, and Pittsburgh went into ecstasies over its first flag. It was an eventful year in baseball, as the National League first introduced the foul-strike rule, making it compulsory for the catcher to remain behind the plate at all times.

Clarke's 1901 champions made up a team that gathered strength as they moved along, and eventually defeated the team from eastern Pennsylvania, the runner-up Phillies, by seven and a half games. The Quakers, weakened by the loss of Lajoie, Bernhard, and Frazer, were also gunning for their first championship. Pittsburgh won 90 games and lost 49; Philadelphia followed with an 83-57 performance.

The New York Giants, who flopped to a dismal seventh at the finish, were the early pacemakers, and for a good part of the season Dreyfuss and Clarke thought they were the team to beat. A young Pennsylvania pitching sensation, Christy Mathewson, was a big early-season winner for the New Yorkers. At the end of May the Pirates were only fourth, trailing the Giants, Reds, and Phillies in that order.

On their first eastern trip the Pirates lost the first game in each of the cities visited and dropped seven games out of thirteen. But when the eastern clubs visited Exposition Park, it was a different story, the Buccaneers winning nine games out of twelve. That shot Clarke's boys into the lead June 15, and they held on to the finish with the exception of a half day on the nation's birthday, July 4.

The Pirates played the Giants at Exposition Park, and Mathewson brought gloom to a loyal morning turnout by defeating Jesse Tannehill and Jack Chesbro, 5 to 3, in 12 innings. The New Yorkers counted three runs in the twelfth, and the Pirates could come back with only one on Matty. That put the Giants back in the lead by a half game, but the Pirates delighted the afternoon holiday throng with a 12-to-0 cakewalk. Sam Leever won the shutout over Dummy Taylor and Ed Doheny, who later came to Pittsburgh. The afternoon win sent the Pirate skull and crossbones back to the top of the halyards, and from then on the Bucs were never headed.

In writing of Pittsburgh's first pennant, Henry Chadwick, known affectionately as "Father" Chadwick, wrote in the 1901 *Spalding's Guide,* of which he was the venerable editor:

The success of the Pittsburgh club in 1901 was mainly due to the pluck, energy and unwonted liberality of financial expenditure in securing a winning team for his club which marked the work of its enterprising and persevering president, Mr. Dreyfuss.

Moreover, it was more harmonious as a team than its adversaries and did less kicking, the latter being a weakness that characterized every team in the league in 1901 to a more or less extent, the rule of the season in this respect being "the more the kicking the nearer to the last ditch" and the less of that nearer the goal.

If the Pirates were commended by Chadwick on their good behavior in a rowdy season, only the quick work of Clarke and Wagner prevented the Pittsburgh and Allegheny fans from roughing up Umpire Elton Cunningham, who supposedly was gunning for the Pirates, as a result of Dreyfuss letting him out after the Louisville-Pirate merger.

The Sporting News gave considerable space to the incident in its issue of June 8, 1901, under a heading: ATTACKED UMPIRE Cunny's Close Call on Pittsburgh Grounds . . .

Clarke and Wagner prevented a mob of 2,000 from beating a N. L. Official . . . There is a difference of opinion as to the cause of the hot time in the old town last Saturday, when 2,000 men and boys chased Umpire Cunningham off the grounds and would have injured him if Manager Fred Clarke and big Honus Wagner had not acted as his bodyguard. Some people say that Cunningham's umpiring angered the crowd, while others claim that the players of both teams worked up the indignation meeting by nagging the umpire all through the game.

The Pittsburgh players were around him twice and made so many noisy objections at various times that when in the ninth Cunningham called Bransfield out when he was safe by two feet on a bunt—that would have come close to winning the game if it had been allowed, the loyal rooters needed only someone to lead them to become a howling mob. Two good policemen would have restored order in a minute or two, but although there is always a large detail from Allegheny head-quarters at every game, not an officer appeared to protect the umpire who could not have escaped injury if the players had not hastened to his rescue. The people in the grandstand were in sympathy with the umpire and one prominent businessman leaned over the railing and shouted "Shame" at the mob until he was hoarse.

Dreyfuss expressed deep regret that the trouble occurred. He thought Cunningham gave the Pirates a raw deal, but said: "Bad umpiring doesn't furnish an excuse for mobbing the umpire."

Barney said the umpire told Leach before the game that he intended to get even with Pittsburgh. Barney hasn't spoken to Cunningham since the Louisville merger. The little pitcher felt he should have been retained with the other stars, and when released to Chicago sent Barney several insulting letters.

Apparently the pint-sized Cunningham was a storm center all over the league, as the same edition tells of Outfielder Jimmy Sheckard, of Brooklyn, (later the famous Cub left fielder) spitting at "Cunny" after the umpire had ruled that "Sheck" had been caught napping. After the nasty incident, Cunningham fined Sheckard five dollars and put him out of the game. Cunningham was quoted as saying: "I don't know what kept me from pitching into Sheckard, but if ever a player does that to me again, I'll pick up a bat and smash it over his head."

3

In the early part of the first flag-winning campaign, the 1901 Pirate champs lined up: Beaumont, center field; Clarke, left field; Wagner, right field; Bransfield, first base; Ritchey, second base; Leach, third base; Ely, shortstop; O'Connor and Zimmer, catcher. In midseason Lefty Davis went to right field, batting after Ritchey, as Wagner took over at third base, and later replaced Ely at shortstop.

Wagner was high man at bat among the Buccos, with an average of .352, but fell to fifth in the National hit parade, which was led by Jesse Burkett of St. Louis, with .382. Ginger Beaumont and Claude Ritchey each hit .328, and Clarke, .316. Tommy Leach banged away at a .298 clip and this time took part in 93 games. We also read: "Leach, who was seldom heard from on the field last year, is now one of the most aggressive of Clarke's crew."

Probably the biggest difference between the 1900 runner-up and the 1901 champions was the acquisition of William Edward "Kitty" Bransfield, from the Worcester club, to play first base. Kitty was a Worcester boy, who had a brief trial with the Boston Nationals in 1898 as a catcher–first baseman. He had a big shock of hair, which dangled down over his eyes, and an Eastern

League batting average of .371 got his name into Barney's dope book. Kitty didn't hit that hard in Pittsburgh, but from the first he was a steady hitter, and a smooth-fielding first baseman.

It was Bransfield's boast, up to the time of his death in May, 1947, that he played a deeper first base—farther away from the bag—than any other player of his day, and most of them since.

"You know, playing back on the grass that way made for an odd situation," Kitty told Al Laney of the *New York Herald Tribune*, the winter before the veteran's death. "I played for several years on the same infield with Hans Wagner, but I never actually saw him make more than a half-dozen great plays. He would cut that ball loose for the bag, and I had to be there. So whenever it was hit his way I was digging for the bag. I knew he would have it there, and I had to arrive as soon as the ball. I never had time to watch him field it. But if you want me to make an affidavit that he was the greatest ball player that ever lived, I'll gladly do it."

Circumstances helped bring in Wagner from right field to the infield and paved the way for his glorious record at shortstop. Ely played shortstop until July, when Dreyfuss heard about his American League affiliations and promptly fired him. Clarke then picked up Lefty Davis to play right field; Wagner was moved to third base, and Leach shifted to shortstop.

Here's Wee Tommy's version of it: "When we were shifted from Louisville, most persons thought of Honus only as an outfielder. I recall in 1899, our last season in Louisville, Fred Clarke was short of players, and he moved Hans to third base and put a catcher in right field. But when we were moved to Pittsburgh, Clarke had plenty of infielders, and Hans seemed destined for a long outfield career.

"However, at the time that Ely was released, Clarke tried to talk Hans into playing shortstop, but it was no go. John said: 'What's your idea in wanting to put me in that position? You know I'm an outfielder.' He finally consented to come in and play third base, with me moving over to shortstop. But Fred said to me: 'Keep talking to the Dutchman and see whether you can't make him switch positions with you. Tell him he can cover more ground than a little fellow like you.' I guess it worked, for after about a week's arguing and conversation, we switched, and that started his great career at shortstop. But I agree with Ed Barrow; it wouldn't make any difference where you would have played Wagner—he would have been the same standout in any position."

Early in the 1901 season, when the Giants looked like the team to beat, the Pittsburgh letter in the *Sporting News*, signed by Duquesne, did a little boasting on the subject of the Pirate pitching staff: "Leever, Tannehill and Phillippe should be able to out-pitch any three men that any other club can boast of, and any New Yorker who would like to do a little speculating in the baseball line would not have any difficulty in getting his money up on a proposition that any member of this trio will make a better record for the season than will the great Mathewson."

Now it is amusing that Duquesne entirely overlooked big Jack Chesbro in tossing bouquets into the laps of Clarke's leading pitchers. However, the big fellow from North Adams came fast that season and led the Pirate regulars with a percentage of .700, winning 21 games and losing 9. Deacon Phillippe worked just a little harder, winning 22 games and losing 12; Tannehill won 18 and lost 10, and Leever trailed the big four with a showing of 14 wins and 5 defeats.

During the season, Ed Doheny, a hefty, hard-living left-hander, was picked up from the Giants. George Merritt, Ed Poole, and Lou Wiltse (an older brother of George, later crack Giant southpaw) pitched in a few games for Pittsburgh's first pennant winner, and Rube Waddell's brief record was no victories and two defeats. Clarke had his fill in trying to manage the big southpaw from Butler. He told Barney Dreyfuss: "Sell him; release him; drop him off the Monongahela bridge; do anything with him you like, so long as you get him the hell off my ball team."

Barney sold Waddell to the Chicago Cubs, where Rube soon got into a fuss with Jim Hart, the Cub president, and jumped to the Los Angeles club of the Pacific Coast League. Connie Mack lured Rube to his Athletics in 1902, and it was in Philadelphia that the eccentric southpaw established his uncanny records. As for Clarke, he fired Rube and soon found he had another left-handed problem child on his hands, in Ed Doheny.

4

Barney Dreyfuss had his first champion; he made considerable money in 1901, but he still had his full share of sleepless nights. With the former immigrant boy from Freiberg, life was just one

Pittsburgh Pirates Publicity Department
BABE ADAMS

National League Service Bureau
MAX CAREY

BURLEIGH GRIMES

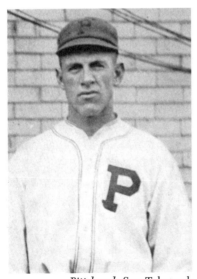

CHARLIE GRIMM

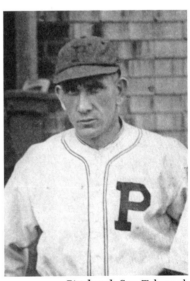

RABBIT MARANVILLE

battle after another. After winning his fight with Kerr and re-
pelling Ban Johnson's raiders, the end of the 1901 campaign
found Dreyfuss in a new fight with Andy Freedman, who first
tried to beat him out of the Sunday dates when Barney headed
the Louisville club.

"Do I always have to fight for what is coming to me? Must
life always be a conflict?" the young owner wailed.

Freedman, the New Yorker, backed by John T. Brush, then
still in Cincinnati, introduced a measure that would have made
the National League a big syndicate. The loop would have
pooled all of its resources, and the profits—if any—would have
been divided among the various club owners at fixed percentages, with New York getting the lion's share. If there were
losses, they would be divided among the club owners of the
entire league.

Dreyfuss felt, and perhaps rightly, that the move was aimed
primarily at him. Of all the National League clubs, the Pirates
were least hurt by the baseball war; Barney made a tidy profit
in 1901, while most of the other clubs lost. But under the Freedman plan, Dreyfuss' profits would have gone into the general pot,
and as the entire league lost money, he would have had no
profit at the end of the season but would have shared in the
National League's losses. And Dreyfuss was further angered by
Freedman because the New Yorker never had paid his share
in reimbursing the former Louisville, Baltimore, and Washington clubs, after they had been dropped from the old twelve-club
league.

The fight centered around the National League presidency,
and Albert G. Spalding, the baseball pioneer and former manager
and owner of the early Chicago White Stockings, was the
Lochinvar selected to rescue the game from what was termed
the evils of Freedmanism. The Pittsburgh, Chicago, Philadelphia,
and Brooklyn clubs, the most opulent clubs, supported Spalding
for the presidency, while New York, Boston, Cincinnati, and
St. Louis went along with Nick Young, president of the league
since 1885 and a man who had grown old on the job. The
presence of the Giants on the "Have Not" clubs was due to the
fact that Freedman had badly mismanaged this valuable property and after seven years had almost run it into the ground with
a succession of feuds, fights, managerial changes, and second-
division baseball.

Twenty-five ballots were taken to elect a president of the National League at the old Fifth Avenue Hotel in New York, in December, 1901, and each time it was four votes for Spalding, and four for Young, with Dreyfuss regularly crying: "I vote for Mr. Spalding, a man who will do honor to the presidency."

After the twenty-fifth ballot, the four Young clubs left the room. Col. John I. Rogers of the Phillies, who was in the chair, immediately called for another vote. And on the twenty-sixth ballot, with Dreyfuss, Reach, of Philadelphia, Hart, of Chicago, and Ebbets, of Brooklyn, supporting Spalding, Al was declared by the chair to have been "unanimously elected." "I am the only man who ever was unanimously elected by four votes in an eight-club league," Spalding once reminisced in one of his lighter moments.

Spalding was called in after the "election," and he noted that Fred Knowles, secretary of the Giants and Freedman's observer, was still in the room. Though Knowles was a subordinate with no authority, his presence made a majority of clubs represented. Spalding whispered to Rogers: "Bring the meeting to order, and call me to the chair."

Rogers got the idea, and Spalding probably made the shortest acceptance speech on record: "Gentleman, I accept the office. Thanks! Call the roll."

The Pittsburgh, Chicago, Philadelphia, and Brooklyn clubs voted present. Knowles did not reply when the New York club was polled, but Spalding ruled the Giants were represented and called for the regular order of business. The Freedman syndicate plan was quickly voted down.

Barney returned to Pittsburgh with a lighter heart. Not only on the ball field, but in the league council halls, he had been on the winning team. Deep down he felt that the Freedman plan was a far greater threat to his club, himself, and the security of his loved ones, than the rival American League. "It was one of the few times I was sorry I was in baseball," Barney once told the author. "If the Freedman plan had succeeded, I would have wanted no more of baseball."

Even so, it was only a partial victory. The Nick Young faction, especially the truculent Freedman and the crafty Brush, didn't take their defeat lying down. Spalding took over the league records and other papers, but Freedman, Brush, Soden of Boston, and Robison of St. Louis refused to acknowledge him as league president. They procured a temporary injunction; the case dragged in the courts until March 29, 1902, when Judge Truex of New York ruled against Spalding.

The sporting-goods manufacturer resigned, and the names of Col. Temple of Pittsburgh, John Montgomery Ward, the former star player and manager, and President Soden of Boston were all put forward as compromise candidates. Even the name of Harry Pulliam, secretary for Dreyfuss' club, first appeared in the public prints as a presidential possibility. However, on April 3, almost on the eve of the second war season, Nick Young was re-elected secretary-treasurer, and it was decided to have a three-man executive committee run the league. John T. Brush of Cincinnati served as chairman, and Soden of Boston and Hart of Chicago were his associates.

It gave the former Freedman faction two members on board, also the chairmanship, and Dreyfuss wasn't satisfied. But Barney always was a patient man and bided his time.

X. BUCS WIN SECOND FLAG BY 27½ GAMES

A SECOND PENNANT came in 1902, and the gallant Bucs won by a margin from here to Christmas. Fred Clarke has called it his greatest ball club, and it unquestionably was one of the top teams of baseball history. Its margin over the second-place Brooklyns was fabulous—a little matter of 27½ games. The club's percentage of .741 was exceeded by only one major-league club in this century—the 1906 Cubs, who soared to .763.

After the early April fighting, Clarke's team quickly sprang to the fore, assumed the lead May 4, and soon the ripsnortin' Pirates were so far in front that the rest of the league couldn't even follow their foam. An indication of the 1902 team's power may be gleaned from the fact that they defeated both the second-place Dodgers and third-place Bostons by the same margin— 14 games to 6, and the fourth-place Reds, 15 to 5. The second-division teams were bowled over as follows: both Chicago and New York, 13 to 7; Philadelphia, 18 to 2, and St. Louis, 16 to 4. Somehow Pirate fans took an almost sadistic delight in the way their pets almost annihilated their Pennsylvania rivals, the once formidable Phillies.

Unquestionably the new devastating raids by the American League in the winter of 1901-02 made this overwhelming victory possible. Those 1902 Pirates were strong enough to have won in most any major league—at any time—but Johnson's raiders made things that much easier for Fred Clarke.

The Phillies were ruined when Elmer Flick, Ed Delahanty,

Frank Donohue, and Monte Cross followed Lajoie and the 1901 jumpers to the American League. Johnson moved his Milwaukee club to St. Louis, and the cream of what remained on the Cardinals, Pitchers Jack Powell, Charley Harper, and Willie Sudhoff; Infielders Rhody Wallace and Dick Padden, and Outfielders Jesse Burkett and Emmett Heidrick, jumped to the new American League Browns. Brooklyn lost Bill Donovan and Jim McGuire, the Bostons, Bill Dinneen (soon to be a decided pain in the neck for Pittsburgh fans), and the Giants, George Davis, Al Selbach, and Frank Bowerman. Even the great Mathewson signed a winter contract with the Athletics but jumped back to New York.

Again a big majority of the Pirates remained amazingly loyal to Dreyfuss and Clarke, and other National League club owners looked at Barney as more or less of a wonder man. "How the dickens does he do it?" they asked. "Does he hypnotize them, or something? We try to hold our best men, but while we talk to them, they have American League contracts in their pockets."

Barney actually gained two American League players at the start of the 1902 season. Catcher Harry Smith, who had gone to the Athletics the previous season, hopped back to Pittsburgh, and Dreyfuss also signed Infielder William (Wid) Conroy, who had played for Hugh Duffy's 1901 Milwaukee team.

However, American League troubles caught up with Barney as the season advanced. In August the little club owner learned that O'Connor, acting for the American League, had talked to most of the stars, and it was common gossip he had signed the pitching aces, Jesse Tannehill and Jack Chesbro, to contracts to play on the New York club, which Ban Johnson planned to put into Manhattan in 1903. Tommy Leach, Wid Conroy, and Lefty Davis also had apparently swallowed American League bait and were expected to flop at the end of the season. O'Connor was dismissed with a stinging rebuke in mid-August, Davis in September, and Tannehill also was notified by Dreyfuss on payday, September 18, that Barney "would have no further use for his services." Jesse won his last game for Pittsburgh that day, defeating St. Louis in ten innings, 7 to 6. O'Connor, Tannehill, Chesbro, and Conroy eventually bobbed up on the first edition of the New York Highlanders, now the Yankees, in 1903.

Dreyfuss had another American League worry, apart from losing star players to the Johnson loop. One reason that he was able to go on under war conditions and still make money was that he had no opposition in Pittsburgh. He had the town to himself, and pennant winners were still new enough for Pittsburgh and Allegheny fans to be a grand and glorious experience. But Johnson now was planning to give Dreyfuss a little competition in his own back yard. In addition to shifting the Baltimore American franchise to New York in 1903, the energetic American League president had a move afoot to transfer his Detroit club to Pittsburgh. The City on the Straits then had a population of only a quarter of a million and was the most backward of Ban's clubs at the turnstiles. Johnson made repeated trips to Pittsburgh, contacting several affluent persons, and a syndicate was formed to back a club. Ban looked over several sites to build a ball park, and even took a quick peep at the locality where Forbes Field is now located. The Pirates were still playing in Exposition Park in Allegheny, and in back of Johnson's head was a selling slogan for the new club, "A Pittsburgh team in Pittsburgh." Allegheny was not incorporated into the present city of Pittsburgh until 1907.

The Freedman plan was beaten; yet here was a new condition to make nightmares of Barney's dreams!

2

In its review of the 1902 National League race, Reach's 1903 *Guide* paid this glowing tribute to Clarke's fast-moving Monongahela River brigands:

> The Pittsburghs owed their wonderful success to the fact that their team entered the race unbroken—and even strengthened, over the previous year. The team was superior to any club in the country in the matter of pitchers, strong in batting, fast in fielding and master of a superb system of team play which its rivals could not fathom, let alone break through.

Inasmuch as *Reach's Guide* was the official book of the American League—still engaged in bitter warfare with the National—the kind words said about Clarke's pitchers, superior to any in the country, were indeed a compliment. The staff of Mack's Philadelphia Athletics, American champions, was headed by the brilliant southpaws, the former Pirate, Rube Waddell, and the Gettysburg collegian, Eddie Plank. There was a bit of talk of having the two Pennsylvania teams meet in a World Series, but with the baseball war still going on full tilt, it never got past the conversation stage.

There were five good reasons for Reach's high estimate of the 1902 Pirate pitching—named Chesbro, Doheny, Tannehill, Phillippe, and Leever. The brilliant quintet grabbed off five of the seven top positions in the 1902 National League official pitching records. Big Jack Chesbro was really magnificent; he had been experimenting several seasons with his spitball and now had learned to control it. He led the league with 28 victories and 6 defeats.

"How did you come to lose the six?" they asked the big man from North Adams.

"Oh, I guess I got a little careless," laughed Happy Jack.

Ed Doheny ranked second in the official figures, with 16 wins and 4 defeats, and his fellow southpaw, Jesse Tannehill, was third, with 20 and 6. Deacon Phillippe was fifth, with 20 and 9, and Schoolmaster Leever seventh, with 15 and 7. In no other major-league race have five pitchers so dominated the pitching records.

Ginger Beaumont had his year in the sun in 1902 and led the National League hitters with .357. Other Pirates high up were: Wagner, .329; Clarke, .321; Bransfield, .308; O'Connor, .292; Davis, .291; Leach, .280.

There was a little surprise package hidden in the official slugging table. The broad-shouldered Wagner, with his heavy bludgeon, was first with his extra base hits adding up to 124 bases. Fred Clarke, heavier and stronger than when he was in Louisville, was fourth, with 104. But guess who was in between? Of all people, the little 150-pounder, Tommy Leach. He ranked third, with 114 extra bases, getting 15 doubles, 20 triples, and 6 home runs. And here was really one for the book! Tommy the Wee's 6 round-trippers made him the home-run king of the National League. It was the lowest number of homers to win the crown in either major league in this century.

Despite the fact that Clarke and Leach apparently had talked Wagner into playing shortstop after Ely's release in 1901, Dreyfuss and Clarke still regarded the Dutchman primarily as an outfielder when the season opened. Wid Conroy, the newcomer from Milwaukee, played 93 games at shortstop, while Wagner played 59 games in the outfield, 31 at first base, and 45 at shortstop. Honus was Clarke's trouble shooter; whenever a key regular was hurt, the versatile Dutchman shifted to his place. Kitty Bransfield met with an injury, playing in 100 games only, which accounts for Honus' stint at first.

Clarke had a great team in 1902, but it seems everybody took a crack at right field. Honus started in the position, after which Davis, Jimmy Burke, the St. Louis–born third baseman, and Jimmy Sebring all took a shot at it. Sebring wound up the season at the position, Dreyfuss snatching him from Worcester in Tim Murnane's New England League.

3

No story of the Pirates' victorious 1902 campaign would be complete without a recital of their Fourth of July program with Brooklyn, the club's leading rival, at Exposition Park. It has previously been said that when the Allegheny River rose, the water frequently engulfed Barney's playing field. Following a heavy rain, water backed through the sewers during the morning game, and when the contest ended, parts of right and center fields were underwater.

By the time the afternoon game started, before a then capacity crowd of 10,290, the water was more than knee-deep in center field, and the miniature lake spread into right field. A ground rule was adopted, allowing only one base on a fair ball that was hit into the lagoon, and a boy was kept busy with towels, drying up the balls as they came out of the water. Umpire Bob Emslie handed the pitcher a dried ball after nearly every other delivery. Yet despite the slippery ball there was only one wild throw, a ball sliding out of Claude Ritchey's hand. Cozy Dolan, the Dodger center fielder, made a sensational catch by dashing into the high water and grabbing Fred Clarke's fly with one hand.

For Pittsburgh, Ginger Beaumont caught two fly balls while knee-deep in the center-field water, and when he caught Dolan's fly for the final out in the ninth inning, ending the game, he fell headlong into the lake, and was drenched from head to foot. Later it was learned that the players agreed that the outfielder making the final out was to let himself go, and that Ginger deliberately took his dive.

Willie Keller, Brooklyn's able right fielder, found a little island of a dry spot inside the right-field lake. He left it only when he waded through the pool to make a try for a ball hit in his direction, but neither of the rival right fielders, Keeler and Lefty Davis, came up with a single put-out in the afternoon game. The center fielders fared better, Beaumont getting two, and Cozy Dolan four. The Brooklyn second baseman was quite appropriately named Tim Flood.

In the face of these ground conditions it was nothing short of remarkable that the two Pittsburgh pitchers who worked the holiday games, Tannehill and Chesbro, should register shutouts. Jesse defeated another left-hander, Eustace Newton, 3 to 0, in the morning, and Happy Jack earned a 4-to-0 decision over Frank Kitson in the afternoon.

4

When the three-man executive committee that ran the National League in 1902 proved a sad fizzle, Barney Dreyfuss was among those who could have said "I told you so." From the start, he recognized that the committee would be a poor substitute for a strong league executive, especially with the National still having the American League war on its hands. In midseason of 1902 the truculent, aggressive John McGraw won Ban Johnson's undying enmity by returning to the National League to take up the management of Freedman's Giants, then in last place. McGraw had been repeatedly in Johnson's doghouse for what Dreyfuss termed "rowdy tactics," and was under suspension at the time he hopped back. He took a parcel of Baltimore stars with him: Joe McGinnity, Roger Bresnahan, Billy Gilbert, Dan McGann, and Jack Cronin.

"I'm glad to see McGraw back in our league," said Dreyfuss. "He'll help the Giants, but no club owner's committee headed by Freedman can ever expect to make McGraw toe the mark."

Matters were somewhat simplified for Dreyfuss when at the end of the 1902 season Andy Freedman, Barney's bête noire, sold the Giants to John T. Brush, and Brush disposed of the Cincinnati Reds to a syndicate headed by August (Garry) Herrmann. Dreyfuss had done some clever spade work, and when it again came time to elect a league president, the Pittsburgh owner put forward the name of his club secretary, Harry C. Pulliam, as a compromise candidate.

"Harry and I have worked in close association in both Louisville and Pittsburgh," Barney told his fellow club owners. "I never had a more loyal man work with me. And I can promise you that Harry Pulliam is the soul of honor. If he is elected president, he will serve the league as faithfully as he has served me. As for me, if Mr. Pulliam is elected, I shall expect no favor —I will want no favors, though knowing Harry I can say with greatest sincerity, he will favor no club in the league above any other."

Dreyfuss' sales talk convinced the league, and Harry Pulliam was unanimously elected the fifth president of the league. The Kentuckian was only thirty-two years old. He didn't favor Dreyfuss but promptly made him chairman of the schedule committee, a post which Barney held tenaciously to the day of his death.

The election of Pulliam to the National League presidency, bringing order and stability to the senior loop, was soon followed with peace for all baseball. At the National League's annual meeting, Frank DeHaas Robison, of St. Louis, who was fighting a losing battle against the new American League Browns, indicated he had enough and suggested that the league appoint a committee to call on Ban Johnson and several of his club owners, who then also were in New York, and ascertain exactly what the American League wanted. Robison's suggestion was warmly supported by Dreyfuss, Herrmann, the new man from Cincinnati, Hart of Chicago, and Rogers of Philadelphia.

The National League committee, of which Dreyfuss was a member, held a preliminary meeting in New York with Johnson, Charley Somers, and John Kilfohl. Johnson quickly vetoed a suggestion by the National Leaguers that the two leagues merge and again form a twelve-club National League, but out of the preliminary New York talks grew the Cincinnati peace meeting of January 5, 1903.

The National League agreed to accept the American League as a full-fledged major, with all the rights and prerogatives of the National. Dreyfuss won the National League's most important concession. The old league agreed to the American League placing a club in New York in 1903, provided Ban Johnson gave his pledge to stay out of Pittsburgh.

A joint committee was appointed to take up the question of disputed players, most of whom had signed two contracts. Here Dreyfuss also fared better than most of his fellow club owners, as the American League grabbed off most of the big names.

Jack O'Connor and Jesse Tannehill, who were released by Pittsburgh, and the great Chesbro did not appear on the disputed list, but the committee ordered Tommy Leach, who jumped after the 1902 season, and Catcher Harry Smith returned to the Pirates, while it approved of Wid Conroy's contract with the new New York Americans.

An indication that Dreyfuss didn't get the worst of it may be gleaned from the fact that Nap Lajoie, Ed Delahanty, Willie Keeler, Sam Crawford, Bill Donovan, Norman Elberfeld, George Davis, and Dave Fultz were all awarded to American League clubs. In addition to Leach and Smith, ordered back to the Pirates, the National League salvaged the great Mathewson, Vic Willis, Rudy Hulswitt, Sam Mertes, and Frank Bowerman.

At first, Brush of New York and Ebbets of Brooklyn, who had lost the great Keeler and Bill Donovan, refused to ratify the peace settlement and filed a minority report. Brush even went into court to try to block the settlement. Only recently he had bought the Giants with the idea of having New York to himself, and resented the terms of the pact. "That Dreyfuss is a smart fellow," he wailed. "It's all right for me to have to buck an American League club on Manhattan Island, so long as he is saved any opposition in Pittsburgh."

Yet, Barney had a greater sense of well being after the peace than any time since he came into baseball. He had the game's greatest team, his own friend as president of the league, and he had done his share in writing the peace. And though he had succeeded in keeping the American League out of Pittsburgh, he did not share the hatred for the new league felt by many of his National associates. He started his baseball with Louisville in the old major American Association, and sensed what the rivalry of two strong, well-conducted leagues could do for baseball.

XI. PENNANT LIGHTNING STRIKES AGAIN

Despite the loss of Chesbro and Tannehill, who won forty-eight games between them in 1902, the Pirates carried on to one more championship before their great string of three straight was snapped. In winning their 1903 flag, the Buccaneers found a little tougher sailing than in the two preceding years, with the Giants, the 1902 tail-ender, offering the stiffest competition.

The Giants, under the high-pressured leadership of the fire-eating ex-Oriole, John J. McGraw, made the amazing leap from eighth to second in one season. Young Mathewson came into his own and won thirty games for New York. Barney still had it in his craw about McGraw practically kidnapping Jimmy Williams off a train when "Mac" was an American Leaguer, and remarked to Fred Clarke: "That McGraw is getting awfully hard to beat. You're not going to let him finish ahead of you, are you, Fred?"

"Not if I can help it," said Clarke, "but he's put together a mighty strong team."

Eventually Fred beat McGraw by six and a half games. Selee's Cubs were also dangerous that year and finished only a game and a half behind New York. The Pirates had their hands full when they played these two tough opponents. They split 20 games with the Giants, while the Cubs took the season's series from Pittsburgh, 10 to 8. The fifth-place Brooklyns were also difficult, and the Exposition Park boys won a narrow decision over the Dodgers, 11 to 9. But the rest of the league was Pittsburgh's oyster. The fourth-place Reds and seventh-place Phillies both were shot up, 16 games to 4, and the sixth-place Bostons and tail-end Cardinals, 15 to 5.

After a particularly rough series with the Giants, Clarke's team cleaned up Philadelphia four straight. "Thank God, the Phillies still are in the league," observed Barney.

The 1903 Pirates started off in an April rush, winning six of their first seven games, but then skidded in their spring warfare and fell back to third place, which they held for over a month, from May 11 to June 15. There was a most distressing game at Exposition Park, May 6, when the Cubs exploded a nine-run ninth-inning rally to beat out the flabbergasted Corsairs, 11 to 4. Clarke kicked over all the benches in the clubhouse and swore a blue streak, while Dreyfuss went through all the agonies of Dante's Inferno as the Cubs put on their nine-run scoring parade at the expense of Deacon Phillippe. What's more, Clarke made the Deacon stay and take his bumps.

However, a different kind of a Pirate pitching performance followed a month later. While the club was still in the third notch, it ran off the believe-it-or-not record of six consecutive shutout victories, which still remains a major-league record. Never before in baseball and never since has there been such a spray of whitewash as that which emanated from the arms of the Pirate pitchers in the week, June 2 to June 8.

All the games were played at Exposition Park, and happily the calcimine ducking began against the already hated Giants. Deacon Phillippe started it with a 7-to-0 dousing of McGraw's New Yorkers, the losing pitcher being Dummy Taylor. The next day Sam Leever repeated over New York, 5 to 0, the great McGinnity going down to the bottom of the sea. The Boston Beaneaters were next dunked in the whitewash pail in an entire series, as Kaiser Wilhelm, Ed Doheny, and Phillippe won their games by scores of 5 to 0, 9 to 0, and 4 to 0. Whitewash Week ended on Saturday, June 8, when Leever defeated the former Pirate, Frank Sparks, then with the Phillies, 2 to 0.

That succession of shutouts set off a Pirate victory rampage that stretched to 15 straight. It shot the Bucs into the lead in mid-June, and from then on Clarke's bold band never surrendered first place.

Though the nominal National League batting leader was Pirate pitcher Bill "Brickyard" Kennedy, with an average of .362 for 18 games, old Honus dethroned Ginger Beaumont as the loop's official batting king and regained his 1900 crown with an average of .355. Wagner just nosed out Mike Donlin of the Giants, while Fred Clarke was a close third with .351. Beaumont, still a man to be reckoned with, was sixth on the list, with .341, and Leach, the little man who was rescued from the American League, just barely missed .300 with .298.

Despite that June string of six successive shutout victories, Clarke's 1903 pitching wasn't overly strong. The jumping of Chesbro and Tannehill left an awful gap in the staff, which was felt even more acutely when Doheny developed a lame arm and became unmanageable late in the season. Leever and Phillippe had almost identical records; both won 25 games, the Schoolmaster lost 7, and the Deacon 9. Doheny was the third-ranking pitcher, with 16 wins and 9 defeats. Brickyard Kennedy could also have been called "Woolworth" Kennedy, as his record was 10 and 5. Fred "Buckey" Vail, Irwin "Kaiser" Wilhelm, and Fred "Cy" Falkenberg, later an American League star with Washington and Cleveland, helped out.

Early in the 1903 season Dreyfuss told Clarke: "Harry Pulliam intends to clean up the National League. He's going after the roughnecks, the rowdies, the umpire baiters, and the men who swear so you can hear them all over the stands. I told him I'm all in favor of it. Now I want you to fight as hard for games as you ever did. I don't want a ball club that will let anyone push it around, but if we lay off Harry's umpires, we make it easier for him."

Reach's Guide for 1904 indicates Barney's counsel bore fruit. Discussing the 1903 Pirate champions, it said: "A pleasing feature of Pittsburgh's work was their season-long abstentation from kicking and rowdyism—misnamed 'scrappy playing'—which formerly had been held indispensable to pennant winning. When necessary to extend themselves, the Pirates always were there."

Elsewhere we read that Pulliam's clean-up campaign was a general success: "Under Pulliam's rule, deportment in the National League was the best since the Brotherhood days."

Furthermore, the first year of peacetime baseball proved most profitable to the three top National League contenders. Brush, the new Giant owner, cleaned up $100,000 with his strong second-place club; Dreyfuss made $60,000 in Pittsburgh, and Jim Hart of the Cubs showed a tidy profit of $50,000. However, two great young players, Hans Lobert and Artie Hofman, were permitted to get away from the Pirates in that successful 1903 season. Lobert became one of the game's top third basemen and speed boys; Hofman was the perfect utility man and later great center fielder of the Cubs.

2

Even though the peace treaty between the National and American Leagues was signed in January, 1903, and baseball was under a national commission form of government, headed by August Herrmann, president of the Reds, there remained a lot of rancor and ill feeling between the two circuits, a holdover from the bitter strife of 1901 and 1902. Brush, who had tried to stop the peace agreement in the courts, and McGraw, his manager, were the leading dissenters. Ban Johnson was scathing in his denunciation of McGraw after John J. left the Baltimore Americans in 1902 to take up the management of the Giants, and Ban's hatred for McGraw was only exceeded by John J.'s hatred of Johnson. Brush and McGraw almost started the war all over again, when they tried to play Shortstop George Davis, awarded to Comiskey's White Sox, after the Tigers traded Norman "Kid" Elberfeld to Griffith's New York Americans. The Tabasco Kid had jumped to the Giants the previous winter but was returned to Detroit by the peace commissioners. It took men with cooler heads, such as Pulliam, Dreyfuss, and Charley Somers, to hold the peace.

When it became evident that the Pirates and Boston Pilgrims would win the pennants in their respective leagues, the writers and many of the fans called for a World Series between the two pennant winners, similar to those played between the champions of the National League and American Association in the eighties, before the Temple Cup series. Some of the die-hards of the National League were opposed to such a series so soon after the war, but Dreyfuss visualized the national interest such a series would engender, and early declared himself in favor of it.

"Sure, we'll play them [the Bostons], if they want to meet us," Dreyfuss told reporters, "and I think we can beat them." In fact, after talking to Fred Clarke, Barney felt sure his team would win and that a victory over the champions of the new loop would add to the prestige of his league and club. Henry J. Killilea, president and owner of the Boston club, who lived in

Milwaukee, came on to Pittsburgh in early September to make the arrangements with Dreyfuss. The two men agreed to a five-out-of-nine series, starting in Boston, October 1, with three games in the Hub, four in Pittsburgh, and two more in Boston, if they became necessary. The two club owners decided to divide the receipts evenly, and to play no player who was not under contract by September 1, a stipulation still in the present-day World Series regulations. The two clubs were to make all pecuniary arrangements with their own players. That was all to Dreyfuss' advantage. His Pittsburgh contracts ran until October 15, whereas Killilea's contracts with the Boston players ran out September 30.

At one time, the players of the Boston club threatened to strike and hold up the entire Series unless they were paid the Boston club's share of the receipts. Killilea mollified them by granting them two weeks' additional salary and a slice of his club owner's share. Both clubs raised their grandstand prices to a dollar, while bleachers and standing room sold for two-bits. An eight-game series eventually drew 100,429 admissions, a lot of people in 1903, and a total gate of $55,500.

Few Pittsburgh fans expected the American League contender, made up largely of National League jumpers, to give the Pirates much of a fight. Of course, they knew the Boston manager, Third Baseman Jimmy Collins, the great Cy Young, Bill Dinneen, Chick Stahl, Buck Freeman, Lou Criger, and other Boston regulars, from their earlier visits to Exposition Park in National League uniforms, but now they were American Leaguers. All during the recent baseball war Pittsburgh had remained a strong—almost 100-per-cent—National League town. What chance would even Young and Dinneen have to stop the mighty Honus, Clarke, and Beaumont, and Pirate rooters still had a great faith in the pitching staff that had pitched the six consecutive June shutouts.

Ralph Davis, of the flowing tie, echoed the town's sentiments when he wrote: "Many persons refuse to believe that the Boston team of today is one whit better than the old Tebeau aggregation, when Cleveland had that crack National League team, and if Cy Young could not win from the team which represented this city in those days, I do not see how he can be expected to do much against the present champions of the parent league! Bill Dinneen is another who never could do anything against the Pirates."

Poor Ralph! He had to eat his words before many days had passed.

3

Clarke took his swashbuckling crew to Boston for the first game, October 1, and the Pirates were in no mood to give any quarter. Certainly they were not of a mind to ask for any. The Freebooters from the Monongahela country stopped at the Vendome in Boston, and they early showed their teeth to the Boston citizenry, who crashed into the lobby to get a closeup of the enemy.

"Well, who the heck are you staring at?" Beaumont demanded belligerently of one of the curious bystanders. Tobacco juice sprayed dangerously near the milling crowds.

"Hey Dutchman, we're going to give you and the Pirates a licking you'll never forget," one of the bolder Boston fans told Hans Wagner.

Honus only guffawed. "Who with?" he asked. "With that old man, Cy Young? Why, we chased him out of the National League years ago."

Other Pirates weren't as polite or as careful in their choice of words. The baseball guides had complimented the Pirates on their good behavior, but that conduct was good only in comparison to deportment that had gone on before. Fred Clarke was still a firebrand and he had no sissies or pantywaists on his ball club. It was still a rough period in baseball despite Pulliam's reforms. Gamblers in the Vendome were flashing handfuls of bills. It was reported that on the morning of the first game $10,000 was bet in the lobby on the outcome of the contest.

Clarke early was concerned about his pitchers. He felt reasonably sure of his two aces, Phillippe and Leever, though Sam was complaining about his arm. Doheny was behaving peculiarly; his arm hadn't been right all through September. Ed came from Andover, Mass., and he began acting up after cronies from his home town started "setting 'em up."

But everybody was pleased when the first game was over. Ralph Davis' words on Cy Young's inability to beat the Pirates, and Wagner's chuckles on what would happen to Boston's "grand old man of the mound," proved no empty boasts when the Pirates, with Deacon Phillippe on the rubber, trounced Young and the Pilgrims by a score of 7 to 3. The victory came even easier than was expected.

A rather unruly crowd of 16,242, a great baseball throng for that period, was on hand. They packed Boston's small Huntington Avenue stands and milled behind ropes in the outfield and along the foul lines. Dreyfuss attended with a delegation of Pirate fans. Joe Smart, the Boston business manager, made Barney pay to get into the Series. Smart also sent no Annie Oakleys to the owners of the Boston Nationals, Arthur Soden, J. B. Billings, and William Conant. It raised a fuss at the time, though today it is a common practice to make everybody but the players, press, and radio pay their way into a World Series game. But the idea then was new, and Barney yelled: "Did you ever hear of such a thing? They make me pay to see my own players."

The Boston club had a noisy band of followers who termed themselves the "Royal Rooters," who were led by Mike Regan, a famous Boston fan at the turn of the century, and "Nuff Ced" McGreevey. The latter was a Boston innkeeper, who would terminate any argument with, "Enough said." So Paul Shannon, the jovial Boston writer, nicknamed him "Nuff Ced" McGreevey, which "Mac" painted proudly on his saloon and printed on his visiting cards. The Royal Rooters were always accompanied by their band, and their inveterate theme song through the 1903 World Series, as well as other Boston Series that followed, was "Tessie."

There was almost "enough said" for McGreevey, or any of the Boston fans, when the Pirates put the wood to old Cy in the first inning and shot him up for four runs. The Pirates then picked up additional runs in each of the third, fourth, and seventh innings, and by that time the crowd was in an ugly mood. It wasn't until Pittsburgh enjoyed a 7-to-0 lead that the Deacon eased up. Boston scored twice in the seventh and once in the ninth, but the Pilgrims closed the day with only six hits, half as many as the profitable dozen that the Pirates prodded out of Young.

Tommy Leach, the wee one, had his own private vendetta with old Cyrus. His little bat fired at regular intervals all through the afternoon, Tommy winding up the day with two triples and two singles. Sebring had three hits, including the first modern World Series home run, so Tommy and Jimmy outhit the entire Boston club. It was a night for jollification and rejoicing.

4

If the Pirates got an idea that the Series would be a lark after their first easy victory over Cy Young, they were brought up sharply by Bill Dinneen, in the second game played in Boston, October 2, before a reduced crowd of 9,415. Bill had improved considerably since Ralph Davis had seen him in Dinneen's National League days. Burly Bill gave a good indication that he intended to be tough when he blanked Pittsburgh with three hits, all singles, and won by a score of 3 to 0. Dinneen also blew down eleven of the Bucs on strikes.

Schoolmaster Sam Leever started for the Pirates and was clipped for two runs in the first inning. He then withdrew because of arm trouble and Buckey Vail finished. The Boston bogeyman was lead-off man Pat Dougherty, who contributed two homers and a single to Jimmy Collins' winning attack.

The two teams were all tied up for the Saturday game of October 3, and it brought out the largest crowd of the Series, 18,801, and the first World Series ticket scandal. Railroads running into Boston ran special trains from points 100 miles away, and some of the early comers moved into reserved seats. Later, when the holder of the ticket for the seat arrived, the squatter refused to be dispossessed. Other choice seats fell into the hands of speculators, after Boston fans were told all such seats had been sold. After the game got under way, the overflow crowd, which was two dozen deep behind outfield ropes, became ill tempered and unruly. Hits into the crowd were ground-rule doubles; the fans tried to open up for Boston outfielders but presented closed ranks when Clarke, Beaumont, and Sebring moved back for fly balls. Even so, Pittsburgh got five of the two-baggers, and Boston only two, as the Pirates won by a score of 4 to 2.

With Phillippe having only one day's rest, Clarke came back with the Deacon. "You stood them on their heads the last time, Deacon; you can do it again," encouraged Fred. Phillippe did all that Clarke asked of him. This time he yielded only four hits, two less than in his first outing. No wonder Ralph Davis went into superlatives in writing of the gamester. He observed that other Pirate pitchers, especially prior to 1903, had been more in the spotlight than the modest Deacon. Davis felt it was because Phillippe went about his business so unostentatiously. "Look up

the record," wrote Ralph, antedating Al Smith, "and you'll find
through Pittsburgh's pennant years, Deacon Phillippe has been
the most dependable pitcher of the bunch."

Jimmy Collins pitched Tom Hughes, his third-best bet, who
had a formidable 21-7 record in the American League. But Long
Tom had nothing in his repertoire to bother the Pirates; they
flayed him early and knocked him out in three innings, in which
Hughes was spanked for four hits and three runs. Collins didn't
quit but called in Young as a rescuer. Cy did much better than
in his first effort, holding the Pirates to three hits and one run
in his six innings. But Cy was behind, 3 to 0, when he took over,
and his good box work was wasted as Phillippe, backed by
errorless support, cast his spell over the Pilgrim bats.

<h2 style="text-align:center">5</h2>

The Buccaneers were a happy band when they climbed on
board their special back to Pittsburgh. "We've got them on the
run and should finish them in Pittsburgh," yelled Kitty Bransfield.

"No use dragging it out any longer than we have to," contributed Wagner. "I don't want to go back to Boston. I got some
hunting I want to do."

"Well, don't forget that second game," said Clarke, overhearing
the remark. "We still got to do our winning on the ball field."

"We'll take care of that Dinneen when we meet 'im again,"
laughed Honus.

An admiring crowd greeted the team on its return to Pittsburgh on Sunday. It rained on Monday, and the Series wasn't
resumed in Exposition Park until Tuesday, October 6. That was
a break for Clarke; it again gave Phillippe two full days of rest,
and as he obviously had the Boston team's number, why not
give them more of the Deacon? It was a happy thought, and
a rather disappointing crowd of 7,600 yelled itself hoarse when
the fans saw Phillippe go out to warm up.

"Make 'em eat out of your hand, Deacon; we'll show those
phony champions what a real championship club looks like,"
shouted a vociferous Pittsburgh fan.

Though the Pilgrims were in hostile National League territory,
they were not without encouragement from the stands, as about
100 of the Royal Rooters had sufficient faith left in their team to

accompany the Collins expedition to Pittsburgh. They cried out happily when Collins picked Dinneen, the second-game winner, to oppose Phillippe. "Just give 'em more of what you give 'em in Boston," encouraged Mike Regan, the Royal Rooter chieftain.

The game proved the high tide of Clarke's 1903 World Series campaign, as the Pirates won again, this time by 5 to 4. Phillippe and Dinneen were not as effective as in their earlier efforts; the Deacon gave up 9 hits and the Boston star, 12. Phillippe struck out only one, and Bill 7. It was anyone's game for 6 innings. The Pirates picked up an early run in the first inning, and then each team tallied single runs in the fifth, giving the Bucs a 2-to-1 lead. The Pirates apparently sewed up the game with three runs in the seventh, when Beaumont and Leach fired devastating triples, but the Pilgrims also had a three-run bomb left, which they exploded in the ninth. The tired Phillippe barely staggered through the Boston uprising, leaving Collins' tying run on base.

What the crowd lacked in size it made up in enthusiasm, and it appeared that almost everyone present was a member of the Loyal Order of Phillippe Admirers. They rushed out on the field after the last put-out, seized the perspiring and happy Deacon, and paraded him around the park on their shoulders. After carrying Phillippe to the clubhouse, the backslappers wouldn't let him dress for another half hour. Each man in the crowd wanted to shake hands personally with the man who had won three World Series games.

Wagner and Beaumont also fared well in this encounter, Honus enjoying his best day of the Series; he hit three singles and stole a base. Ginger belted a triple and two singles. Barney beamed; Clarke's eyes blazed with the excitement of a man who is getting ready for the kill; Wagner laughed out of the sheer joy of living. Yes, everybody was happy!

6

Pittsburgh began to take greater interest in the Series, as the fifth game, on October 7, rolled around. The Pirates needed only two more victories to clinch the coveted title, and Dreyfuss' turnstile count jumped nearly 5,000—to a paid crowd of 12,322. As Exposition Park seated only around 10,000, a part of the crowd was herded behind ropes in both left and center fields, and after Managers Clarke and Collins went into a huddle with

Umpires O'Day and Connolly, they decided that hits into the crowd would be ground-rule triples. And before the day was over, Pittsburgh fans saw enough Boston three-baggers to give them nightmares.

With the Pirates ahead three games to one, and feeling they had the Pilgrims on the run, some wags among the Pittsburgh fans thought it might be fun to make a present to Boston's Royal Rooters. With feigned solemn dignity, they presented Nuff Ced's visiting firemen from Beantown with a many-hued umbrella. It was fun which quickly backfired.

It just wasn't possible for Clark to pitch Phillippe every day, and reaching into his pitching bag, Fred pulled out Brickyard Kennedy. Collins pitched Young for the third time, and while the final tabulation was Boston, 11, Pittsburgh, 2, Kennedy was in no way as bad as this score might indicate. As a matter of fact, Brickyard held up his end beautifully for five innings, during which time neither club scored. Even Kennedy did his best to start a rally in the third; he opened the inning with a double, but the next three batsmen, Beaumont, Clarke and Leach, couldn't move him off second base.

Brickyard gave up six runs in the sixth, when his support came tumbling around his ears like a ton of bricks. The great Wagner booted two chances, Clarke and Leach each one; even Phillippe could not have held up in the face of such support. The Rooters, with their new umbrella, danced happily through the stands, as the Boston runs poured over the plate. They had a chance to stage another demonstration when Jack Thompson, who succeeded Kennedy, was slapped for four additional runs in the seventh. Ten Boston runs in two innings!

When the carnage was over, the Pirates had 6 hits off Young, while Boston had jolted Kennedy and Thompson for 14, including 5 triples. Even old man Young blew himself to a ground-rule triple and a single.

Pittsburgh's pitching was now pretty thin. The erratic Doheny was out of the Series, and for the sixth game, October 8, Clarke took a second chance on Sam Leever. The schoolteacher opposed Bill Dinneen, so it was the starting pitchers of the second game in a return engagement. Though each team bashed out ten hits, the Puritan blows were bunched to better effect off Leever, and Boston won by a score of 6 to 3, evening up the Series. Sam again complained of his arm, but he gave a fair performance.

Dinneen really won on his superior support. The weather had turned quite cold, and the Pirate infielders had more difficulty handling the baseball than the Bostonians. While Pittsburgh messed up only three chances, the boots came where they did Leever and the Pirate crew the most harm. Three Pilgrim runs in the third inning were built around a wild peg by Leach, and another strong-arm throw by Wagner, which landed deep in foul territory, gave Boston a run in the fifth.

Even so, with the score 6 to 0 against them when they went to bat in the seventh, the Pirates gave their chilled fans a chance to shout, when bunched hits by Sebring, Phelps, Beaumont, and Clarke swept three Pirate runs over the plate. Dinneen then pulled himself together in the two closing innings. Beaumont had a field day, even in his team's defeat, and came out of the game with four hits and two stolen bases.

It was getting colder by the minute, and Barney Dreyfuss, deciding it was too frigid for a Friday game, postponed the seventh contest tó Saturday, the tenth. Barney was also playing a little inside baseball. It had been demonstrated that Phillippe was the only pitcher who could stop Boston, and by calling off the Friday game, he gave the Deacon another day of rest. There was some beefing in the enemy's camp, but it was also a smart move from the standpoint of the gate. As Killilea and Smart packed their park in Boston the previous Saturday, Barney now used a shoehorn and squeezed 17,038 into Exposition Park.

The teams were back where they started in Boston, October 1, and everyone sensed this was the game, and that the winner in all probability would take the Series. Realizing this would be their last chance to see Phillippe, win or lose, a delegation of the Deacon's admirers called him to the plate before the game and presented him with a diamond stickpin.

The spokesman said: "We hope this pin brings you good luck today, Deacon, and in your remaining games of the Series, if you again are called upon to pitch."

There is no better way of putting a hex on a player than to give him a trinket, an automobile, or a box of neckties before a game, and the stickpin acted more like a jinx than a luckpiece. Anyway, the gallant Deacon had no rubber arm and was reaching the end of human endurance. He again tangled with Cy Young, and by an odd coincidence the score of the first game was reversed. The Puritans won this time by a score of 7 to 3, and for the first time during the Series, Boston was ahead.

Hits were fairly frequent, and the big crowd saw plenty of action. The Pirates tore into Young for ten hits, but the Pilgrims got eleven off Phillippe, or one more than they did in his first two games combined. The crowd in the field handicapped the Deacon's efforts, as a number of Boston's ground-rule triples were balls that could have been caught on a clear field. While only Bransfield and Clarke reached the three-bagger zone for Pittsburgh, the Bostonians trained their heavy artillery into the overflow crowd all afternoon, as five different Hub players—Collins, Stahl, Freeman, Parent, and Ferris—pumped out triples.

No World Series park was ever such a "Triples Paradise" as Exposition Park in 1903, the four games in Pittsburgh producing 17 three-baggers, 12 of them from Boston bats.

7

Clarke did his best to rally his team, as the clubs backtracked to Boston. Fred now not only had pitching worries, but the Boston pitchers had spiked his biggest gun—Honus Wagner. Wagner had failed to hit in three successive games, and when Hans wasn't hitting, it had an unconscious effect on the entire team's morale. The Series by this time was also dragging on everyone connected with it; fans, owners, players, and writers.

There was another idle Sunday, and then the game on Monday, the twelfth, Columbus Day, was postponed because of rain. The Series was finally concluded on the thirteenth, with Dinneen repeating his second-game, 3-to-0 shutout, but the defeated pitcher, the intrepid Phillippe, won as much glory out of it as the victor.

The fanfare had pretty well gone out of the Series by this time, and only 7,455 of Boston's faithful were on hand when their team scored the clinching victory. The final game saw the Pirates, who started so bravely two weeks before, close in low. Before the contest, Clarke told Phillippe, "Deacon, you're our only hope. But if you pitch as well as you have done, I'm sure the boys will start hitting behind you."

But that was the rub. Phillippe again hurled well enough to win the average game, yielding only eight hits, but Dinneen was at his very best and gave up only four. Again the Deacon's support was erratic, the Pirates being charged with three errors, whereas the Puritans encouraged Dinneen with perfect support.

Poor Phillippe! He stopped the toughies at the top of the Boston batting order but was beaten by the weaker sisters at the bottom. Six of the eight Pilgrim hits went to the last four batsmen. Candy LaChance, the Hub first baseman, who had been easy pickings for the Pirate pitchers all through the Series, broke out with a two-run triple in the fourth inning, which practically spelled curtains for the Pittsburgh cause.

The Pirates had only one real chance to score, and it was broken up with a smart play by Lou Criger, the American League catcher. With Leach on third and Wagner on second, Lou bluffed a throw to catch the Dutchman off second base. But he never completed the throw. Wheeling suddenly to his left, he shot the ball to Jimmy Collins and nipped the surprised Leach off third. That play almost brought tears to Fred Clarke's eyes.

Wagner finally broke his hitless streak with a single, his only hit in his last 14 times at bat. He hit only .214 for the 8 games, and Dinneen closed the Series by curving over a third strike on the baffled Dutchman. That was the signal for the Boston crowd to tumble out on the field. What they lacked in numbers they now made up in noise and enthusiasm, as they sang, shrieked, danced, and fought for the privilege of getting their hands on their heroes. As the Pirate fans rode Phillippe around Exposition Park on their shoulders only a week before, the Boston rooters now rode their entire team around the Huntington grounds.

There were some recriminations on the Pirates. Everybody felt that Clarke's pitching shortage beat the club. Many wondered what had happened to the pitching staff that had pitched 56 consecutive scoreless innings in June; there was criticism of Leever for not having worked more often, and in Pittsburgh the fans threw a few verbal brickbats at Chesbro and Tannehill for jumping the club the winter before, leaving Clarke short of starting pitchers of World Series caliber.

Faithful Ralph Davis spoke for all Pittsburgh when he wouldn't admit the Pilgrims were a better team. He wrote:

It is a pity that the Pittsburgh pitchers were not right for the Series, for, under the present circumstance, there always will be a doubt in the minds of the fans whether Collins' team could have triumphed had the local (Pirate) twirlers been at their best. For myself, I do not think they could.

On all sides, it was admitted that Ed Doheny's breakdown threw the entire staff out of gear. On the very day that the Series closed in Boston, Doheny went entirely berserk and was committed to a Massachusetts insane asylum. An account of his last frightful escapade is told in the October 17, 1903, issue of *The Sporting News.*

The poor fellow is now in the Danvers, Massachusetts, Insane Asylum. Yesterday [October 13] he murderously assaulted Oberlin Howarth, a "faith cure" doctor and nurse, at his home in Andover. He attacked Howarth with a cast-iron stove footrest, inflicting a deep gash in Howarth's head. The victim was unconscious for an hour. His condition is critical, but he may recover.

Doheny was subsequently examined by physicians, pronounced insane and committed to the Danvers Insane Asylum. He had shown signs of mental disarrangement since midsummer, but did not become violent until now. He also attacked his physician, but did not injure him.

The entire country sang the praises of Phillippe and Dinneen; the Deacon for trying to win the Series singlehanded and working in five games, three of them victories. Dinneen won three of his four games, two of them shutouts. Sebring was the batting star of the two clubs, and one of the two regulars to hit .300. Jimmy batted .366; Chick Stahl topped Boston with .309. The mighty Honus had to be content with a lowly .214.

Barney Dreyfuss made one of the finest gestures ever made by a big-league club owner. He tossed his entire club owner's share of the receipts into the Pittsburgh players' pool, with the result that the losing Pirates drew more out of the Series than the winning Bostonians. Each Pirate cashed a $1,316 check, whereas each Pilgrim had to be satisfied with $1,182. Killilea, the Boston club owner, kept his club owner's share of $6,699.65.

"The boys deserved it," Barney told Fred Clarke. "They've won three pennants for me, and they stuck by me during the American League raids. I'm glad to do it."

XII. EVIL FIRST-BASE JINX RAISES ITS HEAD

ALL GOOD THINGS come to an end, and Pittsburgh's great string of pennants ran out in 1904. The Giants, who leaped from eighth to second in 1903, made the top perch in 1904, when John McGraw, the fighting New York chieftain, won his first of ten pennants. McGraw's two pitching aces, Joe McGinnity and Christy Mathewson, blocked the path of further Pirate pennant progress by winning 68 games between them, and losing only 20. Iron Man Joe had a remarkable record of 35 victories and 8 defeats; Matty was right behind him with 33-12.

The Pirate crew was handicapped by a season-long epidemic of injuries and illnesses. Everything broke out on the "Jolly Roger" but scurvy. Second Baseman Claude Ritchey was the only one who escaped, playing in his team's entire 156 games. But the durable Wagner missed 24 games, Bransfield was out of 27, and Skipper Clarke played in only 70 games. During a good part of the season the fighting Buccaneer leader was bed-ridden.

For years Dreyfuss trained his team at Hot Springs, Arkansas, instead of sending the men farther south. Barney liked the baths at the spa himself, and felt they were most beneficial to his players. This spring Clarke had atrocious weather at the resort, and sports columns of the day said Fred started the season with the poorest trained club in either league. A number of early injuries were blamed on the poor condition of the players.

The three-time pennant winners were left at the post in April, and though at times the Pirates showed flashes of their former ability and power, the club had to be satisfied with a fourth-place finish, winning 87 games and losing 66 for a percentage of .569. Not only the Giants, but the Cubs and Reds whizzed by the slipping Corsairs.

Realizing that a shortage of pitchers had cost the club the World Championship in 1903, Dreyfuss and Clarke brought in a whole raft of pitchers that season: William "Doc" Scanlon, Jack Pfiester, Mike Lynch, Lew Moren, Roscoe Miller, Charley Case, Howard Camnitz, and Anthony "Chick" Robertaille were added to the pitching staff. Pat Flaherty, the team's 1900 left-hander, was re-engaged. Lynch was a crafty collegian from Brown University, and Camnitz, nicknamed the "Kentucky Rosebud," developed into one of Pittsburgh's greatest pitchers. Unfortunately, Pfiester, whose real name was Pfiestenberger, Scanlon, and Moren were all permitted to slip through Clarke's fingers. Pfiester, a southpaw, became the famous "Jack the Giant-Killer" of the Cubs. Scanlon was for years a first stringer with Brooklyn, and Moren, a little chap, had his moments with the Phillies. His father then sent him a one-hundred-dollar check whenever he defeated the Pirates.

Following the 1904 season, considerable ill feeling was engendered between the two major leagues because of the unwillingness of the Giants, the new National champions, to accept the challenge of John I. Taylor, new president of the Boston Americans, to play a World Series. It was the year Jack Chesbro, the former Pirate, blew a pennant for the early New York Highlanders, with a ninth-inning wild pitch on the last day of the season, after Happy Jack had won forty-one victories for the New York team.

Barney Dreyfuss, chairman of the National League schedule committee, got very much in the hair of the New Yorkers Brush and McGraw by siding with the American Leaguers. After giving permission to the Pirates to play a fall series with Cleveland, the American League's fourth-place club, he issued a statement that accused Brush of running out on an agreement made by the joint schedule committees in the spring. His statement had McGraw frothing and accusing Barney of licking Ban Johnson's boots.

Dreyfuss had said: "It was the National League schedule committee, or a majority of it, which meant the whole, which passed its word to the American League that postseason games would be played. I never agreed to play Cleveland until now. I agreed to play the team that finished in the same American League notch that my team did. The American League managers understood this, all along the line, I think, and I will keep my word with them as far as the Pittsburgh club is concerned."

The series with Cleveland was interesting largely from the standpoint that it brought together the two outstanding stars of baseball, and batting champions of their respective league, the hefty Honus Wagner and Nap Lajoie, who had jumped the Phillies in 1901. It was an odd series; Cleveland won two games, the Pirates one, and two others resulted in ties. One of the deadlocks was a fourteen-inning affair, with each club having three runs, when darkness engulfed the ball yard. At the conclusion of the not-too-satisfactory series, Ralph Davis was able to write: "Our Hans outplayed Larry (Lajoie) in the field, and outdid the Frenchman at bat, though neither player hit .300."

2

Shortly after the 1904 season, there appeared a headline over Davis' Pittsburgh letter to *The Sporting News:* MCBRIDE AT SHORT-STOP; WAGNER GOES BACK TO FIRST. . . . Bransfield's Batting Not Satisfactory to Clarke, And He May Be Benched. . . .

The story went on to say that Bransfield had tumbled to a batting average of .223, and that Clarke couldn't afford to play a first baseman with such a poor average. Dreyfuss had purchased George McBride, allegedly a fielding wizard at shortstop, from the St. Joseph club, and indications were that Wagner would go to first base, which he could play as well as any other position.

The column was most interesting, if not exactly accurate. Wagner didn't return to first base, and George McBride played only a few games with the 1905 Pirates. With the Washington club he later became one of the great defensive shortstops of the American League, but always remained a lightweight hitter. However, the column forecast one of Barney's worst moves, the trading of Kitty Bransfield, which was to vex Barney for years to come. It almost looked as though the trade put a curse on Pittsburgh's first-base position. Dreyfuss had his scouts scour the country for first basemen; they brought in one minor-league star after another, but just as soon as the newcomer donned the Pirate skull and crossbones, the old jinx clamped down on him. It was a decade and a half before the long search for a satisfactory regular first baseman came to an end.

Bransfield had had some personal problems in his last season in Pittsburgh, and worries off the diamond were a contributing factor in that .233 average, the lowest of Kitty's career. And it was Barney who made the decision to get rid of Bransfield. He told Clarke: "When I go to New York for the December meeting, I'll see what I can get for him."

Now Barney ordinarily was a shrewd trader, and he never tried to trade a nickel for two dimes. When he wanted a particular player or players from another club, he always gave full value, was even willing to give something extra. The Phillies had picked up a hard-hitting, minor-league first baseman, George (Del) Howard. His name had been entered in Dreyfuss' dope book as an especially good prospect. It would seem that an even trade of the experienced Bransfield for the novice, Howard, would have been an even exchange, but Barney was so anxious to make the deal with Bill Shettsline of Philadelphia, that he also tossed in Outfielder Harry McCormick and Otto "Oom Paul" Krueger, a dwarf of a ball player who could play either the infield or the outfield. McCormick, passed on to the Giants, became an outfield regular under McGraw and later the greatest pinch hitter of all time. Though Howard subsequently developed into a pretty good reserve player on Chance's famous Chicago Cubs, the trade proved one of Pittsburgh's sourest deals.

Howard was no great shakes as Pirate first baseman in 1905; he played 90 games in that position, Bill Clancy 52, and Homer Hildebrand, a left-handed pitcher, 19. During the season Dreyfuss also purchased Third Baseman Dave Brain from St. Louis, which enabled Clarke to shift Tommy Leach to center field. And it wasn't long before Tommy the Wee was an even greater man in the middle-outfield pasture than he had been at third base. For many years Pittsburgh sports writers, alone among big-league scribes, called the center fielder the "middle fielder."

Two new catchers came to Exposition Park in 1905, Heinie Peitz, a seasoned veteran, and George Gibson, a sturdy young Canadian from London, Ontario. For many years Peitz caught The Breitenstein in St. Louis and Cincinnati, when the pair made up the legendary Pretzel Battery. Gibson was acquired from the

Montreal club in June; he had hit .290 for the Royals in forty-one games. The brawny lad with the big chest was a little light with the stick when he first reported to Clarke, hitting only .178 with the Pirates for the remainder of the season. But he was destined to become Pittsburgh's greatest all-time catcher, a horse for work, and latter-day Pirate manager. Though George collected quite a few splinters on the Buccaneer bench in his early years, he caught 120 games in 1907, raised it to 140 in 1908, and was almost the entire catching staff, with 150 games, in 1909.

After their slump to fourth in 1904, the Pirates bounced back in 1905 and became the Giants' strongest competitor as McGraw won his second flag in New York. Though at the finish the Giants had 105 victories, 48 defeats, and a percentage of .686 against Pittsburgh's 96 wins, 57 setbacks, and .627, it was a dogfight until the last fortnight of the schedule. On the season's series, the Pirates lost to the Giants by the narrow margin of 12 to 10, but Clarke's warriors overwhelmed everyone else, smearing the sixth-place Cardinals, 18 to 4.

It was a year in which Cy Seymour of the Reds created something of a sensation by muscling in on Honus Wagner's preserve as National League batting champion. Cy was red-hot that year and beat the Dutchman .377 to .363. It was such a sensation that John T. Brush of New York bought the big outfield from Garry Herrmann of the Reds for $10,000. This was considered such a big chunk of money that for years the Giants had the canceled $10,000 check framed in President Brush's office.

Sam Leever was the league's pitching leader, with 20 victories, five defeats, and a percentage of .800; he beat out Mathewson, who worked much harder, winning 31 games out of 40, for a percentage of .775. Looking at the pitching averages at the season's close, Dreyfuss pointed to the name of Mathewson, and said: "That man—not McGraw—prevented us from winning this year. I almost wish we'd let him go to the American League in the peace settlement." And then catching himself, Barney added: "But I'm too good a National Leaguer to say anything like that."

3

The 1905 campaign was a painful one for Dreyfuss; he was in a season-long feud with McGraw and Brush, and only Barney's family and immediate friends knew how much he was hurt over the season's incidents and the insults of the New York manager. He never quite forgave the caustic-tongued McGraw.

From the time McGraw lifted the Giants from a tailender to a contender in 1903, there had been miniature warfare every time the New Yorkers and Pirates tangled in the same arena. "Pittsburgh is the team we've got to beat," McGraw told his players that year, "and no holds are barred." And though the Pirates had been praised several times in the annual guides for their deportment, this referred more to their humane treatment of umpires rather than to their attitude toward opponents. And a team managed by the fiery Clarke could be as tough, if need be, as McGraw's most truculent crew. The Pirates could take it and they could dish it out.

Bad blood between the two teams boiled over in a spring game at the Polo Grounds. Mike Lynch, the Pirate pitcher (who later became a Giant), was taking a drubbing, and as he returned to the bench after a distressful inning, McGraw, who had been coaching on third, yelled: "Stay in there, you big quitter, and take your medicine. You'll get plenty more before this is over."

Clarke, coming in from left field, overheard the remark. He took up the collegian's argument, and soon the two managers were exchanging billingsgate dipped in prussic acid. In a jiffy Fred and John J. squared off and began swinging, but Umpire Johnstone rushed between them before any real blows were struck. Apparently considering McGraw the original offender, Johnstone ordered him off the field. McGraw left his bench but took refuge in a little closet next to his dugout.

"Get 'im out of there! Get 'im out of there!" Clarke roared at Johnstone. "You put him off the field, now have the guts to put him off the grounds."

"He's off the grounds as far as I'm concerned," said Johnstone, and McGraw stayed in his cubbyhole.

Dreyfuss had a few things to say about what he termed "muckerism" and bad sportsmanship at the Polo Grounds. The New York newspapers played up the incident, also Barney's comment, and shortly afterward McGraw's sharp tongue struck at Dreyfuss. Barney was standing near the press gate at the Polo Grounds, chatting with friends, when McGraw appeared on a passageway that ran from the former Giant clubhouse, one floor above the street level. Cupping his hands, McGraw yelled: "Hey, Barney! Hey, Barney!"

BILL McKECHNIE

National League Service Bureau

National League Service Bureau

KIKI CUYLER

Pittsburgh Pirates Publicity Department
PIE TRAYNOR

Pittsburgh Sun-Telegraph
GLENN WRIGHT

Dreyfuss didn't look up, but McGraw continued his taunts. "Hey, Barney! Wanna bet?" With mock seriousness, McGraw defied Dreyfuss to bet $10,000 on the day's game and then dropped innuendoes that Dreyfuss hadn't picked up some markers he had given bookmakers.

Barney was livid with rage, and getting back to his hotel, he immediately wrote a letter to his former protégé, league president Pulliam:

I desire to and herewith make formal complaint against the conduct of John J. McGraw at the Polo Grounds Friday and Saturday, May 19 and 20.

While sitting in a box with a lady and gentleman from Pittsburgh, I was annoyed by McGraw's frequent personal references to me— sneering remarks that I personally be the umpire for the remaining games of the series.

On Saturday, May 20, I was standing in the main entrance of the Polo Grounds, talking quietly to some friends, when McGraw, who had been put off the grounds for using foul language, appeared on the balcony of the clubhouse and shouted: "Hey Barney!"

I did not answer that too familiar greeting and did not respond to any of his several attempts to attract my attention. Then he urged me to make a wager. He was very insistent but I had nothing to say to him. He also made remarks about me controlling umpires and other false and malicious statements. Steps should be taken to protect visitors to the Polo Grounds from insults from the said John J. McGraw.

Pulliam made public Dreyfuss' charges, and then McGraw hit the ceiling. He gave out a blistering statement in which he scorched Pulliam for giving out Dreyfuss' charges without giving McGraw a chance to defend himself, called Harry a "Dreyfuss' employee," and stressed Barney's part in making Pulliam the league president.

"Why, there is no organization on the face of the earth, except the National League, that will convict an accused man without a hearing. We might as well be in Russia," said McGraw. "If Dreyfuss and his employee, Pulliam, can prove that I have been guilty of conduct prejudicial to the best interests of the National League, well and good, but I must insist on having a fair hearing before sentence is pronounced on me."

Pulliam by this time felt the matter had become too hot a potato for him to handle. He called a meeting of the league board of directors for Boston, June 1, selecting the Massachusetts town because of the generally hostile attitude of the New York sports writers. That further infuriated McGraw, who vented his spleen on Pulliam over the telephone. Harry struck back by fining McGraw $150, and suspending him for fifteen days.

New York writers, led by Sam Crane, a former ball player, rushed to McGraw's rescue and printed names, imprecations, and insinuations, which McGraw fired at Dreyfuss and his alleged stooge, Pulliam. The *New York Journal,* with which Sam was affiliated, got up a petition with 10,000 signatures, calling for McGraw's prompt reinstatement, which was presented to the directors in Boston. The petition insinuated that Dreyfuss wanted to weaken the Giants in their pennant fight with the Pirates, which allegation Dreyfuss and Pulliam hotly resented.

At the trial in Boston, Dreyfuss further amplified his accusations against McGraw and charged that the New Yorker had vilified his character. Barney told the directors: "McGraw asked me: 'Is that bet you made with Shad on the level?' I turned and asked: 'Are you on the level?' Then McGraw said: 'How about those markers to the bookmakers? I have nobody chasing me with bad debts on racing bets. How are you on the level?' Then he cursed me and said I controlled umpires."

McGraw, on his part, testified that he had accused Barney of not picking up markers, but denied that he had said Dreyfuss was crooked or had influenced umpires.

The verdict of the directors was a Mexican standoff. McGraw was exonerated of the charges Dreyfuss brought against him, and the Pittsburgher was criticized for what the directors termed "his undignified conduct in engaging in a public altercation with a manager." However, the directors commended Pulliam on his splendid handling of the case. McGraw's fine and suspension stood.

The Giants were scheduled for a series in Boston immediately afterward, and Brush and his attorney applied to Judge Sheldon in Massachusetts Superior Court for an order restraining Pulliam and his umpires from enforcing the suspension. A temporary order was granted, and McGraw, in full uniform, was at the ball park that afternoon, directing his forces.

The "rhubarb" eventually blew over, but for years the controversy was a sore subject with Dreyfuss. One of the most dignified of the club owners, he bitterly resented the directors' finding that his conduct had been "undignified." The incident didn't die for over a decade. Fans, impish writers, players (when they knew they weren't detected), plagued Dreyfuss with cries of "Hey, Barney," when he entered his box in New York, Chicago, St. Louis, and other rival towns. Even at winter-league National League meetings at the old Waldorf-Astoria in downtown Manhattan, some wag would blurt, "Hey, Barney," as the Pittsburgher marched down Peacock Alley. It usually brought a laugh, but for Dreyfuss it was like a piece of barbed wire drawn across his skin. Is it any wonder that his hatred for McGraw became almost as great as that of Ban Johnson for the tempestuous New Yorker?

Yet through all of the bitterness engendered by the Dreyfuss-McGraw feud, McGraw never lost his respect and admiration for Hans Wagner. On a day when he was badgering Honus from the third-base coaching box, the Flying Dutchman was enjoying one of his greatest days. McGraw's pitchers couldn't get him out, and Hans was converting seemingly sure New York hits into put-outs and double plays.

In the eighth inning, as Wagner was returning to the bench, McGraw barked at him, as usual, but concluded: "But Honus, I've got to hand it to you. You're a great player! A great player! I surely wish I had one like you."

"Coming from McGraw, I knew that was a real compliment, and I always was proud of it," reminisced Hans. "McGraw knew ball players as few men knew them."

XIII.   BARNEY GOES HIGH FOR 29-GAME LOSER

"WE'VE GOT TO catch McGraw, I won't let him beat us out again,"
Dreyfuss said to Clarke and Will Locke, his new secretary, at a
conference after the 1905 season. "I've got a new first baseman
from San Francisco, Joe Nealon, who'll fill the bill. Every one
tells me he's a fine hitter. And, I'm working on a deal with Soden
of Boston that'll give us the pitcher we need to regain the championship."

The deal with Boston materialized later in the winter, and it
proved a good one for Pittsburgh, even though some of the fans
were aghast when Barney came up with the 29-game Boston
loser of 1905, Vic Willis. However, Victor had been crucified by
feeble support, and Barney and Clarke considered him one of
the top-ranking pitchers of both leagues. To bring Vic to the
Pirates, Dreyfuss gave up his new third baseman, Dave Brain;
Del Howard, the costly player acquired in the Bransfield deal,
and a young pitcher who had the fancy name of Vivian Alsace
Lindaman. Two new infielders, Tom Sheehan, a third baseman
from Tacoma, and Alan Storke were added, but as Sheehan soon
proved an ordinary performer, Tommy Leach was returned to
third base.

While Dreyfuss and Clarke were concocting plans for stopping
and passing McGraw, a new pennant threat—far more serious
than the Giants—was looming on the National League horizon.
Selee's Cubs had been second in 1904 but dropped back to third
in 1905. Selee resigned because of ill health, and Charley

Murphy, the new Cub president, permitted the players to elect a manager from their ranks. They chose Frank Chance, the aggressive first baseman. Murphy made a few advantageous trades, and almost overnight this Chicago club found itself under the inspiration of its new leaders. The 1906 Cubs, winning the first of a string of pennants, hung up the amazing record of 116 victories against 36 defeats, for a percentage of .763, the major-league record for the century.

We read in *Reach's Guide* that "the Pirates led twice in April, but fell out of the real pennant fight with the Cubs in May, and for the rest of the season they were engaged in battle with the Giants for second place. But, this position eventually went to New York." So, with a .608-percentage club, Barney's Corsairs followed not only in the wake of Chance but in that of the hated McGraw.

Even though the 1906 Pirates finished third, the pitching staff had an admirable season and scored 26 shutouts, a record for a Pittsburgh club. Willis, the newcomer from Boston, did all that was expected of him, winning 23 games and losing 13. Leever again was up there with Mathewson, with a 22-7 record. Leifield, a left-hander from St. Louis, who had joined the Pirates the previous season, came fast and won 18 games, while losing 13. Old Deacon Phillippe still had enough zip on his fast one for a 15-10 performance, and young Lynch won 6 while losing 5.

After yielding one year to the batting pretender, Cy Seymour, Honus clubbed his way back into the National League batting leadership, with an average of .339. There were only a handful of .300 hitters in 1906, but Clarke was in the exclusive circle with .309. Tommy Leach was the third best Pirate, with .286, and Nealon, the new first baseman, was listed at .255.

2

By 1907 it was no longer a case of "catching McGraw." Now, it was stopping Murphy and Chance. The stock of the Cubs went down somewhat when they lost the 1906 World Series, four games to two, to the light-hitting White Sox, but there was no laughing off a team that had just won 116 games. Despite the World Series upset, the Cubs were good, and no one knew it better than Dreyfuss and Clarke.

Dr. Barney decided another trade with Boston was the cure-all for Pirate ills. The transaction of the previous winter for Willis had turned out very well. Dreyfuss now felt Claude Ritchey, one of the few survivors of the "Louisville Guard," was no longer covering the ground that he did, or working as smoothly with Wagner on double plays. He looked with covetous eyes on the Boston second baseman, Ed Abbaticchio. Ed, whose name was shortened to Abby in box scores, was the vanguard of the Italian invasion of big-league baseball. Abby came from Latrobe, in western Pennsylvania; he played for Greensberg, Pa., and as far back as 1898 had had a tryout with the Phillies.

The Boston club had just been taken over by a new crowd headed by two brothers, George B. and John S. C. Dovey. Their club promptly was given the new nickname of Doves. The Doveys were also anxious to show Boston new faces and were agreeable that the black-haired Abbaticchio should become a Pirate, provided Ritchey, Ginger Beaumont, and Pat Flaherty took on the wings of Doves. Some said Barney went too high for the Italian second baseman, but Dreyfuss again got his man. With Beaumont gone, a new batch of outfielders, Art Meier, Billy Hallman, Ed "Goat" Anderson, H. W. Maggart, and Dan Moeller, were brought up. Moeller remained only two seasons and later developed into an American League star in Washington, on the same team with George McBride.

The Cubs didn't win 116 games in 1907 but they were still good enough to pile up 107 victories, and though the Pirates waged a fighting campaign, their strong second-place club came home 113 points behind the brilliant Chicagoans. This time not only the Pirates, but the Phillies, beat out the Giants, and Barney told Billy Shettsline, the Philadelphia club's president: "I didn't win the pennant, but I am happy that two Pennsylvania clubs finished ahead of New York's Muggsy McGraw."

If the Cubs led in percentage, the 1907 Pirates were tops in most everything else. They led in team batting, with an average of .254, and in stolen bases with 264. Most everyone took part in the wholesale larcenies, the Flying Dutchman—by now 33— stole 61 bags; Leach, 43; Clarke, 37, and Abby, the new man, 35. Wagner had no difficulty in winning his fifth batting crown with an average of .350. There were only four .300 hitters among the National League's regular players. Beaumont put on a batting revival in Boston and hit .322. Leach was fourth with .303, and by scoring 102 runs, Tommy the Wee was the only player in his loop to reach the century mark in tallies.

Of course, that old debbil, the first-base jinx, still got in its nefarious work. After Nealon played 104 games and hit an unimpressive .256, he jumped to Oakland of the then outlaw California State League. Storke played 23 games at first, and Harry Swacina, an alleged hard hitter acquired from Peoria, took care of 26 others. Swacina, a St. Louisan, wasn't too graceful as a fielder, but he was a hefty, well-built chap with strong arms and powerful shoulders, and for a while it looked as though he might be the answer to Barney's first-base prayer.

Again the pitching was splendid. Willis repeated his fine work of 1906 with a 21-11 season, and Lefty Leifield was good with a 20-16 mark. The Kentucky Rosebud, Camnitz, developed to a point where he won 13 and lost 8, while the two veterans, Leever and Phillippe, were almost the same; 14-9 for the schoolmaster, and 14-11 for the Deacon. Bill Duggleby, a grizzled veteran, was a waiver pickup from the Phillies.

The pitching would have been even better, and the entire Pittsburgh story different, if Barney had entered the name of a young semipro from Weiser, Idaho, in his little dope book. One of Barney's salesman friends sent him glowing accounts of a youngster, Walter Johnson, who was burning up the mining-town teams around Idaho. If anybody got more than three hits off him, Johnson had a bad day, and his strike-outs averaged 20—if he was lucky enough to get a catcher who could hold him. The salesman could bring the young sensation east, if Barney was willing to send transportation and a little extra for expenses.

Barney, always willing to gamble, probably would have sent the money if the fellow hadn't been so extravagant with his praises. Dreyfuss decided he was laying it on too thick; he was trying too hard to make a sale. Barney didn't send the money. Soon afterward, Cliff Blankenship, Washington catcher–first baseman, out at the time with an injury, took a look at Johnson and signed him to a Washington contract. The Senators were then the American League tailender, with one of the leanest treasuries in the two majors. They snatched Johnson not only from under the nose of Dreyfuss, but from under those of 14 other more opulent big-league club owners. Johnson, a success from the start, became one of the pitching immortals of all time, a man who closed his big-league books with 413 victories. One can only dream of the pennants he might have brought to Pittsburgh.

3

There was a good chance to beat out the Cubs in 1908. From 116 victories in 1906, and 107 in 1907, Chance's great machine subsided to 99 in 1908. The Pirates had plenty of opportunity to pull them down, but at the finish the Corsairs had 98 victories and 56 defeats, which gave them only a second-place tie with New York, a game behind the ever dangerous Chicagoans. It was the greatest race in National League history, for in their last two games of the season, the Cubs, with Mordecai Brown the winning pitcher, knocked both Pittsburgh and New York out of the race.

It was a race of bitterness, rancor, and recriminations. For six seasons the National League's pennant fighting had been between Pittsburgh, New York, and Chicago, and this year the clans of Clarke, Chance, and McGraw got right down into the bull pit and fought it out in hand-to-hand battling with teeth and claws. Gouging and biting were minor infractions.

Speaking of this bitter 1908 fighting, Hans Wagner told a Toronto audience a few years ago:

We went into Chicago at a time when we were neck and neck, and the Cubs were especially rough on us, and I mean rough physically. We lost the series, two games out of three. We returned shortly afterward to Exposition Park for a series with Chicago. Fred Clarke called a meeting in our clubhouse, and said: "I'll give a fifty-dollar bonus to the player who can do the most damage to the Cubs."

One of our pitchers spoke up and asked whether he couldn't get in on the proposition. He suggested that after he'd get "ahead" of the hitter, he'd start chucking at his head. After Clarke's offer, we all wore our longest spikes. And those who didn't have long ones filed the short ones down to a point. I'll tell you we were ready for them. That was managerial strategy in the old days.

It's quite a little different from the way they do things today. A manager calls a clubhouse meeting; we discuss the enemy's weakness and go over their hitters. It's pitch to this one on the inside, and don't groove one to the next, or he'll knock it over the fence. Then after the manager's gone all the way down the line, he'll say: "Now I want you fellows to show me plenty of fight and hustle. Try all the time, but above all play fair." That gives you an idea of the change in a manager's attitude since I played, but I wonder just how we would have reacted if Clarke had told us to play fair with Chance's Cubs and McGraw's Giants.

Wagner himself didn't sign with the 1908 Pirates until the season was four days old. There is a fallacy that the Flying Dutchman signed any contract Barney pushed under his nose, without so much as looking at the figure. That legend is grossly exaggerated. While Hans Wagner unquestionably could have put the squeeze on Dreyfuss during the American League war, he knew he was good when he was batting champion, and was paid the best salary in the National League.

The training season of 1908 was the holdout spring of the batting champions. In the American League the fiery Georgian, Ty Cobb, who had won his first batting title in 1907 at the age of 21, was asking for a salary allegedly as much as Dreyfuss was paying Wagner. However, Honus upped his own demand on Sir Barney to $10,000 and wouldn't take a penny less. Wagner held out during the entire training season, passed up Hot Springs, and was still missing when the Pirates opened the season. It wasn't until April 19, four days after the Pirates opened in Cincinnati, that he reported to Clarke in St. Louis. And he got his $10,000!

He had a business associate and adviser in Carnegie named James Orris, and Wagner rarely transacted any business dealings without consulting Orris. And it generally was believed that it was Orris who influenced Hans in his stand. "I've got not only Wagner, but this other fellow, Orris, holding out on me," sighed Barney, at the time.

Speaking of the incident today, Wagner says: "I really wasn't a holdout in 1908. I was going to retire and go into the garage business in my home town. I had an option on a half square in Carnegie and was going to take it over. But finally Barney convinced me that $10,000 a year in baseball was better than the garage business of that time. He even said he would go in with me at the end of my playing days. But I played ten more seasons and forgot about the garage, though I had a small garage in 1912 and 1913."

Yet those who knew Honus, and how he loved to play baseball, cannot believe he would have retired at that stage of his career. There was an amusing Wagner happening that season. As Pittsburgh didn't have Sunday baseball at that period, it was a common practice for the Pirates to jump to Chicago, St. Louis, and Cincinnati for Sabbath games. To hold down expenses, the Pirate party for these one-day trips usually was limited to 14 players. On the train to Cincinnati, Bill Locke, the secretary, found he was one player short; he had only 13 players on his list, but 14 tickets. He finally showed the list to both Fred Clarke and Wagner, and asked: "Who the hell did I leave off?"

Clarke couldn't find the missing player, and then big Hans ran his thumb down the list of names. He also couldn't name the man who had been left off. It turned out that the missing name was none other than that of the team's most famous player and the National League's greatest all-time star, Honus Wagner.

4

Pittsburgh and Chicago made the pace in early April, 1908, and then it was New York for a few days. The Phillies and Reds had their brief whirl on top in May, while McGraw tumbled into the second division, apparently out of the running. The Cubs led most of the time after that, but on June 29, the Pirates dislodged Chicago for four days, and again from July fifth to eighth. Each time Chance's grim warriors bounced back, but on July 15, the Pirates dragged the Bruins down and held the lead for 36 consecutive days. "I think we're in again," said Barney hopefully.

But the Giants came fast, made up their spring losses, and on August 20, they took the lead for a day. Pittsburgh quickly regained the top perch, but lost it again on August 24, and New York occupied first place continually until September 29, with the Pirates and Cubs alternating in second place, and never more than a few jumps behind.

On September 23 came the famous Cub-Giant game at the Polo Grounds, New York, in which Fred Merkle, young Giant utility first baseman, failed to run to second base, as Al Bridwell hammered in what apparently was the winning run with two out in the ninth. The little second-base crab of the Cubs, Johnny Evers, won undying fame by tagging· his second-base bag for a force-out on Merkle. Hank O'Day, the veteran umpire, allowed the put-out.

Yet the Giants would never have been caught on this play had the New Yorkers been observant and followed the games of their closest rivals, Pittsburgh and Chicago. Tommy Leach recalls how a play at Exposition Park only a few weeks before foreshadowed the more famous Evers-Merkle play:

We played Chicago at home just about two weeks before the Merkle incident, and oddly enough it was also a young first baseman, Warren Gill, who was involved," said Tommy. "The race was so close at the time that we were almost on a three-way tie for first place. In our game with the Cubs we had the bases full and two out with the score tied in the ninth. Chief Wilson hit a clean single to center, and the winning run crossed the plate. Gill ran about halfway down to second and then started to run off the field. Some of us older players on the bench saw what was going on, especially as we heard Evers and Tinker jabbering around second and calling for Artie Hofman, the Cub center fielder, to throw the ball to second base. We started running after Gill, to get him to retrace his steps and touch second, but in the meantime we noted that both of the umpires had walked off the field. They didn't see the play, and apparently were satisfied that Pittsburgh had won. One of the umpires was Hank O'Day. He admitted he hadn't seen Gill's failure to run to second, but said if such a play came up again, he would call the runner out.

Sure enough, it came up in New York on September 23, and under almost the identical conditions. This time O'Day was umpiring on the bases, and when Merkle didn't touch second, Hank was looking for just that play. Looking back over the years, I can see how Merkle could have been saved a lot of grief if the play hadn't first come up in Pittsburgh. At the time, it was a common practice for players to dash for the clubhouse after the winning play had been made, but the Gill play alerted the umpires to watch for just such an omission. It was tough on young Merkle that the game was so vitally important, and that he had to be the first official victim.

With the precedent of the Gill play, which was publicized at the time, it long has been a wonder to the author that the crafty John McGraw, who never missed a trick on the diamond, did not call the play to the attention of his players in a clubhouse discussion and warn them against such a contingency.

If the National League race was tighter than a drum before the Merkle game, it had now become whackier than ever. And it vitally concerned the Pirates. They wanted to know whether they had to beat out Chicago or New York. For a week no one knew who had won the game of September 23; McGraw claimed his club had won a legal victory, and the Cubs claimed the game by forfeit, as the field hadn't been cleared after the O'Day decision, and there had been no chance to complete the game. The board of directors eventually ordered the game replayed on October 8, the day after the close of the National League season.

The Pirates could have made this replay of the Merkle game meaningless, and could have won the 1908 pennant had they won their last game of the season with the Cubs in Chicago on Sunday, October 4. According to accounts at the time, the crowd was 30,647—6,000 more than had ever been in Chicago's old West Side Park. It was a game for blood all the way, with the Cubs defeating the Buccaneers by a score of 5 to 2.

Bill McKechnie, then a Pirate rookie, and other 1908 Corsairs, still say that a decision by Hank O'Day (Hank just couldn't keep out of vital decisions in 1908) cost the Pirates the game, but the Cubs outhit the men of Pittsburgh, 12 to 7, and had the knack of bunching them. They scored single runs in each of the first, fifth, sixth, seventh, and eighth innings. Vic Wallis gave up 9 hits in 7 innings, and Howard Camnitz 3 in the eighth. The Pirates reached Three-fingered Brown for only 7 and had their brief flare-up in the sixth, when they scored 2 runs, and tied the score for a few minutes at 2 to 2. The Cubs quickly regained the lead in their half.

Dreyfuss was heartbroken over the defeat but took it like a real sportsman. Ralph Davis quoted Barney as saying: "Only one team could win, and it wasn't ours. It was too bad. Willis was in grand form and the other members of the team played the game of their lives, but against Brown and the support given him by the Cubs the chances of the Pirates taking this crucial game were indeed slim. I salute a great ball club!"

While victory for the Pirates would have clinched the flag for Dreyfuss and Clarke, there still remained a mathematical pennant chance for Pittsburgh. The Pirates had completed their schedule, and the Cubs had only the replay game with the Giants on Thursday, October 8. But the Giants had to play three more games with the Boston club on October 5, 6, and 7. Should the New Yorkers lose one of the three games to Boston and defeat Chicago in the play-off of the September 23 game, the three leaders would end the season in a three-cornered tie. That would have necessitated a round-robin play-off.

The Pirates kept their eyes glued to scoreboards and the ticker tape throughout the Giant-Boston series. Joe Kelly, an 1892 Pirate and a former teammate of McGraw's on the Baltimore Orioles, was manager of the Boston club, and to his dying day

Joe resented intimations that he didn't try too hard to win a game in this important series. He had the former Pirates, Ritchey, Beaumont, Brain and Flaherty, on a fair .409 percentage, sixth-place club. Nevertheless, the Giants won by comparatively easy scores of 8 to 1, 4 to 1, and 7 to 2, and the third game officially eliminated Pittsburgh.

It made the pennant hinge on the outcome of the October 8 play-off; the Cubs won it, 4 to 2, and came home with a percentage of .643, seven points higher than the .636 of both Pittsburgh and New York.

Actually the Pirates lost the flag as the result of their old first-base weakness. The club had no regular first sacker; Swacina played 50 games at the bag; Storke, 49; Jimmy Kane, 40; and Warren Gill, 25. Many fans sighed: "If Barney had only kept Kitty [Bransfield]." Bransfield hit .304 for the Phillies, one of the league's four .300 regulars, and played brilliantly in the field. A business associate of Dreyfuss brought up the matter of Kitty, and Barney almost snapped off his head with a 1908 version of: "Why bring that up?"

The club also lacked the hitting to back up its fine pitching. Old Honus was up there, as usual, leading the parade with a robust .354. But from there it was a big drop to Clarke's .265 and Leach's .259.

We also read that "outfield weakness held back the club a good part of the season," and that the youngster John Owen Wilson "had difficulty playing center field." Leach played most of his games at third base, and Clarke lined up his best outfield after he acquired the crack Philadelphia center fielder, Roy Thomas, and shifted young Wilson to right. The latter, nicknamed the "Chief," hit only .227 in his first season, but he had an early knack of hitting triples, also a magnificent arm, and soon developed into one of the great right fielders of the game. Gibson, who caught 140 games, advanced in leaps and bounds and was grouped with Johnny Kling and Roger Bresnahan as the great catching trio of the league.

Nick Maddox, the rookie of 1907, flashed like a meteor across the National League pitching sky, winning 23 games in his sophomore year, while losing only 8. Willis also won 23, and lost 11. Camnitz was listed at 16-9; Leever 15-7, but Leifield had a difficult time staying on the right side of .500, with 15-14.

Clarke also had Irving M. Young (Cy II), a left-hander procured from Boston, and Harley E. Young (Cy III) on his 1908 staff.

And Clarke was as severe with himself as with any of his players when he thought he made a bad play. He had the knack of diving in and snatching line drives a few inches off the ground.

In an important late-season game with the Phillies, with the score tied in the late innings and a runner on second, Fred dove in for a low liner. He missed the catch and the ball rolled through him, the runner on second scoring what proved to be the winning run. Had Fred played the ball on the first hop, it would have been a short single, and he could easily have held the runner on third.

There was an awkward silence when the manager came to the bench at the end of the inning. After a few minutes, Clarke blurted out: "Well, what's the matter with you yellow bellies? Hasn't any one of you the guts to tell me I pulled a lousy bone out there? Well, I know it, and I deserve everything you're thinking about me."

XIV.   NEW CASTLE AND NEW PENNANT

No BASEBALL owner had a greater faith in baseball, or a greater prophetic sense of the advances the national game would make in this century, than Barney Dreyfuss. At a time when most of the major-league stands, including those in the big breadwinning cities of New York and Chicago, were still cheap structures of wood, the little Pittsburgh owner conceived the idea of a great three-decked grandstand, which would be a monument to baseball.

Though Barney had won no pennant since 1903, his Pirates annually had been first-division contenders, and Pittsburgh loyally had supported the club in its modest Allegheny settings, and on big days fans stood uncomplainingly behind ropes in the marshy outfield. What's more, Barney was tired of the river backing into his outfield, and players needing rafts to play their positions.

While Charley Ebbets of Brooklyn was still preaching, "Baseball is in its infancy," Dreyfuss showed his belief that the infant at least had reached adolescence by ordering the construction of a new park with a great triple-decked grandstand in that part of Pittsburgh known as Oakland and Schenley Park. The new edifice was named Forbes Field in honor of General John Forbes, who camped his Revolutionary Army in the district when the young republic fought its war for independence.

"When I first selected the present Forbes Field site for our new ball park in 1908, people laughed at me," Barney confessed later in life. "There was nothing there but a livery stable, a hothouse, while a few cows roamed over the countryside. They belonged to the Schenley Farms. A ravine ran through the property, and I knew the first thing necessary to make the field available for baseball was to fill it in and level off the entire field.

"However, I had decided we had to get out of Exposition Park in Allegheny. The game was growing up, and patrons no longer were willing to put up with nineteenth-century conditions. Besides, the park was located in a poor neighborhood, and many of the better class of citizens, especially when accompanied by their womenfolk, were loathe to go there.

"I made several trips out to Schenley Farms, and the more I looked over the property the better I liked it. I had a strong hunch, which amounted to a conviction, that Pittsburgh would grow eastward."

Dreyfuss acquired the ground through Andrew Carnegie, with whom he was well acquainted. The famous steel magnate and philanthropist was one of the executors of the Schenley estate.

In the same year, 1909, that Dreyfuss built Forbes Field, Benjamin Shibe and Connie Mack of the Athletics opened Shibe Park, their concrete and steel park in Philadelphia, but old Ben and Connie were still appealing largely to their two-bit trade. The Athletics built a grandstand seating 6,000, while the park had great concrete bleachers in both left and right fields, taking care of another 14,000 fans.

Not only did Dreyfuss put in 5,000 more seats than the Philadelphians, but the greater part of his new 25,000 capacity was in the higher-priced grandstand seats. His new grandstand was a huge triple-decker, with elevator service to the third tier.

"A park in Pittsburgh, seating 25,000, was considered another of my follies," Barney confessed with a lurking smile. "Why, they told me the Giants don't have that large a park with all New York to draw from. One friend bet me a one-hundred-and-fifty-dollar suit of clothes the park would never be filled. We filled it five times the first two weeks. And I collected not only the suit of clothes, but a nice return at the gate."

Dreyfuss organized the Forbes Field Co. to buy the land and to build his ball park. It is now worth many times the original investment. And Barney was a good prophet in predicting the city would spread eastward. Today the Pittsburgh ball yard is situated in the heart of the cultural, educational, and residential center of Schenley Park. It is flanked on one side by the University of Pittsburgh's great cathedral of learning, and Carnegie Tech and the Carnegie Museum can be seen plainly beyond the center-field fence.

For years no advertising was permitted on the fences; the field had great outfield pastures, and the home plate was 110 feet from the stands. It gave the catcher more room to maneuver after foul flies than in any other big-league park. The park was such a beauty that a Pittsburgh reporter once referred to it as "the Hialeah of major-league baseball," in a talk with the late baseball commissioner, Judge Landis, whose particular bugaboo was horse racing.

"The what?" demanded the Judge.

"Well, Hialeah is just about the most beautiful race track in America," the scribe persisted.

The Judge smiled, and replied: "That's right and Forbes Field is a mighty pretty ball park."

The park was officially opened on June 30, 1909, before a crowd of 30,338 (outfield ropes had to be put up the very first day), and the Cubs, the Pirates' spirited rivals, won a close game by a score of 3 to 2. Vic Willis battled it out with big Ed Reulbach through nine grim innings. Hits were at a premium, Vic giving up only four safeties to five for Ed, but Johnny Evers, the pesky Cub lead-off man, bagged two of Chicago's hits and scored two runs. Reulbach was wild, walking six and hitting a seventh, but the Pirates couldn't hit in the pinches, and they left ten runners on the bases.

"What a shame we had to lose that one," said Dreyfuss, after it was over. "I'd have given my share of the gate to have won on this day."

It was a day that stayed with Barney as long as he lived. Everybody who was anybody in baseball, or in Pennsylvania politics, was there. One of the proud features of the opening-day parade was a march of Pittsburgh's baseball old-timers: Uncle Al Pratt, who once hit five home runs in a single game; John K. Tener, the big pitcher from Charleroi, then a United States congressman; Ned Hanlon, the early center fielder and manager, then owner of the Baltimore Internationals; Eddie Morris, ace pitcher of the original 1887 Pittsburgh Nationals; Sheriff A. G. Gumbert, and a host of others.

Then came the visiting notables: Garry Herrmann, the National

Commission chairman; Harry Pulliam and Ban Johnson, the major-league presidents, and most of the club owners from both big leagues. It took two city officials to get the ball game under way. Mayor Magee, seated in a box in the center of the second tier, tossed out the ball to Public Safety Director Morin in left field. And Morin relayed it to Vic Willis on the mound.

2

Had it not been for the midseason suicide of league president Harry Pulliam, Dreyfuss' beloved friend and former associate in both Louisville and Pittsburgh, the season of 1909 would have been Barney's "year of years." Not only did he open a ball palace that was the game's show place, but his Pirates won all of the year's honors on the ball field.

Yet Pulliam's suicide hung like a dark shadow over Dreyfuss' artistic and financially successful 1909 season. It happened little more than a fortnight after the elaborate opening-day ceremonies at Forbes Field. The 1908 Merkle game and the Giants' loss of the subsequent play-off game had many unhappy repercussions in New York, and in a fit of moody depression Pulliam put a revolver to his head in his New York hotel, July 29, and pulled the trigger.

Dreyfuss was heartbroken and could not have grieved more if Harry had been his own son. "This is one of the game's most grievous tragedies," he said. "Pulliam was a true Kentucky thoroughbred; no finer man ever was born into this world. I am heartsick over what has happened."

However, on the ball field the fates ran with Dreyfuss and Clarke all through the 1909 season. Even though the Cubs won 104 games in their effort to win a fourth straight pennant, the rampaging Buccaneers shot by them like a buzz bomb, with 110 victories, the second-best performance in National League history. It is still a moot question among baseball students which Pirate team was greater, the 1902 entry, which won 103 games and had a percentage of .741 in a 140-game season, or the powerful 1909 club, which won 110 games and lost 42 for a .724 percentage in a 154-game season. Two 1909 games were left unplayed.

The Cubs were handicapped by the season-long holdout of Johnny Kling, their ace catcher. But even without Chattering John, Chicago was five games stronger than in 1908 and still couldn't make it a real contest for Clarke's valiant crew. After Boston and the Phillies held the lead following April skirmishes, when Pittsburgh was as low as fifth, the Bucs snatched first place, May 5, and were never headed thereafter.

Week after week the Cubs engaged in a relentless pursuit, and some of the wise ones predicted Pittsburgh would crack at the stretch. "Watch the Cubs put on a great September drive," was one of the forecasts, but by the time the race reached Labor Day, the flying Pirates were so far in front that even the Cubs had all but given up hope.

Particularly pleasing to Clarke was the way his boys fought off the Chicago toughies themselves. Even though the Pirates lost the big dedication game to the Cubs at Forbes Field, the Buccos won the year's series from Chance's stubborn warriors, 13 games to 9. The third-place Giants were again difficult, and Clarke got only an even break with McGraw in twenty-two games. But from there on, the Pirates fairly feasted on their rivals, winning 15 games from each the Reds and the Phillies, 18 from each the Dodgers and the Cardinals, and 20 from the Braves.

Clarke made several changes in the club's personnel, especially in the infield. Bill Abstein, a former St. Louis sand lotter, who had been briefly with the club as early as 1906, took over at the jinxed first-base spot. A tall, lanky kid from Kearney, N. J., Jack "Dots" Miller, with only a little experience with Easton, Pa., and McKeesport in the O. P. League, won the second-base job from Abby. Pittsburgh fans immediately took the kid to their hearts, and for several seasons Dots could do wrong. Honus also took an early fancy to the loose-as-a-goose youngster and taught Jack all he knew about infield play. Miller worshiped old Honus, and they became an adept double-play combination.

Fred started the season with a pint-sized French Canadian, William Joe "Jap" Barbeau, at third base. Jap, who measured only five feet, four and a half inches, had come from Columbus, Ohio, after he had been up briefly with the Phillies and Cleveland. Barbeau was a difficult little monkey at the top of the batting order, but late in the season Dreyfuss and Clarke procured the man they wanted in peppery Bobbie Byrne, an aggressive St. Louis Irishman and one of the league's best third basemen and base runners. Byrne came from the Cardinals, August 29, in a swap for Barbeau, Alan Storke, and a little cash.

The 1909 National League season again produced only four

100-game players in the .300 class, and Honus continued the old Wagnerian custom of being boss man of the hitters, with .339; he remained sufficiently agile to steal 35 bases. Chief Wilson improved 100 per cent over his freshman year, and Gibson established two major-league records for that time by catching 150 games, 133 of them in succession. Clarke had two other catchers, Paddy O'Connor and Mike Simon, but it was a rare day when Pirate fans could find either of them in a box score. Even after Pittsburgh clinched the flag, Gibby worked every day, just as though the pennant were still at stake. And the Pirates came up with one of the game's greatest pinch hitters, Hamilton Hyatt. Hyatt was listed as an outfielder–first baseman, but he wasn't much of either. He was distinctly "good hit; no field," but that season, whenever Clarke needed a hit, Ham was the boy who could deliver it.

The 110 victories of Pittsburgh's new champions were made possible by the superb work of the pitchers. Clarke picked spots for the gallant survivors of the early titleholders, Leever and Phillippe, who still had creditable marks of 8-1 and 8-3, respectively. Howard Camnitz tied the great Mathewson for the league's leadership, with 25 victories and 6 defeats; Lefty Leifield won 22 victories and suffered 11 defeats. Nick Maddox fell off somewhat from his great record of 1908, but still won 13 games out of 21.

The newcomer of the staff was a handsome, likable Hoosier from Tipton, Ind., by the name of Charles Adams, but he never has been known as anything but "Babe." He was a babe of that pitching staff of veterans, though not as young as many fans believe. Actually he was 26 and made a National League appearance with the Cardinals as far back as 1906. Clarke had the kid on his squad for a short time in 1907, and in 1908 Babe was farmed to Louisville, where he won 22 games and lost 12. Brought up by the Buccos in the exciting closing days of the 1908 race, the young Hoosier won two games out of three. Commanding a veteran staff, Clarke used Adams rather sparingly in 1909, but he was the "Baby on the Spot" whenever Fred called on him, winning 12 games while losing 3.

3

No story of the Pirates' 1909 pennant race is complete without a recital of the dramatic game of August 16, when Red Murray, Giant right fielder, made one of the greatest catches ever seen on Forbes Field, also one of the most picturesque and dramatic in baseball history. With Mathewson pitching against Willis, the score was 2 to 1 in favor of New York, as the Pirates came to bat in the second half of the eighth inning. It was evident a severe storm was about to break; there were rumbles of thunder, and it was so dark that electric lights had been turned on in the grandstand. Klem and Kane were the umpires, and though it had started to rain, Bill, working behind the plate, was giving Pittsburgh every opportunity to take "its lick."

Clarke sent Hyatt to bat for Willis, and Ham came through with his usual brilliance, slashing a triple to right. Abby ran for him and scored the tying run on Barbeau's fly to Seymour. Leach doubled, and after Clarke popped to Bridwell for the second out, the Dutchman was intentionally passed.

"Now, you break it up," Wagner yelled at his young buddy, Dots Miller.

No one ever tried harder, and when Miller sent a terrific drive screeching for the pocket in deep right center, it looked like two runs and the ball game. Rain was now falling heavily, and in the darkness the fans could scarcely make out the ghostlike figure of Murray. Then a great flash of lightning illuminated the park, and the 10,000 fans beheld a remarkable—though unwelcome—sight. Murray, running full tilt into right center, stuck out his bare hand and snatched Miller's line drive about three feet off the ground.

The Murray catch retired the side, and Klem called time before the Pirates could take the field. The downpour lasted a half hour, but by the time it stopped the field had become a quagmire. Further play was out of the question, and Klem called the game. Red Jack's circus catch in the lightning flash gave New York a 2-2 eight-inning tie; it also enabled Matty to tie the Kentucky Rosebud for the league's 1909 pitching honors. Had Miller's ball gone safe, Mathewson would have had an additional defeat.

From the time that Fred Clarke tossed Dreyfuss out of the clubhouse in their first season in Pittsburgh, 1900, Barney never invaded the sacred domains where the Pirates took off their skull and crossbones, plunged into their showers, and dressed their spike wounds. But after the pennant-clinching game, Barney stuck his head through the clubhouse door and called to Clarke: "Can I come in?"

"You bet you can," said the happy manager.

"I want to say that you're not only a great team but a fine bunch of fellows," said Dreyfuss. "I congratulate everybody."

XV. BABE ADAMS BASKS IN
NATIONAL SPOTLIGHT

HAVING SAFELY tucked away the 1909 flag, the Pirates' next objective was the coveted World Championship, the prize that had eluded them in 1903. Dreyfuss, Clarke, Honus, and Tommy the Wee all figured they had a few scores to settle with the American League. Ban Johnson's champions were Hughie Jennings' Detroit Tigers, three-time winners, with their great star Ty Cobb, who had won his third American League batting title with the smart average of .377. The Tigers had been easy World Series pickings for the Cubs in 1907 and 1908, getting only one victory and one tie out of the two Series, but the Detroit club had been strengthened considerably since 1908. Through trade and purchase, Jennings had entirely remodeled his infield since his 1908 defeat, and showed the aggressive George Moriarty at third; Donie Bush, a latter-day Pirate manager, at shortstop; Jim Delahanty at second, and Tom Jones at first. With George Mullin, Bill Donovan, and Eddie Summers heading their pitching staff, and an outfield trio of Davey Jones, Ty Cobb, and Sam Crawford, the Tigers were nobody's push-over, as the Pirates soon discovered.

Thanks to Barney Dreyfuss' large new park, the 1909 World Series was the first to reach big baseball arithmetic—certainly for that time. The gate for seven games was $188,302, with an attendance of 145,807. The three games in Pittsburgh attracted 82,885, or more than the total attendance in the Cub-Tiger Series in either 1907 or 1908. The fact that the two batting champions

of the majors, Hans Wagner and Ty Cobb, were on rival sides
helped steam up interest in the Series.

Barney Dreyfuss was in a lucky year, and in a preliminary
World Series meeting in Garry Herrmann's room, he rightly
called the coin when he and Frank Navin of Detroit tossed for
who would stage the first game. It gave Barney the first and
second games at Forbes Field, for Friday, October 8, and Saturday, October 9.

During the league season, Howard Camnitz, Vic Willis, and
Lefty Leifield had accounted for sixty-six of Pittsburgh's victories,
and it naturally was assumed the mighty trio would take care of
the bulk of Clarke's Series pitching. As events turned out, not
one of the three won a game. Camnitz, the 1909 ace of the staff,
had an attack of quinsy before the start of the Series. It was a
tough break for the Rosebud, but maybe it turned out for the
best for Pittsburgh and the Pirates.

Late in the season, John Heydler, a former Washingtonian,
who had succeeded Pulliam as acting president of the National
League, had seen an American League game in which Dolly
Gray, pitcher for the last-place Senators, had held the Tiger batsmen helpless for eight innings before losing the game, 3 to 1,
when Detroit scored two unearned runs in the ninth. Heydler,
a former National League umpire and an earlier amateur star,
knew his baseball and had observed that there was a strong
similarity between the deliveries of Gray and of Clarke's pitching
youngster, Babe Adams.

Looking up Clarke before the first game at Forbes Field,
Heydler remarked: "Fred, I don't know who you're going to
pitch in your first game, but I saw Detroit play a late September
game in Washington, and they couldn't touch Gray. Dolly pitches
very much like Adams; I think Babe is faster, and he should give
those fellows a lot of trouble."

With Camnitz still bothered by his quinsy, Clarke played the
hunch, and the 29,577 crowd that attended the first game was
rather surprised to see Adams warm up to face George Mullin,
the Tiger ace, and a 29-game American League winner.

"Aren't they sending a boy on a man's errand?" and "Do they
expect that kid to hold off Mullin?" were some of the pregame
comments from loyal National League sympathizers. But they
didn't know their boy! Doubters sang a different story before the

afternoon was over, as Babe triumphed brilliantly by a score of 4 to 1.

It was a stunning and emphatic National League victory and assuredly got the Pirates off on the right boot. It was a light-hitting game; the Pirates made only five hits to six for Detroit, but the Buccaneers bunched their blows to good advantage, and one of the Pittsburgh hits was a homer by Fred Clarke. Fred had an odd series, banging only four hits in the seven games, but two were damaging round-trippers.

Getting his World Series baptism, Adams did well to survive a shaky first inning with only one run scored against him. For a few minutes it looked as though Detroit might open with a parcel of runs, but Babe remained cool under fire. The Hoosier started wildly by walking Jones, and after Bush sacrificed, Babe also gave four balls to Ty Cobb. That brought up the dangerous Sam Crawford, and Hugh Jennings, on the third-base coaching line, beseeched his Nebraska barber to drive home the runs. But the crowd gave a spontaneous yell of sheer joy when Crawford poked the ball back at Adams, and Babe tossed it to Byrne for a force play on Jones at third.

There was still trouble, as Jim Delahanty, a Tiger thorn all during the Series, lashed a single to left, scoring Cobb, and on Clarke's futile peg to the plate, Crawford made third and Delahanty second. Moriarty punched another ball toward left field, but it hit Delahanty on the leg, automatically retiring Jim for the third out.

Cobb's run was the only tally for Detroit, as Babe grew better with each succeeding inning. He was backed with brilliant error-less support, the particular gem being a miracle catch by Tommy Leach on Cobb in deepest center, robbing the Georgia firebrand of a home run with Davey Jones on first base.

Clarke's vigorous home run thrust into the left-field bleachers tied the score for Pittsburgh in the fourth inning and Pittsburgh fans had a lot of fun riding Jennings and Cobb, after fumbling Detroit fingers helped the Buccos to two soft tallies in the fifth. Delahanty permitted Bill Abstein's grounder to roll through his legs, and when Cobb also fumbled the ball in right field, Bill never stopped running until he reached third base. "What's the matter, Ty? Got lard on your glove?" sympathized the right-field bleacherites.

Mullin struck out Chief Wilson, but Gibson pumped out a

double, scoring Abstein. Bush wrestled with Adams' grounder all around the infield; that put the bulky Gibson on third, from where he ambled home on Leach's long outfield fly. The fourth Pittsburgh run was aided by the fourth Tiger error in the sixth. Wagner made his first World Series hit since 1903, a slashing double to left. The Dutchman took a long lead off second base and coaxed Dutch Schmidt, the heavyweight Tiger catcher, to throw down to the bag. Schmidt's strong-arm peg landed out in center field, Honus taking third, from where he scored on Abstein's infield out.

2

The second game was played on a beautiful mild Saturday before a crowd of 31,114, a record World Series turnout for that era. It was a good day for Jennings' second-best pitching bet, the veteran Smiling Bill Donovan, who needed a good warm sun to loosen the sinews in his right arm. Bill spoiled the fun for the partisan Saturday throng that started the day in a holiday mood, by tying up the Series for the American League, winning easily by a score of 7 to 2.

Clarke, who had held back Camnitz because of his throat trouble, took a chance on the Rosebud in the second game, but the attack of quinsy had taken a severe toll on Howard, and he was far from his usual self. After Camnitz had yielded six hits and five runs, Skipper Fred pulled him in the third and sent in Vic Willis, who fared much better.

Much of the excitement for the Pittsburgh fans came in the very first inning, when the Pirates scored their two runs on Donovan, and the right-field bleacherites were asked to "call" a batted ball hit into the sun seats, one of the believe-it-or-not World Series decisions. It was the first time four umpires were assigned to a Series, but only two worked the game; the others looked on from a field box. Jim Johnstone and Silk O'Loughlin had umpired the first game, and two novices, Billy Evans and Bill Klem—both destined to be great umpires—took care of the second game, with Evans behind the plate.

Donovan had difficulty at the start, as he walked Bobbie Byrne and the St. Louisan scored on Tommy Leach's double. Clarke sacrificed Tommy to third, but Donovan mowed down Wagner on strikes. Dots Miller followed with a stinging line drive, which was headed for a low temporary bleacher deep in right field, and almost at the foul line. Part of the bleacher was in fair territory and part on foul soil. As the ball headed toward the stands, the crowd stood up and hid the sphere from the two umpires.

Evans stood at the plate for a few moments, trying to collect his wits, and then talked it over with Klem, who was umpiring the bases. "Did you see it, Bill?" he asked.

"No, I was hoping you'd seen it," said Klem. "What'll we do?"

Evans trudged slowly out to the bleacher, trying to formulate his plan, Klem walking a few steps behind him. As they approached the place where the ball had disappeared, the loyal Pittsburgh fans began to yell: "It was a homer! It was a homer!"

"Let's ask them where the ball landed," Evans said to Klem, and the young National Leaguer gave his assent.

Evans raised his hands and asked the bleacherites: "Just where did the ball land?"

Several men in the front row pointed to a spot just inside fair ground. "It landed here—right here!" they shouted.

"That's just what I wanted to know," said Billy. "If it landed there, it must have hit in fair territory and bounded into the crowd, so it's a ground-rule double." Leach's run was allowed, but Miller was sent back to second.

Clarke came running out and demanded: "Why isn't it a home run?"

"Because your own fans out there showed me it was a ground-rule double," snapped Evans.

When play was resumed, Abstein vexed Dreyfuss by striking out, one of his numerous whiffs with runners on base during the Series.

After that big Pittsburgh first inning, the game was a lark for Bill Yawkey, the playful former president of the Tigers, and his delegation of Detroit rooters. Donovan yielded only three more scattered hits, while the Michigan Felines started to go to work on Camnitz in the second inning. With two down, Moriarty and Tom Jones bashed singles, and the pair scored the tying runs on big Schmidt's long double.

The Tigers kayoed the Rosebud in the third, with a three-run barrage. Abstein dug the pit for Camnitz when he muffed Byrne's throw on Davey Jones. To the distress of the great Pittsburgh throng, a single by Bush and a pass to Cobb filled the bases. The crowd gave a little sigh of relief when Camnitz retired the clouting Crawford on a short fly, which Clarke snared on the edge of the infield. But Delahanty was tougher, shooting a long single to left, on which Jones and Bush scored and Cobb sped to third. By this time Clarke had seen enough of Camnitz. He came tearing in from left field, shooed the Rosebud off the rubber, and motioned to the bull pen for Vic Willis to take over. Almost immediately Vic was the victim of a fresh humiliation. With Moriarty at the plate, Cobb took a long lead off third base and made a clean steal of home, sliding into the sputtering Gibson ahead of Willis' pitch. Just to give Donovan a bigger margin to work on, Charlie Schmidt knocked in another pair of runs with a crashing single in the fifth, scoring Crawford, who had doubled, and Tom Jones, who reached first on a walk.

There was an interesting sequel to the Evans odd first-inning decision, which has left its imprint on present-day World Series umpiring. After the game, the old National Commission summoned the young umpires Evans and Klem to their headquarters, and Ban Johnson pontificated: "Now will you men tell us just what happened on that ball that Miller hit to right field?"

Evans explained the umpires' dilemma to the best of his ability, and though only twenty-five, the brash Billy had the audacity to tell the rulers of the game how to use their World Series umpires to better purpose. "Gentlemen, you are paying four umpires, but every day two of us watch the game as spectators in a field box," he said. "Why not put these extra men out on the foul lines so they can see what happens on just such a play as Miller's line drive." The august commission didn't adopt Billy's wise suggestion immediately, but by 1910 two umpires were assigned as so-called "foul-line patrols." Today three men are assigned to the bases, but the first- and third-base umpires are stationed so far back that they can keep their eyes on anything that happens along the foul lines.

3

By the time the third game was played on Monday, October 11, the scene had shifted to Bennett Park, Detroit. Frank Navin's seating capacity was then little better than 10,000, but by using a shoehorn in his little grandstand and standing thousands in his outfield, Frank squeezed in 18,277, far above any Tiger crowds in the Detroit-Cub Series of 1907 and 1908.

There was no Sunday ball in either Detroit or Pittsburgh at

that period and the idle day gave both managers Clarke and Jennings a chance to regroup their forces and establish new battle lines.

"I guess Detroit will give us more trouble than they made for the Cubs the last two years," Dreyfuss remarked to Clarke on the trip to Detroit.

"Yes, they're stronger; Cobb is a better player, but we'll beat them," Fred replied.

The game started out as a Pittsburgh picnic; the Pirates knocked out Kickapoo Eddie Summers in a third of an inning, scored five runs in the first, took a 6-to-0 lead in the second, and eventually staggered through to a desperate 8-to-6 victory. Nick Maddox, who weakened perceptibly at the finish, just barely survived the Tigers' last desperate rally. And if the second game was Ty Cobb Day, this one strictly belonged to Hans Wagner. The big Dutchman reached base five times, knocked out three hits, and stole three bases.

The Buccaneers lost no time in starting operations, and they fired a withering broadside before the startled Tigers knew what had struck them. Bobbie Byrne opened the game by beating out a bunt and sprinted to third on Leach's single to center. Clarke hit to Summers, and Byrne was run down, but not until Tommy reached third and Fred second. Wagner next hit to Bush, who fumbled ingloriously, Leach scoring. The Dutchman stole second, and when Schmidt hurled the ball into center field, Clarke tallied and Hans pulled up at third. He scored a moment later on a wild pitch.

"Keep the rally going!" Clarke yelled at Dots Miller, as the second baseman strode to the plate, and Dots followed instructions by working the jittery Summers for a pass. Abstein singled to center, and when Crawford threw wildly to nip Miller at third, the ball rolled to the stands, Dots scoring and Abstein reaching third. By this time the sight of Kickapoo Summers in the box had become an eyesore for Jennings and he called in Ed Willett. Before Eddie could retire the side, Wilson bumped him for a single, and Abstein crossed the plate with the fifth run of the inning.

It looked as though Willett had declared a personal war on the Pirates in the second inning, when he hit both of the first two men to face him, Leach and Clarke. Wagner forced Fred, Tommy advancing to third. As Wagner went down to steal second,

Schmidt let go a good throw to Moriarty and caught Leach off third. Tommy made a dash for the plate and made it when Willett, covering the scoring dish, dropped Moriarty's throw, giving the Buccos that early 6-to-0 lead.

Maddox had pitched shutout ball for six innings, and Clarke patted him on the back as he came in from the sixth inning, as he said: "Nice going, Nick, you've got them eating out of your hand."

Therefore, a four-run Tiger flare-up in the seventh, cutting the Tiger lead to two runs, came like a bolt from the blue. An error by Abstein hurt the Pirates again, and made Barney wince. The ever troublesome Delahanty opened with a double, and George Moriarty hit to Miller, but the play at first was lost when Abstein dropped the throw after a little smashup at first base. It started a merry rumpus. Johnstone first called out Moriarty, whereupon he had Jennings, the aggressive George, and half the Tiger team snarling and clawing at him.

Johnstone then changed his decision, claiming he thought he had got the sign from O'Loughlin, the American League umpire behind the plate, that there had been interference. Now Clarke tore in from left field, and half the Pirate team was yipping around Johnstone, insisting that Moriarty had bumped deliberately into Abstein and knocked the ball out of Bill's hand. But the decision stood, and Delahanty was on third and "Morey," on first with none out.

The delay while the bickering was on didn't help Maddox. In a jiffy Tiger hits were bouncing all over the green, and singles by Tom Jones, Davey Jones, and Cobb produced four runs. Then with the tying runs on base, the stands in a bedlam, and Jennings giving his weird cry of "Ee-yah," the slugging barber, Sam Crawford, ignominiously popped a dainty fly to Abstein.

Pittsburgh propped up the tiring Maddox with another pair of badly needed runs in the ninth. By this time Ralph Works, Jennings' third pitcher, was pitching; later Ralph became a sports scribe, and the Pirates promptly gave him something to write about. Byrne birched out a single and took third on Leach's double. Clarke sent Bobbie home with a long outfield fly, and the Dutchman whizzed a single past Bush's ears, scoring Wee Tommy.

The Pirates combined to make it tough for Maddox in the Detroit half, and the Tigers scored two more runs before it was over. Poor Abstein was again the culprit. After Mullin struck out, batting for Works, Bill muffed Wagner's throw on Davey Jones, and a moment later Byrne gave Bush a life with a wild throw to first. Then Cobb almost ruined Pittsburgh's victory party with a savage drive to deep right. On a clear field it would have been a homer, but the ball landed in the overflow crowd and was ruled a ground-rule double, Dave Jones and Bush scoring. The partisan crowd was yelling itself hoarse, but Nick had just enough left to dispose of Detroit's two clean-up toughies. He got rid of Crawford on a grounder to Wagner, and Clarke clutched Delahanty's fly for the last out.

The last play seemed almost a signal for the rain god in the sky to cut loose. As the happy Clarke was running off the field with the victory ball clutched in his hand, the leaden clouds that had hovered over the park all afternoon opened up and drenched the big crowd as it was leaving the park.

Following the rainstorm that drenched the third-game crowd, the temperature dropped to freezing, and the thermometer read 32°, as the rival pitchers, Lefty Leifield and George Mullin, warmed up for the fourth game, played in Detroit on Columbus Day, October 12. A strong biting wind, which blew across the field in vigorous gusts, had the players jumping up and down to keep warm and chilled another good Detroit crowd of 17,036 to the marrow.

This time again it was Detroit's day, as Mullin proved a splendid cold-weather performer. Backed by errorless support, big George showed the Pirates the stuff that had made him a 29-game winner in his loop. He struck out ten of the Buccaneers, yielded only five hits, a double by Byrne and four scattered singles, and won by a score of 5-0. If the Tigers were good, the Pirates were bad and were guilty of six errors, two each by the butter-fingered Abstein, Jack Miller, and Deacon Phillippe. The Deacon, however, enjoyed a flash of his 1903 glory and gave up only one hit and no runs in his four innings.

All five Tiger runs were jolted off Leifield's left-handed delivery. Two of the Felines tallied in the second, when Lefty plunked Jim Delahanty in the ribs, and the growling Moriarty singled. On Tom Jones' tap to Leifield, "Del" was caged between third and home, but he eluded his Pirate captors long enough for Moriarty to get around to third and Jones to second. Both scored when Oscar Stanage lined a long single to right.

Leifield sailed safely through the third inning, but he was in fresh difficulties in the fourth, when the Tigers hung three more runs on the scoreboard. And Lefty got into his big trouble after Honus apparently had rescued him with a brilliant double play. After Tom Jones opened with an infield single, the Dutchman grabbed Stanage's hot shot, tagged second for a force play on Tom, and then doubled the catcher with a snap throw to Abstein. With the bags empty and none out, Leifield walked George Mullin and Davey Jones singled to center. Both Bush and Cobb, left-handed hitters, then pulled outside pitches down the left-field foul line, as Mullin, Jones, and Bush scored.

For a few minutes in the second inning it looked as though Pittsburgh might win the game by forfeit. Donovan came from the Tiger bench to talk to Detroit's third-base coach, apparently to relay some instructions from Jennings. He lingered so long that Klem walked down and told him to "break it up" and "get back to your bench." The usually amiable Donovan wouldn't budge, telling Klem: "I'm talking to this man. You go on with your umpiring business, and I'll look after my business."

"My business is running this game, and you can't stand out there and talk all afternoon," shouted Klem. Donovan stood his ground, and the partisan Detroit crowd bellowed its encouragement.

Klem pulled out his trusty timepiece and told Hugh Jennings: "I'm giving Donovan 30 seconds to get off this ball field. If he isn't off by that time, I'll forfeit the game to Pittsburgh. And if I've got to do that, I wouldn't like to be in your shoes when you're up before Ban Johnson." Wild Bill departed.

5

The 1909 Series was following an odd pattern. After four games the Pirates had taken all the odd-numbered contests, and the Tigers the even-numbered games. The pattern wasn't broken when the Series returned to Pittsburgh for the fifth game, October 13. The cold, windy weather of the Detroit battles accompanied the baseballers back to the Monongahela, and the attendance for the third game played at Forbes Field fell off sharply to 21,706. The cold weather was no particular handicap to gallant Babe Adams, who brought in his second victory of the Series with a six-hit job. His victory margin was 8 to 4. His opponent, Eddie Summers, gave Babe an argument until the seventh inning, when the Pirates blew Ed's knuckler all over the park. Fred Clarke, who hadn't collected a single since he homered off Mullin in the opening game, helped himself to two hits in as many official times at bat, one of his blows being a three-run round-tripper. Wagner bungled two chances in the field, but Honus made it up with some scintillating base running.

Adams got off to a rough start, when lead-off man Davey Jones pumped a homer into the left-field bleachers. Clarke ran in from left field to the edge of the infield to yell a few words of encouragement: "Don't let that bother you, Babe. We'll get plenty of runs for you." The Pirates did just that, picking up single tallies off Summers in each of the first three innings.

Wagner unwillingly helped Detroit to tie in the sixth, when Cobb singled to right and came home on Crawford's long double to center. Honus then threw Delahanty's grounder to the grandstand, and the Nebraska barber scored the run that knotted the score at 3-3.

Detroit's Summers wilted in the seventh, and the crowd's triumphant roar rumbled over Schenley Park as four Pirates dented their spikes into the plate. After Adams fanned, Byrne singled, and on a hit and run play, Leach stabbed a single through the shortstop zone as Bush ran over to cover second base. Clarke seized this opportunity to explode his second hit of the Series, again a homer into the center-field bleachers, which scored Bobbie and Tommy ahead of him.

Wagner then had Pittsburgh fans in guffaws as he stole a run right from under Dutch Schmidt's big nose. Hans was hit by a pitched ball, stole second and third, and scored when the frantic Schmidt threw into left field trying to break up the second theft.

The Tigers had one good kick left in the eighth, when Sam Crawford hit a terrific home run deep into the left-field bleachers for the longest hit of the Series. But the Pirates promptly got this run back for Babe in their half, when Chief Wilson doubled and scored on Gibson's single. It wasn't until Gibby's hit that Jennings finally yanked the battered Summers.

Bennett Park in Detroit was the scene for the sixth game, played on October 14. The Detroit crowd had dwindled to 10,535, and those who stayed away missed the Tiger thriller of the Series. Pittsburgh lost a heartbreaker, 5 to 4, yet it was one of the epic games of blue-ribbon competition, which left victor and vanquished exhausted when it was over. But the rule of rotation was still on, and the Tigers won the even-numbered jamboree. The Pirates had chances aplenty to bring home the clinching game; they had Mullin dangling on the ropes in both the first and ninth innings, but couldn't deliver the knockout. Clarke was bitter at his team's failure to win, but he couldn't help but hand it to Mullin. "That Mullin's a lionhearted so-and-so," said Fred. "Hanged if he isn't."

Vic Willis was the Pirate starter in the sixth game. "I've been holding you back just for this one, Vic; you can wind it up for us," Fred told his twenty-two-game victor. But Willis blew his early lead and was followed by Camnitz and Phillippe.

The Pirates started in as though it would be a lark; they had three runs in and a runner on third before a man was out as the disconsolate Tiger rooters slumped in their seats. Byrne crashed a single to left, and Leach's hot shot to Tom Jones was scored as an error. Clarke lined a long single to right, scoring Byrne, and when Wagner rifled a long double to deep left, Tommy and Fred scored, and the Dutchman took third on a useless throw to the plate. How long had this been going on? It looked like a breeze.

It was at this point that Mullin made his first stouthearted stand. With the infield drawn in, Delahanty tossed out Jack Miller; Mullin whizzed a third strike over on Abstein, and then tossed Wilson's tap to first. Then, from the second to the eighth, Mullin was invincible, as the Tigers started coming from behind and forged ahead in the fifth inning.

Bush got one run back for the Navin-Jennings clan in the first when he walked and tore all the way home on Crawford's two-bagger. The Felines tied with two in the third, and but for a great throw by Wilson to third base, the damage would have been greater. Crawford walked and took third when that pain-in-the-neck Delahanty stabbed a long single to right. On a hit and run play Moriarty also drilled a single to right, scoring Crawford, but Wilson's great peg to third, a "perfect strike" in the lingo of baseball men, shot down Delahanty. However, Tom Jones plunked a single to left, and when Manager Clarke, to his disgust and dismay, let the ball roll through his legs, Moriarty scored.

The Tigers clawed their way to a one-run lead with a fourth run in the fifth, when they finished Willis. Bush led off with a single and reached second on Cobb's out. Crawford's terrific line smash sailed directly into Wagner's big hams of hands, but the Dutchman dropped it. He recovered in time to throw Sam out at first, but had Wagner held the ball it would have been a double play, as Bush was well off second at the time. It cost Pittsburgh a run, as Delahanty's double scored Donie.

Camnitz was Clarke's starter in the sixth, and it proved almost the subject for a quiz-program question how Detroit could score only one run on a single, double, walk, steal, and outfield error. Yet out of these ingredients the Tigers concocted what proved to be their eventual winning tally.

Big Schmidt opened with a single to right and took an extra base on Wilson's fumble. He was shot down on Mullin's tap to the Rosebud, and Davey Jones forced the Tiger pitcher at second. Davey stole second, Bush walked, and Cobb's double to left brought in Jones. Camnitz retired the menacing Crawford, leaving Feline runners on third and second.

From the start it had been a bitter, fighting Series, and it grew in intensity as it neared its conclusion. Such players as Clarke, Byrne, and Leach on the Pirates, and Cobb, Bush, and Moriarty on the Tigers were no shrinking violets, and conversation bristled with sulphur, brimstone, and billingsgate.

Once, after Cobb reached first base, he yelled to Wagner: "I'm coming down on the next pitch, you big krauthead."

"I'll be waitin' for you," called Hans. As he took Gibson's throw, Wagner tagged Cobb so vigorously in the mouth that he loosened several of Ty's teeth.

"But Cobb was a good sportsman," said Hans in a later-year conversation. "He wanted the base line, demanded the base runner's right of way, and usually got it. He sharpened his spikes, but then we all did that. But Moriarty was the one we really thought was the mean Tiger in that Series."

Tempers rose and spikes rode high as Pittsburgh made its final ninth-inning rally in the sixth game. Miller and the abused Abstein opened with singles, and Wilson tapped a sacrifice bunt in front of the plate. Schmidt pounced on it and threw down to Tom Jones at the first, and the ball, the runner, and the first baseman all reached the bag around the same time. Wilson collided forcibly with Jones, knocked out the first baseman, and as the ball rolled away, Miller scored, Abstein pulled up at third, and Wilson was safe at second.

After a ten-minute delay in which all kinds of questionable compliments passed between the two clubs, Tom Jones was carried off the field, though it later developed he wasn't hurt as badly as was first reported. Crawford moved in to first base for Detroit, and Matty McIntyre went to the outfield.

When play was resumed it was a situation much like the first inning, as Mullin was again in a bad hole, with runners on third and second, and none out. But again Mullin held! Gibson hit a fairly short fly to Crawford, and the Pirate coach yelled for Abstein to hold his base. But Bill, taunted by the Tigers for his errors and repeated strike-outs in the pinch, set sail for the plate. Schmidt had it well blocked off, but Abstein rode in with spikes high, and Charlie was rather badly spiked as he retired the first baseman. The two men kicked at each other on the ground and got up swinging, but Evans, the athletically built young American League umpire, rushed between them.

Abbaticchio batted for Phillippe, and the count dwindled down to two strikes and three balls. Mullin swept by a fast ball for a third strike, and Wilson, trying to steal third, was doubled at third base on Schmidt's throw to Moriarty. The Detroit third baseman was spiked on the final play, and Morey yelled: "I'll get you guys before this is over!"

6

When a Series was tied after six games in that baseball era, it was the common practice to flip a coin to decide the location of the seventh game. Because of the larger stands and the somewhat warmer weather in Pittsburgh, most of the baseball men were rooting for the deciding game to go to Forbes Field, but this time Barney lost when they flipped a half dollar in chairman Herrmann's room. Frank Navin called the turn and won the privilege of staging the seventh game. After a one-day delay, the Series finale was played in Detroit, October 16. The entire nation was absorbed in the event; the Pirates had won games 1, 3, and 5, and Detroit 2, 4, and 6. Was this strange sequence to continue? The answer was Babe Adams.

"You'll pitch the final one for us, Babe," Clarke told the young Hoosier the night before. "You're the only pitcher I have who has tied up Jennings' hitters. Don't think it is the deciding game of a World Series. Just think you are out there to pitch tomorrow's game, and that you have eight men in back of you."

The Pirates had a good ally that day in Detroit weather, especially in the cold blasts that blew down from Lake Huron. The temperature at game time was 40°, anything but Bill Donovan weather. There was no warm sun to thaw Bill's arm, such as prevailed at the Saturday game in Pittsburgh. But Jennings felt he had to sink or swim with his second-game winner, holding the hard-worked Mullin in reserve.

Detroit, encouraged by its team's dramatic sixth-game victory, had become a vast lair of Tiger and baseball enthusiasm. Another crowd of 17,562, which spilled all over Bennett Field, was on hand to root the Bengals to victory, but they sat in at a Tiger wake. All of the fun in the stands went to Dreyfuss and his Pittsburgh henchmen.

For such a Series the finale was almost an anticlimax. If anything, Adams was even better than in his first and second starts, and Babe won even greater national distinction by winding up with an 8-to-0 shutout. Donovan never did get his arm loosened, and he lived up to his early Brooklyn sobriquet of "Wild Bill" Donovan. In his three innings he walked six and put a seventh Pirate on base by hitting him with a pitched ball. Even so, Donovan left the game with the score only 2 to 0 against him, the last six runs being scored on Mullin. The Pirates outhit Detroit by only seven to six, but ten bases on balls made Pittsburgh scoring easy. A tip-off on the game was that Fred Clarke wasn't charged with an official time at bat even though he was up five times; the skipper had four walks and a sacrifice bunt, scored two runs, and stole two bases.

The ill feeling of the sixth contest carried over into the seventh game, with Moriarty again the American League storm center. There was a violent outbreak in the very first inning. Bobbie Byrne, first man up, was hit by a pitched ball, and advanced to second on Leach's sacrifice. While Clarke was up he gave Bobbie the hit-and-run sign, but Fred missed the pitch, and that left it up to Byrne to try to steal third on his own. Schmidt shot the ball down to Moriarty, who blocked off the bag as Byrne slid in reaching for the base with his spiked shoe. The feud boiled over again as the two players fell to the ground, Moriarty on top of the smaller Pirate. Byrne's ankle was badly sprained in the mix-up, and it was necessary to carry him off the field. The Pirates all blamed Moriarty. George didn't escape himself; he remained in the game long enough to hit a double in the second inning, and then his foot became so badly swollen that he, too, limped out of the game.

Donovan escaped in the first inning despite a hit batsman, two walks, and Clarke's steal, but Wild Bill lost his rabbit's foot in the second, when the Pirates scored two hitless runs on the veteran's continued wildness. Abstein walked and stole second, and on Wilson's sacrifice bunt Schmidt threw too late to third to get Abstein, and everybody was safe. Gibson popped to Bush, but when Donovan dished out four balls to his pitching opponent, Adams, the bags were jammed with run-hungry Pirates. Hyatt, who had taken Byrne's place in the batting order, drove in Abstein with a long fly to Crawford. Donovan continued his base-on-balls parade, and walks to Leach and Clarke forced Wilson over the plate. With a chance to break up the game then and there, Wagner left three runners when he lined to Cobb.

However, there were plenty more runs where those second-inning tallies came from. George Mullin tried his luck in the fourth, and he showed quickly he wasn't the Mullin of the earlier games. He walked Hyatt and Leach singled, and both advanced on Clarke's sacrifice. A pass to Wagner filled the bases, and Miller's steaming single sent in two runs.

All doubts that the Pirates would keep the World Championship in the National League were removed in the sixth inning, when the Buccos reached Mullin for three additional runs. Leach whacked George for a double, and Clarke walked again. Wagner drove in two runs with a howling triple to left and made the plate himself on Davey Jones' wild return.

6

Despite their scars and scalp wounds, it was a merry Pirate party that wended its way back to Pittsburgh. They well could sing: "Three dead Tigers on a dead man's chest. Yo ho! And a bottle of rum!" The skull and crossbones of Sir Barney was in the ascendancy, and how proud he was of his boys!

Babe Adams became a household word, and they remembered the Hoosier's three 1909 victories over the Tigers long after he retired from baseball. As for the contest between the two batting champions, all honors went to old Honus. Wagner led the new

World Champions at bat with a smart .333, against a lowly .231 for Cobb. Ty was overshadowed by Jennings' second baseman, Jim Delahanty, who led both clubs with .346, and hammered out the most hits—nine, including four doubles.

Remembering old Ed Delahanty, the former great Phillie slugger of their younger years in the National League, Hans Wagner laughingly remarked to Clarke: "Say, Fred, we kept worrying what we should pitch to that young squirt, Ty Cobb. We ought to have known better with a Delahanty in their line-up. He was the one to watch; why, he almost beat us. Those Delahanty boys really can hit."

The National League merry-go-round on Jennings catchers, which had helped the Cubs to their easy victories over Detroit in 1907 and 1908, continued in 1909, as the Pirates stole 18 bases on Schmidt and Stanage, to six that the Tigers filched on Gibson. Old Honus matched those six Tiger steals himself.

The winning share for each of the Pirates was a nifty $1,825.22, the biggest collected by any victorious World Series players up to that time. With a new park to pay for, Barney couldn't afford to toss in his club owner's share, as he had done in 1903. The rules now provided for the distribution of the receipts, and Barney's own take was $51,273.00. Yes, it was a good world to live in, and if it hadn't been for the summer suicide of his friend Harry Pulliam, Barney really could have let himself go. As it was, he remarked a little sadly: "I only wish Harry could have lived to see us celebrate our new park with a World Championship."

Pittsburgh celebrated its baseball triumph in fitting fashion. As soon as Babe Adams had retired the last Tiger in the Saturday game of October 16, Mayor W. A. Magee proclaimed Monday, October 18, a general holiday in which Pittsburgh would do honor to its new World Champions.

In the early evening Barney Dreyfuss provided grog and fancy victuals to his swashbuckling Buccaneers and the town's sports scribes, at a victory banquet held at the Fort Pitt Hotel. This was followed by a great baseball parade from the downtown district to Forbes Field. All municipal authorities, from Mayor Magee down, were in line, as were two regiments of the National Guard, political clubs, and hundreds of amateur and semipro baseball and football teams from western Pennsylvania, West Virginia, and eastern Ohio.

On a platform at Forbes Field, Congressman James Francis

Burke, Pittsburgh's silver-tongued orator, called up each member of the team, recited his heroic deeds, and then handed the athlete his World Series check. Naturally the fans put on their greatest demonstration when Burke summoned Babe Adams. They almost raised the roof, and it was 15 minutes before the noise abated sufficiently for Adams to say a few words. And his stock didn't go down any after his remarks. "At my farm home in Tipton my father always taught me to finish any job I started," he began.

"And you surely finished this job," yelled the crowd.

One of the best hands was given Bill Abstein, the erring first baseman, who despite the fact that he was on a winner, generally was picked as the goat of the Series. Bill struck out nine times, usually in the pinch, and was guilty of five errors, all of them muffed throws. But in a holiday mood the crowd tried to let Bill know they were with him, and realized he had done his best. He was twice called to the platform.

Barney Dreyfuss wasn't so forgiving; a few days after the big party, he released Bill Abstein to Jersey City. The Pirates were World Champions, but again they were without a first baseman.

⊖

XVI. CORSAIRS ENLIST FLEET-FOOTED
DIVINITY STUDENT

⊖

"FRED, I guess we have a team that'll stay up there for some time, like our team of 1901," Barney said to Fred Clarke, the winter after the great 1909 victory. Fred was making a visit from his Kansas horse and mule ranch.

"That's right, boss," replied Clarke. "There are a few of us getting older, but those Cubs aren't getting any younger, either. We're a great team, and there's nothing in sight that should finish ahead of us in 1910."

Yet something went out of the pennant winners of 1909 from one season to another. The 1910 Cubs, by an odd coincidence, won exactly the same number of games as they did when they finished second to Pittsburgh in 1909—104; it gave Chicago an easy pennant victory, as the Cubs topped the second-place Giants by 13 games and the third-place Pirates by 17. While Chicago stood on an even keel, the Pirates fell 24 victories below their 1909 total, and the Pittsburgh percentage slumped .162 points.

"Our 1910 team was my biggest disappointment in baseball," Dreyfuss once remarked to the author. "Never did I see a great team fold so quickly."

The team broke well from the starting post in April, and as late as the middle of May the Pirates bobbed in and out of first place with the Giants and Phillies. But after the Cubs bumped Pittsburgh off the top, May 25, Chance's team was never headed. The Pirates then ran second most of the season, but the club caved in on its last eastern trip, and Dreyfuss also had the painful experience of seeing McGraw finish ahead of his 1909 champions.

Clarke's troubles were largely on the mound, as the former ace pitchers could no longer deliver. Camnitz, Willis, and Leifield, who brought in 66 victories in 1909, slumped to 36 for the trio, while Nick Maddox, who won 23 games in 1908 and brought home the second 1909 World Series victory, won only two games and lost three. On the brighter side was the real oldster and the youth of the staff—Phillippe and Adams. Though used sparingly, the venerable Deacon won 14 games out of 16, while Adams won 18 and lost 9. A newcomer from Boston, Kirb White, took up some of the slack and broke even in 22 games. Kirb came in a spring swap for Sam Frock, another young pitcher, and First Baseman Bayard "Bud" Sharpe.

With the release of Bill Abstein, first base was the same old problem. Sharpe played the position in April and May, but after the trading of Bud to Boston, Jack Flynn, a likable chap purchased from St. Paul, took over. For a spell it looked as though Jack might be the first-base answer. He was a pretty good fielder and hit .274 in 93 games. A kid first-sacker, Kading, joined the club in the early fall.

For only the second time since 1903, Pittsburgh fans saw another name ahead of Wagner in the batting parade. Sherry Magee of the Phillies beat out Wagner, .331 to .320. Clarke was frequently out of the game, as the old man with the scythe started to crowd the 38-year-old Kansan. Dots Miller was out for over a month with an injury, playing in only 119 games. It gave Bill McKechnie, the lad from Wilkinsburg, a chance to fill in at the keystone sack for 36 games. After playing three games for the Pirates in 1907, Bill had been farmed to Canton in 1908 and Wheeling in 1909.

Two outfielders of unusual promise were brought up in the 1910 season, Vince Campbell and Maximilian Canarius, better known to millions of fans as Max Carey. Both were young men of good education, antelopes on the base paths, and born ball players. Campbell was a St. Louisan with good family connections, who had attended Vanderbilt University. He was signed by the Cubs in 1908, but Charley Murphy optioned Vince to Decatur in some sort of an illegal deal, and the old National Commission made the young outfielder a free agent. Signed by Dreyfuss, Campbell hit .326 for 74 games, second only to Magee.

Carey came up in the fall from the South Bend, Ind., club, and played in two Pittsburgh games, in which he batted .500, getting three hits in six times at bat. Max is still hurt that the National League doesn't include these two games to make him eligible for the league's gold pass, which is granted to players who have played 20 seasons of major-league baseball.

Max was born in Terre Haute, Ind., January 11, 1890, and was educated to be a Lutheran minister. He attended Concordia College in Fort Wayne, Ind. for six years and later matriculated at Concordia College, St. Louis. However, the boy was fast as a deer, and baseball was in his blood.

His conversion from the ministry to a big-league career was brought about in an interesting manner. Max was home at Terre Haute on a summer vacation, and he and a friend went over to South Bend to see a Central League game. South Bend had just sold its regular shortstop, Kelly, to Washington, and the semipro Claffey, who tried to fill the position, had a difficult afternoon. Carey, who was a shortstop and pitcher for St. Louis' Concordia team, remarked to his pal: "Say, I can play shortstop a lot better than that fellow." The more Max contemplated it, the more the thought ran through his mind: "If I couldn't play better shortstop than Claffey, I'd play for nothing."

A daring thought entered his mind to barge into the clubhouse and tell the South Bend manager, Aggie Grant, that he was a shortstop and would like a crack at the job. But at the last moment he lost his nerve. But later he trailed Grant to a downtown hotel, and plucking up his courage, he braced Aggie in the lobby and told him of his speed and ball-playing ability. For reference he showed Grant a gold medal he had won in an intercollegiate 100-yard dash.

After Claffey's showing that afternoon, Grant didn't need a great deal of convincing. "Come out tomorrow before the game, and I'll take a look at you," said the manager. Carey followed instructions and made such a favorable impression in his workout that Grant put the young divinity student in the game at shortstop that day, and Max played the position for South Bend for the remainder of the season.

Even then Carey hadn't yet decided to give up the ministry. He didn't rejoin the South Bend team until he was through with his studies in the seminary, in June, 1910. By that time the club had a new manager, Eddie Wheeler, and a new shortstop, Alex

McCarthy, who incidentally moved up to the Pirates a few months later in the same deal with Carey.

"You've got no chance to play shortstop with McCarthy playing that position," said Wheeler. "He's the best in the league. But I've a catcher playing left field, who isn't doing us any good. Go out to left field, and see what you can do."

Carey played left field that day. He played with such skill and zest that Pittsburgh purchased him before the 1910 season was over. Eighty-six stolen bases in ninety-six games helped get Maximilian into Dreyfuss' dope book.

"It was as a flychaser that I went up to Pittsburgh," reminisced Max, "but oddly enough, Barney Dreyfuss was told to keep working me out at short, even though McCarthy, the South Bend shortstop, went to the Pirates with me. 'Doc' Carson, who was president of the Central League, told Dreyfuss: 'Stick with Carey in the infield, and you'll find Hans Wagner's eventual successor.' But as time went on, the baseball people lost sight of the fact that I ever had been an infielder. After I was sold to Pittsburgh I decided not to return to the seminary, having come to the realization that baseball, rather than the ministry, was to be my life's work."

Doc Carson was right in one respect. While Max's big-league career was in the outfield and he never approached Wagner as a batsman, he was to succeed Honus as the all-round star of the Pirates. Fleet and graceful as an antelope, Carey developed into one of the game's immortal outfielders. His nickname was "Scoops" from the manner in which he could scoop in low-line drives; an earlier big-league first baseman, George Carey, had also been nicknamed "Scoops." At the zenith of his glory they called Max the "Tris Speaker of the National League." "The heck with that," said loyal National Leaguer Eddie Brannick, secretary of the Giants. "Speaker is the Max Carey of the American League." Carey holds a major-league record for having handled 400 or more put-outs in six seasons, with a high of 450 in 1923.

Max batted from both sides of the plate, shifting to the right side when the rival pitcher was a left-hander. He was a good batsman but not a great one, with a lifetime average of .285. His highest average was .343 in 1925, made in his sixteenth season in the league—counting the few games of 1910. An ideal lead-off man, he scored as many as 140 runs in 1922, and a flash on the bases, he holds the modern National League record for stolen bases, with 738. His best season was 61, in 1913.

The 1910 season was famous for what probably was the most tied-up ball game in all professional history. It was with the Dodgers at Forbes Field, August 13, and the umpires called the game after nine innings because of darkness, with the score tied at 8 to 8. Yet that wasn't all; each team had 38 times at bat, 8 runs, 13 hits, 27 put-outs, and 13 assists. Each manager used two pitchers, and the pitchers of the two teams had the same number of strike-outs, 5; bases on balls, 3; and hit batsmen, one. And even the rival catchers were guilty of one passed ball each.

2

In many respects the season of 1911 was a 'carbon copy of 1910. Dreyfuss and Clarke again thought highly of their prospects in the spring but once more had to be satisfied with a third-place finish and a percentage even ten points lower than the year before. The club won one less game than in 1910 and lost two more. After a lapse of six years, McGraw of the Giants was back on top in the annual three-cornered struggle among New York, Chicago, and Pittsburgh. For the first half of the season the race was a real humdinger; after the July 4 holiday games, a blanket could have covered the five leading teams: the Giants, Phillies, Cubs, Pirates, and Cardinals. The Pirates broke out from the pack to lead for a day, August 9, but it was their high tide; from that point they receded rapidly, and the former champion Cubs beat them in the fight for second place. While the Pirates divided their 22 games with Chance's team, it gave Dreyfuss many a headache when he saw his team become a football for McGraw's new champions. The Giants overwhelmed Pittsburgh in the year's series 16 to 6.

"Fred, why don't we do better against the Giants?" Barney demanded irritably of Clarke, after the Pirates had lost an entire series.

"I'll tell you how it is, Barney," said Fred, feigning seriousness. "They score the most runs."

"Fred, you can go to blazes, and take your whole club with you," Barney shot back.

Even so, Barney did his best to prove to Pittsburgh, and all the world, that he was trying to give Pirate fans the best baseball money could buy. On July 20, 1911, he startled the baseball universe by purchasing the pitching wizard of the minors, Marty

O'Toole, from the St. Paul club, for $22,500. And so that Marty would have a catcher who knew the tricks of his elusive spitball, Dreyfuss also purchased O'Toole's catcher, Billy Kelly, for an additional $5,000. In 1911 the O'Toole price tag was considered fantastic, something out of this world. In 1908 the Giants had made the nation's headlines by paying $11,000 for Rube Marquard of Indianapolis, the then record price for a minor-league rookie. Mack and the Shibes of the Athletics boosted that by a grand when they paid $12,000 for Pitcher Lefty Russell of Baltimore, in 1910, but Barney nearly doubled that in outbidding the Giants and other clubs for O'Toole.

O'Toole, a product of South Framingham, Mass., had once been the property of the Boston Red Sox. In 1910 he had attracted national attention by striking out 18 batsmen in a Western League game, and after joining St. Paul in 1911, Marty fanned 17 Milwaukee batsmen in an American Association game. A fortnight before he was sold to Pittsburgh, O'Toole won a sensational 1-to-0 16-inning game from Toledo. Marty was only moderately successful after joining Clarke's crew, and it was explained he was trying too hard and that he was suffering from too much publicity.

Actually another young right-handed spitball artist, Claude Hendrix, with far less of a build-up, showed a lot more, though in 1911 he was credited with only four victories in ten games. And the club permitted Sherrod Smith, a Georgia left-hander, to get away after a brief trial. Sherry later pitched in two World Series for Brooklyn, and was also a winning pitcher with Cleveland.

Honus won his eighth and last batting championship with a mark of .334. Clarke had his last big average, .324, but was finding it more and more difficult to drive his aging legs; he played in only 101 games. After Vince Campbell failed to get the salary he wanted, the brilliant rookie of 1910 held out until July 10, while he engaged in the brokerage business. The deer-footed St. Louisan hit .312, but participated in only 21 games. Barney was so peeved at Campbell for his long holdout that he traded the promising youngster to the Braves for Outfielder Mike Donlin, McGraw's former slugger.

And the first-base parade went merrily on. Fred Hunter, procured in a Kansas City deal for three secondary players, guarded the bag in 61 games, Bill McKechnie in 57, and Wagner in 28.

3

The season of 1912 brought forth Pittsburgh's last great club of the Clarke-Wagner era. While the Pirate runner-up finished ten games behind the champion Giants, it was an exciting, nerve-tingling season for Forbes Field fans. Aided by the brilliant work of the lanky left-hander Rube Marquard, who ran off a winning streak of 19 straight, and the effective work of a new spitball ace, the Missouri mastodon Jeff Tesreau, McGraw ripped the league apart in the first half of the season, and New York's winning margin promised to be as great as Pittsburgh's in 1902.

However, after Jimmy Lavender of the Cubs broke Marquard's streak on July 8, the Giants floundered for weeks in an acute slump, while the Pirates and Cubs leaped forward. At one time, New York's 16½ Fourth of July lead was clipped to three games, but the Giants got their second wind in September, and eventually won by a comfortable margin over the Pirates. An oddity of the race was how each of the three top teams knocked each other off. Pittsburgh defeated the third-place Cubs 13 games to 9, and Chance's club took its New York series by the same margin. That would have been fine for Pittsburgh but for the Giants licking Clarke's Corsairs, 14 to 8.

The 1912 Pittsburgh club made its strong showing despite the fact that Wagner was out ten games with a sprained ankle and Charley horse; Clarke suffered a broken toe; Byrne was out for a month with a misery, and the expensive O'Toole was held back by rheumatism. Even so, the team was strong in hitting, batting .284 against .286 for McGraw's champions. In an early-summer effort to bolster the Freebooters, Dreyfuss traded faithful Tommy Leach, who had been with Barney and Clarke since Louisville, to the old enemy, the Cubs. Tommy and Lefty Leifield went to Chicago for Artie Hofman, the Cub center fielder, who had been a Pirate fledgling in 1903, and Leonard "King" Cole, Chance's pitching sensation of 1910. Neither of the Cub pickups was of much help and soon moved to other pastures.

Clarke thought up a new solution for his first-base problem, switching Jack Miller from second base to the jinxed bag, while Alex McCarthy, Carey's teammate in South Bend, McKechnie, Art Butler, a shortstop purchased from Kansas City, and young Jimmy Viox, all tried their hand at second. Max Carey quickly soared to stardom, hitting .302 and stealing forty-five bases, while all baseball acclaimed his defensive skill.

On the bases Scoops quickly became the Ty Cobb of his league. Unlike the reckless, daring Tyrus, who danced nervously up and down the base line and frequently challenged opponents by saying he was "going down," Carey did his stealing inconspicuously and in businesslike fashion. Quite methodically he took the longest lead of any player in baseball. There he balanced himself on his toes to go either way. If the pitcher threw to hold him on the bag, he merely wasted his energy. Max always got back. Making as much a study of the pitchers as did Cobb, Carey learned their peculiarities and mannerisms, and at the right psychological moment, he was off. And comparing his percentage of steals to that of his attempts the former was amazingly high. On the hit-and-run play, no player could fly from first to third as quickly as the former Concordia comet.

Chief Wilson went absolutely three-base loco in that second-place season. Owen found the triple alleys in left and right fields with amazing frequency, and hammered out 36 three-baggers. No other player of this century has come closer than within ten of that mark. Twice Wilson bashed out three triples in one game.

Claude Hendrix, the sturdy spitballer, was the particular darling of the Pittsburgh fans, winning 24 games and losing only 9, for a percentage of .727. What's more, Claude always gave Clarke a ninth hitter at the bottom of the line-up. Hendrix was used frequently as a pinch hitter and batted .322, only two points behind Honus. Camnitz had his last big season, winning 22 and losing 12. Hank Robinson, a new left-hander, had a 12-7 record, and Babe Adams was only moderately successful at 11-8.

O'Toole naturally was the pitcher that Pittsburgh—and the entire country—was most interested in. Would the publicized New Englander be worth his then fabulous price tag? Marty, bothered with his rheumatism, had only flashes of brilliance, but the Buccos had difficulty scoring behind him. He just missed breaking even, winning 15 and losing 17. In the early part of the season, when Marquard was on his record run, the Rube's two games with O'Toole were sellouts after tremendous build-ups. But O'Toole was on the wrong end of a 4-to-1 game at Forbes Field and then lost, 5 to 4 in 11 innings, at the Polo Grounds.

4

Fred Clarke had finally decided to call it a career as a player. He was forty years old as the curtain was rung down on the 1912 season, and had played a lot of baseball after moving out of Ed Barrow's newsboy league in Des Moines. Fred had to push himself hard to play even a few games in 1912.

"I'll have to run the team from the bench this year, Barney," he told Dreyfuss, at the start of the 1913 season. "The old legs just won't hold up any longer."

"Well, you're the manager and know what you're doing," said Dreyfuss, "but it'll be hard for you to be a bench manager. You're too active."

Dreyfuss was right. It was a tough assignment for Fred to sit it out and watch a half-dozen guys mess things up in his old job. Max Carey and Chief Wilson took good care of two of the outfield beats, but an assortment of rookies and veterans took their turn in left field: Eddie "Midget" Mensor, Fred Kommers, Everett Booe, Artie Hofman, and Mike Mitchell, the latter picked up from the Reds. The old war horse, Clarke, played nine games himself.

Booe's introduction to the National League is one of the most amusing of Pirate stories. The name is pronounced "Boo," with the final "e" silent. It was before ball clubs enjoyed the luxury of a paid announcer, and part of the job of an umpire was to announce pinch hitters and new players as they entered the game. Clarke sent up young Booe, a Texan, acquired from Petersburg, Va., to bat for Camnitz.

When the youngster walked up to the plate, Bill Klem, the umpire, asked: "What's your name, sonny?"

"Booe," said the rookie.

"What's that you're giving me?" demanded Klem.

The kid raised his voice and fairly shouted: "Booe!"

"What are you trying to pull on me, you fresh busher," yelled Bill. "You're out of the game!"

It was necessary for Wagner to come out of the dugout and explain the situation. Klem said, "Nobody has such a name," but Hans insisted, and Klem, still only half convinced, permitted Booe to bat.

Clarke's role as bench manager didn't make for a happy season. The Pirates receded from their strong 1912 runner-up position to fourth in 1913, winning only seven more games than they lost, for a percentage of .523. The Giants won again, and the Phillies— of all teams—gave McGraw his toughest fight. Chance was out in Chicago, but the Cubs, playing under the little Crab, Johnny Evers, crowded past Clarke into third place.

If Father Time had pushed Clarke to the bench, he was also crowding Wagner. An injured knee limited the Dutchman's play to 114 games, and his batting average fell to an even .300. It was John's seventeenth successive .300 National League average and his last. An even more damaging injury to George Gibson, who suffered a broken ankle, side-lined the hard-working catcher for much of the season. Gibby took part in only 48 games, while Mike Simon and Billy Kelly, O'Toole's St. Paul battery partner, rattled in his shoes.

One of the pleasant features of the season was the development of Jimmy Viox into a crack second baseman and .317 hitter, while the old favorite, Babe Adams, had a return to his best form. The modest Hoosier won 21 games and lost only 10, and was ranked behind only the great Mathewson in low earned runs with 2.15.

Camnitz, on the other hand, had frequent lapses; he had a horrible year, winning only 9 games and losing 20, and late in the season the Rosebud and Byrne were traded to the Phillies for third baseman–outfielder Cozy Dolan, later McGraw's "I can't remember" coach.

A young left-hander, Arlie Wilbur Cooper, of Bearsville, W. Va., began to show great promise. He was destined to become one of the great southpaws, not only of the Pirates, but of both major leagues. Wilbur was acquired late in 1912 from the Columbus, Ohio, club. The boy had been developed in Marion, Ohio, of the Ohio State League in 1911, at a time when Warren G. Harding, owner of the town's newspaper, was the largest stockholder of the ball club. After Harding became President, he knew Cooper's Pirate record to the minute. A youthful, fine-looking right-hander, Albert Mamaux, a Pittsburgh lad who attended Duquesne University, also attracted attention. They said the kid had a fast ball like that of Joe Wood, when Smoky Joe first came to the Red Sox. Mamaux spent his summer vacation in 1912 at Forbes Field, and during a good part of the 1913 season the young right-hander was farmed to Huntington, W. Va.

Prior to the game of September 10, 1913, Wagner was called to the plate and presented with a bat carved from a piece of timber taken from Commodore Perry's flagship, the *Niagara*, which was sunk in the Battle of Lake Erie, September 18, 1813. Dave Davies, sports editor of the *Dispatch*, made the presentation and expressed the wish the Dutchman would be around for another hundred years.

"But the bat," said Honus. "Do you think there are a few good base hits in it after being under water all that time?"

One of the old fellow's droll plays occurred that season. As Hans slid into third base, the ball ended up in his armpit. The sphere seemed to have been swallowed up in the very bowels of the earth. The third baseman and shortstop of the opposition searched frantically for the ball, while the umpire looked stupidly on, wondering what had become of it. One of the axioms for an umpire is: "Never take your eyes off the ball."

Wagner got up from the tangle, completed the journey to the plate, and then as he walked away he nonchalantly opened his arm and permitted the ball to drop near the Pirate bench. By this time the umpire had collected his wits, and watching Honus from the corner of his eye, saw the ball fall. He came over and yelled at the Dutchman, "Wagner, y'ur out!"

"Honus was most displeased with the decision and kicked up quite a row," recalled Max Carey. "The play was more or less of a playful gesture, characteristic of Wagner. The ball stuck in his armpit, and why should he tell the whole ball park where it was. I still think the umpires missed the play. The worst they should have done to Honus was to have sent him back to third base.

"You know that big fellow never hurt anybody. Many a time I have seen him slide away from an infielder so as not to hurt him, when he could easily have cut him down if he wanted to. He is a player who never could be replaced. There could be only one Honus."

XVII. "FIVE FOR THREE" DEAL BACKFIRES

⚾

"WE'VE GOT TO DO something about that McGraw. He's making a monopoly of the National League race," Dreyfuss told Fred Clarke, before the National League's annual meeting in New York, December 13, 1913. "The Pirates have fallen into a rut, and I'm going to do something drastic to get them out of it."

That something drastic was one of the biggest deals ever swung in the National League, later known in Pittsburgh as the famous—or infamous—"Five for Three Deal." Miller Huggins, the midget second baseman and manager of the Cardinals, attended the meeting, and in the player mart he represented the comely woman owner of the St. Louis club, Mrs. Helene Hathaway Britton. Mrs. Britton was the daughter of Frank deHaas Robison and a niece of Stanley Robison, former St. Louis owners, and while she had baseball in her blood, she was smart enough to let little "Hug" do her trading.

There was quite a bit of swapping at that 1913 meeting, and Sir Barney looked with covetous eyes on three outstanding Cardinals: First Baseman Ed Konetchy, Third Baseman Mike Mowrey, and Pitcher Bob Harmon. Konetchy was one of the league's best first-sackers and a hard clean-up hitter, Mowrey was a cat around third base and a dangerous clutch hitter, and Harmon had won as high as 25 games for second-division St. Louis clubs. Again Dreyfuss was willing to give full value for the material he was after.

"I want those three players, Huggins, and I can give you good value for them, players that might make your club in St. Louis," Barney told the pint-sized Cardinal chief. He handed Huggins a list with twelve names on it, players he had discussed with Clarke as men who might be used in a trade. "You might like something I have here," he added. "Of course, you can't have them all, but if you do business with me, you'll find me reasonable."

Huggins put the list under his pillow, slept on it, and the next afternoon he gave it back to Barney with checks against the names of: Outfielder Chief Owen Wilson; Infielders Jack Miller and Art Butler; Third Baseman–Outfielder Cozy Dolan and southpaw Pitcher Hank Robinson. The pair haggled a little over some of the names, but eventually Dreyfuss shook hands and said: "Huggins, it's a deal."

At the time the big swap was made, most fans and critics felt Barney had hornswoggled Huggins. In St. Louis they accused little Miller of sacrificing the cream of the Cardinals for a batch of players Dreyfuss and Clarke were ready to toss in the discard.

Barney, himself, was elated, and beamed as he announced the deal, commenting: "At long last we again have a high-class first baseman." Pittsburgh felt a bit unhappy over the trading of the popular Jack Miller and Chief Wilson, the triple king of 1912. Jack apparently had played a satisfactory first base in 1913, and was a hustling, aggressive player. Clarke explained that while Wilson was a capable player, the Chief lacked fire and never could get himself sufficiently aroused at a ball game. "Wilson can't get sore enough at rival players—or umpires," said Fred.

When the 1914 Pirates won 15 games of their first 17, Pittsburgh fans were in the seventh heaven. Babe Adams won the club's thirteenth victory in a brilliant 1-to-0 pitching duel from Larry Cheney of the Cubs. On every side, Barney was being congratulated on his sagacity in obtaining Konetchy, Mowrey, and Harmon. Barney was enjoying a few chuckles at his old enemy McGraw, who apparently had been left at the post. No one gave even a thought to Stallings' Braves.

Then there came a few setbacks, but Clarke apparently got the craft righted, and by late May the club was still far in front, with 21 victories and 9 defeats, for a percentage of .728. No club was near the Pirates, and some slap-happy fans asked: "Isn't anybody going to give us a battle?"

Then some gremlin or other sprite pulled out the cork, and

soon the unsteady Pirates tumbled through the hatch like a gang
of soft landlubbers. They never stopped skidding until they hit
the lower depths of the second division, and about the time the
Braves picked themselves off the cellar floor for their history-
making 1914 drive to the pennant, the Pirates settled in seventh
place, their eventual resting place. And to make it look even
worse, Huggins' Cardinals, the 1913 tailenders, strengthened by
the five Pirates, fought their way to third place, the highest
position for a St. Louis National club since their second-place
position in 1876.

Dreyfuss was heartbroken. It was his first second-division year
in Pittsburgh, something of which a man had to be ashamed. He
couldn't understand it. It was the first year of the Federal League
war, when he had a quasi-major-league rival playing at the old
Exposition grounds. All ball players were upset by the big bank
rolls that Jim Gilmore and his Federal League plutocrats were
dangling before the eyes of big-league stars. In a way, it was a
return to 1901-02, when Dreyfuss had to fight the American
League raiders. Though the Pirates had dropped to a poor last
in team batting, with .253, Dreyfuss felt the team wasn't hustling
or trying for Clarke. He vented his spleen particularly at the new
first baseman, Konetchy, whose average had fallen to a sickly
.249.

It has already been told how Clarke had forbidden Dreyfuss
access to the clubhouse. But after Barney could stand it no longer,
he sneaked around to the clubhouse entrance, opened the door,
thrust his head in, and shouted: "K-witters! And for you, Konetchy, it goes double." Then he ran away.

For years thereafter, Pirates of the 1914 team greeted each
other with the watchword, "K-witters," Barney's quaint pronunciation of "quitters." It used to get a smile from Konetchy to
the day he died, in 1947.

However, Clarke was beset with many difficulties. Mowrey, the
new third baseman, was an even greater disappointment than
Konetchy. Mowrey pulled a tendon in his leg early in the season,
and though he was sent for treatment to the miracle worker of
Youngstown, Bonesetter Reese, Mike played in only 79 games,
hitting .254. Carey seemed unable to shake off a season-long
slump and hit a feeble .243. While Wagner participated in 150
games, the great Dutchman's average melted to .252. Even so,
when Wagner was out for a few days, Ralph Davis wrote: "One

dreads the thought of what will happen ten years hence, when
Wagner will have to quit the game." Honus then was 40; Davis
apparently expected him to go on until he was half a hundred.

Harmon, the new pitcher from the Cardinals, failed to win in
Pittsburgh as he had in St. Louis, bagging 13 victories against 17
defeats. That was practically Babe Adams' record—13 and 16.
Cooper hurled valiantly, but just barely beat .500 with 16 and 15.
O'Toole had a painful year, winning only 2 and losing 9, and
Barney gave up on his expensive investment. On August 14,
Marty, the $22,500 pitcher, was sold to the Giants for $6,500
under a provisional deal. But the costly spitballer couldn't win
for McGraw, either; he was returned to Dreyfuss, who disposed
of Marty to Columbus at a bargain sale the following year. Two
new pitchers, Joe Conzelman and E. L. Kantlehner, were picked
up in 1914.

Adams lost the season's heartbreaker, a 21-inning duel with
Rube Marquard at Forbes Field, July 17. Pittsburgh lost by a
score of 3 to 1. Larry Doyle broke it up in the twenty-first, when
he cracked a homer to deep right with a runner on base. Babe
had such wonderful control he didn't give a base on balls during
the long grueling contest. That really had Clarke raving. "Babe
pitches his heart out," Fred exclaimed. "He don't give a base on
balls for 21 innings, and you yellow so-and-sos let him down and
score only one run for him."

It was a tragic season, but it had its fun. Following an exhibition game at Marion, Ind., Wagner and two young Hoosiers,
Carey and Kantlehner, were invited on a night fishing trip on
a private lake. The lake turned out to be a park pond, on which
the lights had been turned off. Wagner had been furnished with
nets and other illegal fishing paraphernalia.

Just as Wagner was bringing in a fish in his net, someone blew
a whistle, and ten deputies who were surrounding the lake pulled
out flashlights and closed in on Hans. He was told he was under
arrest and was hustled into town for speedy trial in the night
court. Acting with great sternness, the judge fined Wagner $100
and sentenced him to 30 days in the county jail.

"Have you anything to say?" demanded the judge, after he
passed sentence.

"I want to get in touch with Barney Dreyfuss," said old Honus.
"He'll get me a lawyer. I can't go to jail; I got to play ball."

"Dreyfuss can't get you out of this," snapped the judge, "and your team will just have to get along without you. You fellows can't come in this town, break our laws, and expect to get away with it."

Just as they were leading Wagner to the hoosegow, the court relented; there were a few snickers, and then they confided to Honus it was all a gag. Hans gave a great sigh of relief. The reason it all went off so letter-perfect was that the night before, the Marion pranksters had practiced the arrest and trial on two unwary salesmen. And just so that Wagner would leave in a real good humor, they presented him with some fishing tackle.

2

Dreyfuss didn't have to worry any longer about looking at Konetchy and Mowrey, after the sad seventh-place finish of 1914. By the following spring, both of the ex-Cardinals jumped to the Pittsburgh Federals. It left Barney with only Harmon to show for the five players he had sacrificed in his historic 1913 swap with Huggins. It meant the club was back at scratch in its search for a first baseman. Wheeler "Doc" Johnston, a left-handed thrower and batter, was acquired from Cleveland for the inter-league waiver price. Oddly enough, Doc's home town also was Cleveland—Cleveland, Tenn. A newcomer, Douglas Baird, was engaged to plug the vacant gap at third base.

The 1915 club snapped back two positions, and Barney lost his coveted place in the first division by the mere matter of a half game. The Cubs were fourth with .477, having one uncompleted game. The Pirates were fifth with one more defeat than Chicago, at .474. That vexed Barney, for to him the second division was like living on the wrong side of the tracks.

Credit for the improvement belonged almost entirely to the handsome kid from Duquesne, Al Mamaux. Overnight, Al—and his crackling fast ball—became a sensation and the talk of the league. Used sparingly in 1914, Mamaux had won three games and lost two, but he was a flashing, pitching meteor in 1915, with the amazing record of 21 victories and 8 defeats. In earned runs, his 2.03 was third to the famous Grover Alexander and Fred Toney. Fans flocked to the park whenever word was passed out that the sensational Mamaux would pitch. The entire league was speaking of him as the "new Mathewson."

Mamaux's pitching could have sent the 1915 team into the race if it hadn't been for Cooper's near collapse; the southpaw had his poorest season, winning only 5 games and losing 16, and while Kantlehner was fifth in earned runs, he couldn't win, winning only 5 and losing 12. Adams broke even in 28 games; Harmon was just one shy of .500, with 16-17, and George McQuillan, released back to his old team, the Phillies, late in the campaign, won 12 and lost 13.

Wagner, now 41, had a really remarkable season, playing in each of his team's 156 games. He also lifted his average to .274, a gain of 22 points, while he was still sturdy enough to knock out 32 doubles, 17 triples, and 6 home runs.

Fred Clarke took part in one game, got one hit in two times up, for a .500 average, as he poked out his 2703rd National League hit. And Fred finally called it quits with the man for whom he had worked 22 years. Fred had been a small stockholder in the club, and there were reports that Barney reduced Clarke's salary. Dreyfuss corroborated that in some degree at the December National League meeting, when he told reporters: "Fred Clarke can't expect a first-division manager's salary when he finishes in the second division."

Anyway, the pair parted amicably, as Clarke announced his duties on his Kansas ranch would take his full time. He went extensively into mule raising, and later into oil. "After handling ball players for many years, handling mules should be easy," said Fred.

If the Pirates lost Fred Clarke in 1915, they gained Charles (Chilly) Doyle. Chilly never played any position for the club, but no one ever suffered with more anguish when the Pirates lost, or soared higher when the Buccaneer craft blew other teams out of the water. A former sports editor of the Sharon, Pennsylvania, *Telegraph*, Chilly followed the unfortunate Jim Jerpe as the *Sun-Dispatch's* baseball writer. Jerpe lost his eyesight in 1913. Through storm and high water, Chilly Doyle (now of the *Sun-Telegraph*) has been with the Pirates ever since, and though he hasn't been above taking a few pot shots at the Pittsburgh management, no more loyal Pirate ever climbed a mizzenmast.

The season of 1915 also saw Dreyfuss lose one of baseball's greatest prizes, George Harold Sisler, in an adverse decision by the old National Commission. There is no doubt that the Pittsburgher was given a raw deal, and his subsequent bitterness and refusal to forgive the old Commission chairman, Garry Herrmann, was easy to understand.

At a time when Sisler was a scholastic baseball wonder boy at Akron, Ohio, High School, he was signed by the Akron club. George never reported to Akron but went to the University of Michigan, where he became the nation's foremost collegiate baseball star. In the meantime, the Akron club sold Sisler's contract to Columbus, O., and Columbus in turn sold it to Pittsburgh. Under all baseball law, Gorgeous George was Barney's property. But after Sisler's graduation from Michigan in 1915, he was signed to a St. Louis American League contract by Branch Rickey, then manager of the Browns, and a former Michigan coach. With both the Pirates and Browns claiming the Michigan prize, the case went to the National Commission for adjudication. The two league heads, Governor Tener and Ban Johnson, each voted to award Sisler to the clubs of their respective leagues. The important deciding vote rested with Herrmann, and he cast it on the side of Johnson, so the great Sisler was ordered to play with the Browns.

Barney almost blew a cylinder and shouted to the high heavens that "I wuz robbed." He got out a full newspaper page of his grievances, which was sent to baseball men and sports writers all over the country. And as Sisler became one of the game's brightest luminaries, a .400 hitter and a first baseman ranked with Chase, Barney's suffering grew proportionately. He started a one-man crusade to unseat Herrmann as chairman of the Commission, gathered a few supporters as he went along, and finally had partial revenge on Herrmann when the Cincinnatian was ousted in 1920, and Judge Landis later elected to the job of Overlord of Baseball.

3

Jimmy Callahan, a doughty former American Leaguer, was Clarke's successor as skipper of the Pirate craft in 1916. Originally from Fitchburg, Massachusetts, Jimmy's career was spent largely in Chicago, where he was a well-known figure. Jim was a crack pitcher on the Chicago Nationals, when he jumped to the White Sox with Clark Griffith in 1901. When "Griff" was made manager of the early New York Highlanders, Comiskey elevated Callahan to the White Sox management. He ran the club for two years, when he gave way to Fielder Jones. By this time, Jimmy's pitching arm had gone back on him, and he went first to third base and then the outfield. Callahan ran a strong semipro club in the Chicago suburbs, the Logan Squares, for four seasons, but again was called back to the White Sox management in 1912, leading the club three seasons. In 1915 he was Comiskey's business manager.

Callahan had all of Fred Clarke's fiery nature, but like John McGraw, Jimmy was a relentless slave driver and never tired of cracking the whip. If a pitcher made a mistake, it wasn't unlike "Cal" to chase the unhappy culprit into the clubhouse, casting imprecations upon his entire house. Jimmy was no miracle worker, and the 1916 Pittsburghs skidded to sixth place. Again the old enemy, the Cubs, just nosed the Pirates out. Chicago was fifth with .431 and Pittsburgh sixth with .422.

Mamaux was good again, but not quite as effective as in 1915. While the youngster again won 21 games, he lost 15 in his second season as a regular. The old first-base trouble was back, for after Doc Johnston played 110 games, Wagner took over at first. In a midseason trade, the Pirates gained Frank "Wildfire" Schulte, the old Cub right-field star, along with Catcher Bill Fischer for Catcher Art Wilson.

Schulte was acquired with the hope he would put some kick into the outfield punch, as weak hitting by the flychasers had much to do with the Pirates' puny club-batting average. But the great Wildfire was pretty well burned out by the time he reached Pittsburgh, just as was Art Hofman in 1912. A whole raft of out-fielders were trotted out: Danny Costello, Floyd Farmer, Ed-mund Barney, Sebastian Compton, Bill Hinchman, and Carson Bigbee. Hinchman was a member of a baseball family, as he and his brother Harry, an infielder, formerly played with Cleveland. Bill is now a Pirate scout. Bigbee, a product of the University of Oregon, was a speed boy like Carey, and was to develop into one of Pittsburgh's better outfielders.

Gibby was beginning to slow up behind the plate, and there was a batch of new catchers. Bill Fischer was picked up in the Schulte swap, and the club acquired Walter Schmidt, brother of Charley Schmidt, who had caught for Detroit against Pittsburgh in the 1909 World Series. Walter bought his release from the San Francisco club and received a sizable bonus when he signed with Dreyfuss. Walt wasn't as strong or colorful as his better-known older brother, but was a better journeyman catcher. And Honus saw another Wagner appear in the Pittsburgh line-up, William "Bull" Wagner, a catching acquisition from Burlington, Iowa.

Joe Schultz, father of Joe Schultz, present-day Brown catcher, Hoke Warner, and Jimmy Smith were added to the infield. Jimmy, a native Pittsburgher, was strictly "good field—no hit"; he developed into one of the most serpent-tongued bench jockeys in the National League. Jimmy became the father-in-law of Billy Conn, the heavyweight, and in later life Smith made the sports pages by tangling up with his fistic son-in-law.

If the 1906 Pirates established a record for the club by winning 26 shutout victories, the Buccaneers of ten years later established a whitewash record in reverse. Callahan's 1916 team absorbed 28 shutouts. Jimmy Callahan no doubt got shutout in his eye, and it seemed an excuse for a short bender. Anyway, when some friends bobbed up in Philadelphia, Jimmy left with them, and when the Pirates opened a series at the Polo Grounds, New York, "Cal" was missing. He was absent for several days, as Wagner ran the team, and secretary Peter Kelly and the newspapermen made efforts to cover up the manager. Kelly said at the time of Callahan's disappearance: "Barney will have to hear it from someone else other than me."

Barney did hear it, and after the season he fired Kelly for his loyalty to the manager. "Peter supposedly was working for me, not for Callahan," he said.

4

The Pirates had trained at Hot Springs, Ark., ever since Barney took over, and he tried to change its luck by pitching his training camp in Columbus, Ga., in the war year of 1917. But the luck ran from bad to worse, as the Pirates plunged to the very depths. It was 30 years since Pittsburgh had been admitted to the National League, and the once great team burrowed deep into the subcellar. Not only were the Pirates last, with 51 victories and 103 defeats, but they finished 20½ games below the seventh-place Dodgers. Yet it was to be Pittsburgh's only tailender of the Dreyfuss dynasty. It was a year of bitterness and recriminations, in which Dreyfuss not only had a bad ball club, but the owner was subjected to considerable criticism in the Pittsburgh press, and by the fans.

Part of it was due to the owner's sharply cutting Wagner's salary, and the Dutchman's long holdout, which did not end until the late spring. Following Wagner's holdout in 1908, which won him a $10,000 salary, he was paid that amount each year until 1917. A few years before that the club owners evolved the idea of making the reserve clause in the player's contract legal by stipulating in the contract that part of the sum was for salary and part for an option on the player's services for the following season. As a consequence, in 1914 the Dutchman's contract provided for a $10,000 salary and a $25 addition as an option for 1915. In 1915 it was a $10,000 salary and a $50 option, but by 1916 Wagner signed for a $9,000 salary and $1,000 as an option on 1917.

By 1917 Barney offered the fading veteran a contract for a $4,500 salary and $900 for the reservation option—$5,400 in all—which the Dutchman spurned and steadily refused to sign. It wasn't until June 6 that he scrawled his signature on a contract with the understanding that he would play first base. Honus then signed for $750 a month for the remainder of the season and $250 additional per month for the reservation option.

Callahan went out as manager on June 30, and after considerable persuasiveness and pressure on the part of Dreyfuss, Wagner consented most reluctantly to take up the management. "But I don't want to manage the club. I never was cut out to be a manager," Hans persisted to the last.

Nevertheless, the club issued a statement: "Hans Wagner has consented to assume the management of the Pirates on agreement that he would be relieved of the business duties connected with the position. He will handle the team on the field and will direct it from first base. Hugh Bezdek, athletic instructor of the University of Oregon, and well known as a college coach (who has been acting as scout for the Pittsburgh club), will assist Wagner in the management of the team, and will serve as the club's business representative."

On Saturday, June 30, the day Wagner took over, the Pirates vanquished the Reds at Forbes Field by a 5-to-4 score. They jumped to Cincinnati for a Sunday double-header and were defeated twice by scores of 4 to 1 and 5 to 1. On Monday and Tuesday, July 2 and 3, the Pirates, back in Pittsburgh, were trounced by the Cardinals, 6 to 4 and 8 to 6. By this time Wagner had enough, and tendered his resignation. And he meant "positively." Dreyfuss now decided that Wagner was very right; nature never had intended for him to be a manager, and the resignation was speedily accepted.

Hugo Bezdek, who never had had a moment's experience handling professional athletes, was the new manager. A 240-pound Chicago Czech, Hugo had been a college football player and wrestler, and his first interest and love had always been football.

While Dreyfuss was suffering with his club wallowing deep in the cellar mire, Pittsburgh wasn't holding Barney entirely blameless in this year of Pirate woe. He often had been arbitrary and tactless in his contacts with the press and public, and now some of the chickens were coming home to roost. Callahan had his defenders, and it was said that Jim had been made the goat for front-office incompetence and interference.

The *Pittsburgh Press* printed a front-page story blaming Barney for existing conditions, and voiced the emphatic demand that "Dreyfuss must go." The story went on to say that minority stockholders were much dissatisfied with the way the club's affairs were conducted, and quoted one of them as saying that a change in the ownership of the Pirates apparently was the only thing that would bring a turn for the better.

President Oliver S. Hershman and Business Manager Miholland of the *Press* were stockholders in the Pirates, and no doubt were the minority interests mentioned. At one time they hobnobbed with Barney to such a degree that the *Press* was considered the Pirates' official mouthpiece. And when Harry Pulliam was elected president of the league in 1903, Dreyfuss selected the *Press'* sports editor, Will Locke, as secretary. Relations between the club and the *Press* continued very close, until Locke left the Pirates in 1913 to become president and part owner of the Phillies. But a chill developed after Dreyfuss appointed Leslie Constans, Locke's brother-in-law, as Will's successor to the Pirate secretaryship. A dinner was given to Callahan by some of the anti-Dreyfuss faction, in which Jimmy issued a statement in his defense.

5

Hard luck quickly struck the new manager, Hugo Bezdek. In scoring his first victory as manager over the Phillies in old Baker Bowl, July 6, Hugo tried a daring play—the double squeeze. With Wagner on third and Hinchman at second, both got into motion as Bigbee bunted. Wagner scored as Catcher Jack Adams threw out Bigbee. Hinchman also made a dash for the plate and tried to slide in ahead of First Baseman Luderus' return throw. He collided forcibly with Adams, and was carried off the field with a broken leg, which side-lined Bill for the remainder of the season.

One of the reasons for the nose dive of the 1917 Pirates was the almost complete fade-out of Al Mamaux, 21-game winner of each of the two previous seasons. Handsome Al, a gay blade and at the impressionable age where a young man likes to have his fun, won only 2 games and lost 11.

Another consistent loser on the 1917 Pirates was a chesty, outspoken spitballer from the north woods, Burleigh Grimes. He was Burleigh in name, and burly in build. He had come up in the fall of 1916 from Birmingham, and though Grimes showed unquestionable ability, he brought in only three wins and suffered 16 defeats in that tail-end year. And he had one of baseball's most famous fights with the new manager, Hugo Bezdek.

It took place on one of those Saturday-night hops to Cincinnati for a Sunday game. A group of Pirates, Grimes, Max Carey, Carson Bigbee, and Bill Fischer, were grousing in the washroom in one end of the Pullman. Chilly Doyle, the writer, was also there. They beefed as any last-place club is likely to beef, and Dreyfuss, the front office, and the management came in for their full share of complaints. Bezdek came into the little room; the other players piped down, but Grimes, sitting on a window sill, kept up his tirade. He was especially bitter, being on an 11-game losing streak.

"You're getting paid every two weeks; aren't you?" said Hugo.

"Well, so are you," was Burleigh's snappy rejoinder.

The exchange of words became bitter and personal, and Bezdek hauled off and clipped Grimes on the chin. It was a blow that would have felled the average athlete, but Burleigh came back fighting. There wasn't room for much swinging, so soon both men were wrapped in a tight embrace, like two large bears.

Bezdek got his fingers in the corner of Grimes' mouth and started to tighten the screws. They couldn't do that to Burleigh; he almost bit off his manager's finger.

As both big men were bleeding profusely, other players tore them apart, but it was only the first round. From the other end of the car, Bezdek soon shouted: "For a thousand dollars, I can lick that —— ——!"

With his hands full of bills, Grimes came charging down the car like a fighting bull, yelling: "I'll take you up on that." But again other players forced the grapplers apart.

Sam Walters, the road secretary, then asked Bezdek: "Shall I put him off at the next station?"

"No," said Hugo, "if he shows the right spirit, I'll pitch him tomorrow."

Grimes' bloody shirt had been torn to tatters, and he came to Cincinnati wearing his pajama coat. True to his word, Bezdek, his finger taped, pitched Grimes that day.

The 1917 season was the one in which the great Honus Wagner sang his swan song. The holdout for the first two months of the season was now 43, and the most glorious career in National League history came to an end as Hans played 74 games and hit .265. By an odd quirk, the greatest shortstop of all time, who broke in with the Louisville Colonels in 1897 as an outfielder, played his last league game twenty years later at second base.

The dreary 1917 season also saw the annual renewal of the Pirate first-base parade: Honus played the jinx bag in 47 games, Fritz Mollwitz, a Red pickup, in 36, Bunny Brief in 34, and Bill Hinchman in 20.

PAUL WANER

Pittsburgh Pirates Publicity Department

LLOYD WANER

Pittsburgh Pirates Publicity Department

Pittsburgh Pirates Publicity Department
BILL BENSWANGER

DONIE BUSH

Pittsburgh Sun-Telegraph

XVIII. BANJO CHARLEY CHASES
FIRST-BASE HEX

⊖

FOLLOWING FOUR YEARS of dismal, second-division ball, and a forlorn tailender in 1917, Barney Dreyfuss, the first-division man, bounced back strongly in the war year of 1918, and Pittsburgh fans enjoyed another twelve-year sojourn among the "upper crust" of the standings. Barney didn't go, but kept striving to give his Forbes Field patrons bigger and better baseball.

From the depths of the coal hole, the 1918 Buccaneers leaped to fourth and lost third place to the Reds by a mere two points— .531 to .529. On January 8, Dreyfuss made a startling deal: Pitchers Al Mamaux and Burleigh Grimes, and Chuck Ward, promising but erratic-throwing shortstop from the Northwest, to the Dodgers for Second Baseman George Cutshaw and Charles "Casey" Stengel, the frolicsome outfielder. Barney knew he was giving up two of the best young pitchers in the country, but he weakened on Mamaux after Al's 2-11, 1917 season and decided Burleigh was too hotheaded to break bread in the same hold with Hugo Bezdek.

Another smart move was the acquisition of Outfielder Billy Southworth, present-day competent manager of the Boston Braves, in midseason from the Birmingham club, with which the Pirates then had a close affiliation. Billy formerly had played with the Cleveland Americans and was the nominal 1918 National League batting leader, with a .341 average for 64 games. As the major leagues played a curtailed season that year, and Zack Wheat of Brooklyn, next on the list with .335, had partici-

pated in only 105 games, many Pittsburghers felt young South-
worth was entitled to Hans' Wagner's old crown. But John
Heydler, the league head, placed it on Zack's Missouri brow.
Barney also displayed astuteness in picking up Earl Hamilton,
the former St. Louis Brown left-hander, who won six games for
Pittsburgh before he went into the Navy. Fred Mollwitz, the
1917 Red pickup, played most of the season at first base, and
Bill McKechnie, regained from the Reds for the waiver price in
March, played the club's entire 126-game schedule at third base.
A spectacled pitcher, Carmen Hill, helped, while Cy Slapnika,
later legendary business manager of the Cleveland Indians and
now a scout for that team, was another war-year pitcher. And
as such famous Cubs as Artie Hofman and Frank Schulte played
with the Pirates in the twilights of their careers, so Jimmy Archer,
the catcher who could peg his clothesline throws from his squat-
ting position, caught 21 games for Bezdek, before moving to
Brooklyn.

By the end of the 1918 season, the Pirates had one of the
biggest service lists in the two majors and one of the few base-
ball casualties—Marcus Milligan, a pitcher formerly optioned to
Birmingham, who was killed in an air crash. Another Pirate
pitcher-aviator, Elmer Ponder, was wounded and received the
French cross for valor. Other Pirates in the services were: Carson
Bigbee, Fred Blackwell, Jimmy Caton, Hal Carlson, Williams
Evans, Lee King, Walter Mails, Zeb Terry, Hoke Warner, and
George Winn, who wore Army khaki; and Normal Boeckel, Earl
Hamilton, Ray Miller, Casey Stengel, and Billy Webb, who
joined the Navy.

2

Few men in baseball looked into the crystal ball in the winter
of 1918-19, after the first November 11 Armistice Day, and
foresaw the tremendous boom that baseball, along with all sports,
would enjoy with the dawn of peace. In fact, the shortsighted
club owners were so timid about their first peace season that they
reduced the normal 154-game schedule to 140 games.

But the crowds, hungry for baseball, rushed back into the nation's ball parks, including Forbes Field, and Barney ruefully
rubbing his hands, moaned: "If only this season I had a championship team!" Bezdek's 1919 entry again finished fourth, winning three more games than it lost, for a percentage of .511. Weak

hitting held down the club; it was last in that department, with .249.

The 1919 postwar year may best be remembered as the season in which the long search for a first baseman finally came to a happy end in the last fortnight of the campaign. Mollwitz started again at the hexed bag but soon was shipped to St. Louis. Vic Saier, Chance's successor as first baseman of the Cubs and at one time a dangerous home-run man, was next engaged, but he failed to make the grade. Then, late in the season, Barney bought the very left-handed and jovial Charley Grimm from the Little Rock club.

Charley brought a banjo with him as part of his equipment, but he hit .318 in his 14 games and played the bag like a fellow who had the real know-how. A St. Louisan, Grimm had been a scorecard vender at Sportsman's Park. Connie Mack picked him up in 1916, when Charley was only eighteen, and the kid played in a dozen American League games. Two years later Grimm played 50 games for the 1918 wartime Cardinals. A young frolicsome fellow, with a zest for life, fun, and mischief, Grimm wasn't exactly the type of player to steady Dreyfuss' nerves, but for the first time since Barney traded Bransfield in 1904, he was cured of his first-base headache.

When Jolly Cholly first joined the Pirates he was a bashful lad of limited experience. At his first training camp with the Bucs at Hot Springs, Arkansas, he was having breakfast at the Hotel Eastman with Bill Hinchman. While the rookie's attention was diverted elsewhere, Big Bill slipped a toy balloon into his own cereal. Then while talking to young Charley, Hinchman innocently fished the little balloon out of his oatmeal with his spoon. Placing the cream-covered elastic toy on the edge of his plate, Bill went on talking and eating.

"You're not going to eat that oatmeal after what you found in it, are you?" asked Grimm, with wide-open eyes.

"It isn't poison, Charley," said Hinchman. "But there is no telling where these kids of today will lose their toys."

Charley, who was afflicted with a weak stomach, took one more look at Bill scraping the oatmeal off the side of the balloon—and apparently enjoying it—and then bolted out of the dining room, leaving the rest of the meal untouched.

In a subsequent spring, when the Pirates were conditioning for a week at West Baden, Indiana, Grimm was the fall guy for another dastardly prank by his playful fellow Pirates. In the spacious atrium of the hotel were numerous benches, one of which had been electrified by some of the boys for the benefit of unsuspecting guests. By sitting on a raincoat or allowing the feet to rest on rubber heels, one could avoid feeling a shock when the current was turned on.

Grimm was as innocent as a newborn lamb when he sauntered past two of his teammates seated on the charged bench, while a third stood near by, his finger on a push button concealed in the wall. Responding to an invitation to sit down, Cholly sat—but not for long. The fellow by the wall pressed the button and Charley, letting out a scream, slid off the bench and landed on the marble floor, while players, seated around where they could see the fun, fairly rocked with mirth. Gathering himself up and wondering why the other two Pirates had not felt the shock, the victim gazed at them and remarked: "For what I ought to do to all of you, I probably would get myself fried in a hotter seat than that one."

Grimm was not long in adjusting himself to such situations, and he took keen delight in framing jokes on his pals to get even for the early times he had been hazed. Occasionally, after their side had had a hard-fought game and then boarded a train, the boys amused themselves with a sham battle in the Pullmans. Going into the washroom, they saturated newspapers with water and pressed them into ball-shaped missiles to hurl at one another. Grimm was a dead shot, and when he heaved one of those moistened wads at somebody's head, the target had to duck with great haste or suffer a beaning that was like being hit by a pitched ball.

Deciding one zany on a ball club was enough, about the same time that Barney acquired Grimm, he traded Casey Stengel to the Phillies for George Whitted, a Tarheel who was equally at home in the infield or the outfield. But the newcomer was soon to play a gay role in "Grimm's Follies." Norman "Tony" Boeckel, a third baseman who liked the bright lights, was sold to Boston.

One of the reasons the 1919 club didn't fare better than fourth was Max Carey's season-long indisposition. The former divinity student had more boils than were inflicted on Job and participated in only 66 games.

Babe Adams was getting along, but still was quite a pitcher, as his 17-10 won and lost and 1.98 earned-run records will attest.

And Babe, who felt guilty if he crushed a fly, finally deliberately hurled a ball at a batsman. The player was Greasy Neale, a rough-and-tumble collegian from West Virginia, later to win fame as a football coach. A brash youngster, in 1919, Neale was right fielder of the Reds, World Champions of that year, and a talkative, fighting ball player. Greasy had little respect for big baseball names or reputations. As he stood tauntingly at the plate, facing Adams, one of the older Pirates called from the bench: "Knock that fresh busher down, Babe. Knock 'im down!"

Greasy guffawed at the remark. "That old geezer out there couldn't hurt anybody, even if he hit him on the head."

Adams sent a fast ball flying at Neale's head. As the player, an eel on the football field, quickly dropped to avoid the pitch, the ball hit the peak of his cap. But thereafter Neale refrained from any further chiding remarks on Babe's speed.

3

By 1920, the Buccos again had a new skipper, the veteran catcher George Gibson. Bezdek had shifted his football coaching job from Oregon to Penn State, where he soon was to turn out some of the Nittany Lions' greatest teams. For a while there was some thought of big Hugo trying to arrange his schedule so he could work both jobs, but it just couldn't be done. Anyway, Bezdek was primarily a football man.

Gibby was all baseball, and Pittsburgh fans loved him for it. The big Canadian was one of the smartest men in the game, his particular forte being the development of young pitchers. Since leading the Pirates in 1916, he had been with McGraw of the Giants as third-string catcher and bull-pen coach on the 1917 champions, and in 1918 he gained some managerial experience by leading Toronto. George's appointment was warmly received by Pittsburgh rooters.

Oddly enough, Gibson's first club of 1920 was almost a carbon copy of Bezdek's gang of the year before. The club finished fourth, with a percentage of .513, two points higher than the fourth placer of the preceding season. Again the Pirates, who once fired the big guns in the league, trailed in club batting. That annoyed Barney, who wailed to Gibby: "Why can't we get more hitting?"

Gibson replied: "I guess you just have to get me another Wagner."

The 1920 Pirates were nosed out for third place by Jack Hendricks' Reds, as the result of losing two out of three games in a triple-header, October 2. It was only the third time in National League history that three championship games were played by two teams on the same day, the first being in Brooklyn on Labor Day, 1890, when Guy Hecker's terrible Pittsburgh tailender lost three games to the Dodgers. Only the first three clubs took cuts out of the World Series melon in 1919, so by special dispensation of league president John Heydler, the Pirates and Reds battled it out for the third-place purse on the final Saturday of the season. The outcome was a bitter disappointment to Pirate fans and players. The show started at Forbes Field at noon, and Cincinnati won twice, 13 to 4 and 7 to 3, before Johnny Morrison pitched a 6-to-0 six-inning shutout, halted by darkness.

Adams continued his brilliant pitching into 1920, and his earned-run average of 2.16 was second only to that of the great Alexander. Though Fred Nicholson, a new outfielder from Detroit, was no Max Carey in the field, Freddy batted .360 for 99 games and was the runner-up to Hornsby. Max got over most of his 1919 maladies, again participating in 130 games; he hit .289 and stole 52 bases. Billy Southworth had a highly satisfactory season, hitting .284.

XIX. PLAYFUL RABBIT MOVES INTO
FORBES FIELD

ALWAYS THE GAMBLER, Barney Dreyfuss made another of his daring trades at the February, 1921, meeting of the National League. Again he was willing to go high for the man he wanted. Since Wagner's decline, an assortment of run-of-the mine players had tried to play shortstop: Zeb Terry, Chuck Ward, Jake Pitler, a pint-sized Pittsburgher—now a Brooklyn scout—Jimmy Caton, and Walter Barbare.

Barney then went after the best and most colorful shortstop in the National League, Walter "Rabbit" Maranville, of the Braves, and gained possession of the Rabbit in a deal for Outfielders Southworth and Nicholson, Infielder Barbare, and $15,000. Maranville, though a great player, who rarely missed an inning, was at that stage of his career one of the game's most impish playboys, as famous for his extracurricular activities as for such tasks demanded of him in his baseball contracts.

Dreyfuss gave away good talent to get the Rabbit. Southworth was one of the game's topnotch outfielders; Nicholson had displayed a real punch at the plate, while Barbare was a fair-to-middlin' infielder. In acquiring Maranville, Barney hadn't added much to Pittsburgh's offense, as the little Rabbit had been a .265 hitter in Boston, and eventually closed his National League books with a lifetime average of .258.

Shortly after the deal with the Braves, Maranville was brought to Pittsburgh as honor guest at a public gathering of fans. Barney Dreyfuss usually spoke in a low tone of voice, and at times it was

187

difficult to follow him. When Maranville was called upon for a talk, he began by saying: "At first I had some difficulty in understanding what Mr. Dreyfuss was saying to me when he discussed the deal and my new job. But when he handed me my new contract and I saw the fine salary he had written into it, we understood each other perfectly then and there."

Yet the deal was an inspiration, and one of the most profitable that the veteran owner ever made. Chilly Doyle said: "It made Barney a million dollars," which was somewhat of an exaggeration, but Maranville put a quick spark into the club and became an even more colorful star at Forbes Field than he had been in Boston. With the exception of the immortal Honus, no shortstop ever could pack 'em in as did the playful New Englander. A five-foot, five-inch mite from Springfield, Mass., there never was any telling what the little guy would do, from pulling the hidden-ball trick to diving between the outstretched legs of the austere umpire, Hank O'Day, in making a steal of second. On another occasion when an argument was in progress over a disputed play, the tiny New Englander crept on all fours and, with elbows on the ground, rested his head on his hands, directly between the knees of the irate umpire. And in 1921 and 1922 Maranville reached averages of .294 and .295, the highest in his 23-year career.

However, if the 1921 Maranville-inspired Pirates made rich dividends for Dreyfuss and finished second, the highest since 1912, that campaign still is recalled as one of the darkest in Pirate history. The club had its fifth pennant within easy grasp, only to have Barney's old foe, the ever troublesome McGraw, dash the cup of victory from the Pittsburgher's lips.

Maranville wasn't the only infield replacement. James Arthur "Cotton" Tierney, a Kansas City boy, acquired from Tulsa, joined the club in the late weeks of 1920. So did Clyde Barnhart, a Pennsylvanian from Buck Valley. Clyde had been picked up as a free agent, and developed in Williamsport and Birmingham. Cotton and Clyde quickly won jobs as infield regulars.

In 1920 the club also had purchased an infielder who was destined to become one of Pittsburgh's all-time greats, Harold Joseph "Pie" Traynor, an intelligent high-class youth from Framingham, Mass. Both Boston clubs had given young Pie the bum's rush when he tried to convince their respective managers that he was a ball player, yet Traynor became baseball's greatest modern third baseman and one generally rated on a par with Jimmy Collins, Boston's candidate for the third-base post on the mythical All-Star Team of All Time. He was called "Pie" because of his early fondness for that savory New England dish. Dreyfuss purchased young Traynor as a shortstop from Portsmouth, Va., in 1920, and Hal played in 17 Pirate games that year. During most of 1921 he was pastured in Birmingham, but was recalled in the fall for the hot September fighting with the Giants.

Pittsburgh also added a rookie right-handed pitcher, Whitey Glazner, who was a freshman star in 1921, along with Jug Handle Johnny Dewey Morrison, who saw service on the Pirate craft late in 1920. Johnny was a curve-ball pitcher, who acquired his nickname when his curve transcribed an arc that resembled the handle of one of the mountain-dew jugs used in Morrison's home town, Pelleville, Kentucky. Other new pitchers who helped were Chief Moses Yellow Horse, an Indian, and Jimmy Zinn. Tony Brottem was acquired as an aid to Walter Schmidt behind the plate, and in the fall Johnny Gooch, another catcher, was advanced from Birmingham. To help the outfield punch, Davey Robertson, the former Giant, was purchased from the Cubs, July 1. Lyle Bigbee, a pitcher-outfielder formerly with the Athletics and brother of Carson, was another midseason pickup.

With a rejuvenated, youthful club, the 1921 Pirates at one stage promised to win by a wide margin. The Corsairs led most of the season, and by the time they reached the Polo Grounds, August 24, for a five-game series, they were comfortably cushioned on a seven-and-a-half-game lead over the second-place Giants. With the race only five and a half weeks to go, Barney had ordered his pennant pole.

In an effort to keep within striking distance of the runaway Pirates, McGraw had made some frantic and criticized deals within the league. He had a $100,000 deal cooked up with Garry Herrmann of the Reds for Heinie Groh, Cincinnati's holdout third baseman, but Judge Landis nixed that one, and McGraw then worked another with the Phillies for Second Baseman Johnny Rawlings. However, the transaction which really was to wreck Pittsburgh was the Emil "Irish" Meusel deal of the last week in July. Bill Baker, the Phillie owner, said in a statement he "no longer could endure the sight of Meusel," so he shipped

Irish to McGraw for Outfielder Curt Walker, Catcher Butch Hen-line, Pitcher Jesse Winters, and $40,000.

The Giants were strengthened, yes, but not even the faintest Pittsburgh heart expected the detonation that blew the Pirate ship right out of the Harlem River. Ed Ballinger had written: "If the worst comes to the worst, and the Pirates lose two out of five, they'll still leave New York six and a half games to the good."

But something far worse happened. Before the startled Pirates knew exactly what struck them, they blew the entire five games, and in four brief days their apparently foolproof lead had shriveled to a mere two and a half games.

Two torpedoes were exploded under the Pirate craft in a double-header, August 24, before a packed house of 35,000. Adams' nine-straight winning streak was rudely interrupted in the first game, when Art Nehf, helped by George Kelly's twenty-second homer, won easily by a 10-to-2 score, and in the nightcap, Phil Douglas, the big Alabama spitballer, won a 7-to-0 shutout from Cooper and Lyle Bigbee.

Gibson tried to rally his forces in the clubhouse the following day. "All right, we looked lousy yesterday and lost two games, but we're still five and a half games in front and finishing the season at home. Now let's go out there and win today."

But the Pirates lost again on August 25, 5 to 2, as Fred Toney, the man mountain from Tennessee, was the big obstacle in the Pirate path. Not only did the big mountaineer outpitch Morrison, but his terrific three-run homer off Jug Handle Johnny was a devastating blast.

McGraw came back with Phil Douglas in the fourth game, August 26, and Earl Hamilton, the former American Leaguer, gave Shufflin' Phil a classic argument. Earl faltered only once, in the fourth, when the Giants scored twice on a pass to Ban-croft, Frisch's triple and Young's single. Those two tallies gave Douglas the ball game, 2 to 1.

By this time an orderly Pirate retreat had become a rout, and Art Nehf, who was poison to Pittsburgh all season, made it five straight by winning the August 27 game from Hal Carlson, 3 to 1. After the second inning, Art hexed the Buccos to such a degree that only one Pirate reached base. The big Giant gun all during the five games was Irish Meusel, the former Phillie. Standing on his seat in the Polo Grounds press stand, Chilly Doyle denounced the Meusel deal and all those even remotely connected with it, with all his Irish vehemence.

The Pirates had a sizable lead left, and with the Giants scheduled for an arduous September western trip, Gibson's players still had much in their favor. But Pirate morale had been badly shot during the Polo Grounds debacle, and Gibson just couldn't put back the old zip into his shattered forces. By the morning of Labor Day the Pittsburgh lead had shrunk to one game. There was good news on the scoreboard, which showed the Braves had defeated New York, 6 to 5, in the morning game, whereupon the Pirates proceeded to lose a heartbreaker to Cincinnati as Eppa Rixey wore down Morrison and Hamilton, 2 to 1. Cincinnati's winning run hurt like a sore tooth, as it was scored on Bohne's walk and steal, and successive errors by Catcher Art Wilson and Traynor, the kid from down East playing third base.

Both the Pirates and Giants won their afternoon games, and on the Tuesday after the holiday the Pirates had 80 victories and 51 defeats, and the Giants 80 wins and 53 setbacks. The Pirates held on to this slim margin until September 21, when the Giants leaped in front by crushing the Dodgers under a 20-hit barrage, as the former New Yorker, Rube Marquard, then with the Reds, stopped Hamilton, 4 to 1. At the finish New York won by winding up with 94 victories to 90 for Pittsburgh.

What especially made Dreyfuss see red was that of the Pirates' last eleven games with New York, they won only one. He didn't yell "K-witters" into the clubhouse as in 1915, but he was very, very sore. He always blamed the loss of the 1921 pennant on the shenanigans and horseplay in the club. When such congenial, fun-loving spirits as Charlie Grimm and Rabbit Maranville appeared on the same roster, something simply had to happen. Two other funsters, George Whitted and Cotton Tierney, joined them in their frolics. They got up a quartet, with Whitted singing baritone and Grimm bass. They even had a tidy offer to go into vaudeville if Pittsburgh won the pennant.

All had characteristic nicknames. Grimm, the St. Louis German, was "Krauthead"; Maranville, of course, was "Rabbit" because of his outstretched ears; Tierney was "Cotton" because of his thatch of light blond hair, while Whitted, a Carolinian, answered to "Possum" and "Poffin' Belly." Tierney was the wittiest of the four, and drank little. Grimm and Whitted sang best when they sprinkled their tonsils with lager; the Rabbit often preferred a stronger potion.

At a time when post-World War I flappers instituted their mode of rolled-down stockings, Grimm, Maranville, Tierney, and Whitted took batting practice with their socks rolled down. They also sang some of their ditties in the batting cage before games. It led to McGraw's apt remark: "You can't sing your way through this league." That's one time when Barney was in hearty accord with New York's truculent manager.

Although the famed baseball quartet splashed color all over the Pittsburgh scene as well as the National League, Gibby's quaint 1921 team had other characters who would have been headliners except for the three-sheeted publicity of the singers. One of these was Chief Moses Yellow Horse, a full-blooded Pawnee brave with flowing black hair and a sense of southwestern humor that reminded listeners of the late Will Rogers, who was also of part Indian extraction.

Until he threw his arm out, Yellow Horse had a fast ball that might have won him enduring fame. His manners were charming even when he indulged in a few beers, but on one occasion the Chief got into a row just before midnight in the vicinity of Forbes Field. It was during prohibition, and one evening somebody made the mistake of passing a bottle of bootleg TNT around a group after Chief Moses had enjoyed a few beers.

About an hour later, the usually good-natured Pawnee was howling war whoops and biting the tops off beer bottles, being unable to find an opener. In doing so, he cut his lip and was bleeding when he got into an argument with a fan on a crowded corner. There was a report that Yellow Horse pulled a knife in the ensuing fight, but this was a libel. Most of the spattered blood was from his own cut lip. As the Chief told a cop who came to the scene: "I'm an honest Injun—I don't use—or need, any knives, but I can use my fists." With the blessing of the cop, a Pittsburgh fan, another Pirate led Chief Moses away and soon had the Indian pitcher tucked in his bed.

The next morning Yellow Horse was up and in Barney Dreyfuss' office at 9 A.M. He told his boss: "Mr. Dreyfuss, I got off the reservation for a few hours last night and got into a couple of fights. You no doubt will hear about it, so I thought I should tell you about it first."

Barney was so impressed with the Chief's forthrightness on

that occasion that he let him go with a mild lecture—and no fine.

However, that same season, Yellow Horse and Maranville, one of his boon companions, really got the goat of Owner Dreyfuss on a diner, an hour after the Pirates had completed a game in Chicago. Barney took in the game and decided to return to Pittsburgh with his athletes. The train's departure time left little opportunity for larks, but the players had just enough time to snatch a few beers near the station before they rushed into the diner.

Rabbit and Yellow Horse were in rare form after those quick beers on their empty stomachs. They beheld Barney in the far end of the car and decided to take their boss for a little ride. Rabbit knew all about Yellow Horse's mix-up near Forbes Field, and the Chief was equally familiar with some of "Rab's" escapades.

Others in the diner, in addition to the athletes, were startled as the Chief arose, lifted his hand for silence, and announced: "Ladies and gentlemen, I would like to introduce Rabbit Maranville, that great shortstop of the Pirates, and a sweet little fellow who always minds his own business and has never been known to get into any jams."

Rabbit arose, solemnly took a few bows, and then shouted: "And now, folks, it gives me great pleasure to introduce Chief Yellow Horse, who not only is a mighty fine pitcher, but the best scrapper in Pittsburgh."

The entire show was put on for Barney Dreyfuss' benefit, and he didn't like the act the least bit. In fact he told his manager, Gibson: "George, your players are getting away from you; you'll have to do something about it."

Yet with all their clowning, the singing quartet played great ball. Maranville hoisted his average to .294 and handled 854 chances at short. Grimm played a bang-up game at first and hit .274, while Tierney ranked third among the regular Pirates with .298. Whitted hit a satisfactory .280. Carson Bigbee had a grand season, hitting .322, while southpaw Cooper won 22 games in his effort to give Barney another winner. Whitey Glazner, the brilliant yearling, and Babe Adams, the veteran, also did their level best; both had identical records, 14 victories and 5 defeats.

2

The Pirate collapse of the last six weeks of the 1921 season carried over into the first half of the 1922 campaign. There were more recriminations and charges that some of the players had let down Gibson. Gibby himself chafed at assertions, especially in the Eastern press, that the Pirates had turned "yellow" when the 1921 pennant goal was in sight. Some thought Gibby hadn't been sufficiently severe in enforcing discipline on the playboys, or successful in inspiring the team when the retreat was on.

As a consequence, the first week of July saw another of Pittsburgh's sensational managerial changes. Almost without warning, Gibson threw up the job, and Dreyfuss put the canny coach, Bill McKechnie, the home-town boy from Wilkinsburg, in charge. In his statement to the press and public, Barney was careful to explain that Gibby hadn't been fired. He said George's resignation was as much of a surprise to him as to anyone else. As for Gibby, he held a meeting with his players in the clubhouse, saying he thought it for the best interests of the team that he step down. He slipped quietly out of town without giving any newspaper explanation for his action.

After McKechnie wound up his playing career with Minneapolis in 1921, where he was still agile enough to hit .321 in 156 games, Wilkinsburg Bill was engaged as Pirate coach, his third Pittsburgh engagement. "Bill knows baseball and is a good man to have around," Barney said at the time.

Never an outstanding player, McKechnie's baseball wisdom had long been recognized. As far back as 1915, the oil millionaire Harry Sinclair took cognizance of it, when he put Bill in charge of his Newark Federal League team. Bill couldn't hit the way Wagner could or play third base like Heinie Groh, but nothing that took place on the ball field ever escaped his intelligent brown eyes. An elder, and member of the choir of his church in Wilkinsburg, the shrewd McKechnie was immediately dubbed the Deacon. No man of finer principles ever held the reins of a big-league ball club.

Shortly after Bill's appointment, several hundred of his neighbors and friends massed behind a band and paraded from Wilkinsburg to Forbes Field to let the whole wide world know of their esteem for their fellow townsman. The delegation presented the Deacon with a jeweled watch, which is still one of his prized possessions.

Whereas the 1922 Pirates were an in-and-out aggregation during the first half of the season, the club perked up from the day Bill took hold of the tiller. Gibson had been handicapped by the three-month holdout of Walter Schmidt, his first-string catcher. McKechnie quickly straightened things out between Dreyfuss and Schmidt and brought the San Franciscan back to the fold. During his sojourn in Minneapolis, he had observed the hitting of Ewell "Reb" Russell, former southpaw White Sox pitcher, who had turned outfielder. Bill recommended Russell's purchase, and Rebel was an immediate success in Pirate toggery, hitting .368 in 60 games, second only to Hornsby.

When Bill McKechnie took over the Pirates he knew he had a problem with his songbird quartet, Yellow Horse, and several other rough and ready characters. Wilkinsburg Bill was slated for his first eastern trip in command, when Dreyfuss called him into his office.

"Well, have you figured how to make your players behave?" blurted Barney. "I suppose you realize you have a couple of wild Indians on your club—Yellow Horse and that Irish Indian, Maranville."

Skipper Bill was all smiles. "Everything is hunky-dory, Mr. Dreyfuss," he said with a wink. "I'm going to room with that pair."

The first stop was New York, where the Pirates then put up at the Ansonia Hotel, a pretty hostelry where players shared small apartments. McKechnie held a meeting before the first game with the Giants and laid down his disciplinary law. He was emphatic about bootleg liquor, the hour the men should be in bed, and that sort of thing.

When the team checked in, McKechnie shared his suite with his two Indians. Bill was quite a guy for going to an early movie before the hour when his playboys were likely to get into mischief. So the first night in New York he took in a show and returned to the hotel about ten. Obtaining some reading matter, he went to his room to await the arrival of Chief Moses and Rabbit. He wanted to check them and ascertain whether they would try to beat his new midnight curfew.

But a big surprise awaited him. As he turned on the lights, he heard loud snoring. Peering into the adjoining room, he saw his two Indians—Yellow Horse and Maranville—sound asleep.

"Well, this won't be so tough," thought the Deacon. Apparently "Rab" and the Chief had eaten, then done the round of near-by "speaks," got their fill of needled beer, and dozed off early.

McKechnie started to undress. He opened a closet door and almost toppled over as a flock of trapped pigeons flew into his face. Bill recovered and, madder than a hornet, he shouted so loud that he awakened Maranville. "What goes on here, Rabbit?" he demanded.

Rabbit blinked and replied: "Hey, Bill, don't open that other closet. Those pigeons that got out belong to the Chief—mine are in that one over there."

With popcorn and other tempting goodies, the two Pirate zanies had coaxed many pigeon residents of the district from a perch high up on the hotel into Manager Bill's apartment.

McKechnie was also the first to recognize Traynor's great third-base possibilities. Earlier in the season Pie had played a little at shortstop, with Maranville moving to second. The Deacon sent the Rabbit back to his regular position, settled Pie at third, returned Tierney to second base, and shifted Barnhart, the former third-sacker, to the outfield. All clicked. Jewel Ens, a latter-day Pirate manager, was an infield reserve. Barney broke up Grimm's quartet by releasing Whitted to Toledo, while Dave Robertson was also cast adrift.

From the time McKechnie took over, the Pirates moved faster than any club in the league, and at one time there were high hopes Bill might overtake McGraw. But the finish was again disappointing. By hard driving, McKechnie moved the club into second place, September 3, and the Pirates held the runner-up spot until next to the last day of the season. Then the Bucs were nosed out by one game by the Reds, as Pittsburgh fell back to a third-place tie with the Cardinals. Only a game separated the three clubs that followed the Giants; the second-place Reds won 86 games and lost 68; the Pirates and Cardinals each won 85 and lost 69.

Pleasing to Dreyfuss was the knowledge that his boys held their own with McGraw. The 1922 Pirates divided their 22 games with the champion Giants and second-place Reds, and won from St. Louis, 13 to 9. The Buccos fairly feasted on the seventh-place

Phillies, 19 to 3, but lost second place by their inability to do better with the last-place Braves, winning from the tailenders by only 12 to 10.

With the coming of the Babe Ruth period, the powers in baseball jazzed up the ball in both major leagues, and Pirate batsmen prospered as did all others. There was no Wagner on the 1922 Pirates, but their club average soared to .308, the highest it had been up to that time. Carson Bigbee fairly sizzled that season, hitting .350, fourth among the 100 game players. Barnhart hit .330, while Carey was a point below him. Max also stole 51 bases. Young Traynor showed a natural batting form and wound up with .281 for 142 games.

Cooper was again brilliant, with 23 victories and 14 defeats, while Morrison also was a consistent performer with 17-11. Age was catching up on Adams, who won only 8 and lost 11, while Glazner, the wonder boy of 1921, subsided to 11-12. Yellow Horse showed flashes of real ability, but never developed into a Pittsburgh Chief Bender. One of Pittsburgh's best baseball stories is how Rabbit Maranville was sent to bring Chief Moses back to Barney's reservation. We leave the rest to the reader's imagination.

3

It is odd how, through the years, one Pirate team has so frequently duplicated the record of the club that preceded it. In McKechnie's first full season in charge, 1923, it was the 1922 race all over again. The Pirates won two more games than in 1922, and again finished third to the Giants and Reds.

However, for a good part of the 1923 campaign the club was close enough to make every Giant visit to Forbes Field miniature warfare. Unlike 1922, this time it was inability to win from the two top teams that proved the big stumbling block. The Giants regained their 1921 supremacy and licked McKechnie's band, 13 to 9, and the Reds won their Pittsburgh series, 14 to 8. After a fair start, the Buccaneers alternated between second and third for most of the season. They trailed only the Giants during the better part of July and August, but Cincinnati crowded McKechnie in the fall, and Pirate fans saw their team in second place for the last time, September 16.

Dreyfuss went all out in his effort to bolster the pitching staff. On May 23 he traded Cotton Tierney and Whitey Glazner, the young stars of 1921, to the Phillies for the spectacled hurler, Lee Meadows, and Second Baseman Johnny Rawlings. Meadows was one of the outstanding pitchers of the league but long had been dissatisfied with conditions in Philadelphia. Everyone in the Quaker City knew he wanted to get away, but Baker, the owner, repeatedly asserted: "Meadows will have whiskers down to his knees before I trade him." When Dreyfuss tossed in a $50,000 check along with Tierney and Glazner, Baker lost all further interest in Lee's beard.

Meadows started well; including his April and May games with the Phillies, the right-hander won 17 games and lost 13. This was a year Johnny Morrison really had his curve breaking, for under McKechnie's careful tuition, he won 25 games and lost 13. Cooper was down to 17 and 19, but Adams reversed 1922, winning 13 and losing 7. In a further effort to strengthen the staff, Dreyfuss procured the original Jim Bagby, a 31-game winner in 1920, from the Cleveland Indians, but by this time Sergeant Jim was well on the way out.

The play of the 1923 Pirates was again featured by the club's terrific slugging. While they receded somewhat from their .308 team average of 1922, they lost the club-batting leadership to the Giants by a silken hair—.2953 to .2945. Charley Grimm fairly leaped forward to .345, and young Traynor skyrocketted to .338. Barnhart, playing in the outfield, poked the ball for .324, and Carey .308. For the second straight year, Max stole 51 bases. Wallie Mueller, a young flychaser, hit .306, but Bigbee receded from his brilliant .350 of 1922 to .299.

Another young outfield star, Hazen "Kiki" Cuyler, came up from Nashville in September and clicked immediately. A right-handed hitter, brilliant fielder, and a whippet on the bases, Kiki came from Harrisville, Michigan, and was picked up as a green rookie from the Bay City club three years before. He was groomed for his Forbes Field berth in Charleston, South Carolina, and Nashville. A star in the making, his meteoric career was to flash over the Pittsburgh skies for only four brief but tumultous seasons, when the brilliant Cuyler was to become the fickle Dreyfuss' gift to the Chicago fans.

4

The 1924 season was another heartbreaker and one in which Dreyfuss said he sweated blood. It wasn't too easy on the Deacon either. It was another season when the pennant lightning nearly struck, and again the flag was blown in a late-season series at the Polo Grounds. McGraw won his fourth straight pennant, beating Brooklyn by a game and a half, and Uncle Robbie's Dodgers had a similar game-and-a-half edge on the Pirates.

Substantial improvement was wrought on the club. The Pirates came up with another gem of a shortstop, Forest Glenn Wright, a handsome Archie, Missouri, boy, who was acquired from Kansas City. He was a rangy lad, with an arm of steel. "The greatest since Wagner," wrote Chilly Doyle enthusiastically, and he wasn't much out of the way. In Glenn's first season, the sparkling youngster handled 601 assists, 67 more than the second-best man, Travis Jackson of the Giants.

With Wright giving Wagnerian performances at shortstop, Maranville was moved to second place, where the agile Rabbit established a former fielding record for second base by handling 933 chances, 365 put-outs and 568 assists. As a second-base combination, Glenn and the Rabbit were a fan's dream.

Two new pitchers were added to the staff, Emil Yde, a left-hander, and Remy (Ray) Kremer. Yde, whose home was in Great Lakes, Ill., and who came from Oklahoma City, was an immediate success, winning 16 games and losing only three. It's still a mystery how scouts overlooked Kremer so long, as Remy, by this time 28, had browsed 7 seasons with the Oakland Coast League club. He made one training trip with the Giants, after which the astute McGraw turned thumbs down and sent Kremer back to California.

Bill McKechnie scouted Kremer personally. Late in the 1923 season, Dreyfuss sent him to the Coast to look at two expensive infielders, including Willie Kamm, San Francisco's crack third baseman. Bill learned the White Sox had the inside track on Kamm, and the other wasn't available. Bill didn't want to go back empty-handed and recommended Kremer.

"Why, that guy is 50 years old," they kidded Bill in the Pirate office.

"If he's 60, he's still a good pitcher," countered Mac.

Dreyfuss put through a deal with Oakland, whereby he procured the minor-league veteran for Infielder Spencer Adams, Pitcher Earl "Pinches" Kuntz, and $15,000. Kremer won 18 and lost 10 that season, and was Pittsburgh mound ace for the next half-dozen years.

Jeff Pfeffer, a former Brooklyn pitching ace, was purchased from St. Louis, while McGraw's former outspoken catcher, Earl Smith, was acquired from the Braves. It took McKechnie a little while to appreciate Cuyler, as Kiki didn't become a regular until June. When the black-haired boy got in, he hit .354 for 117 games. On August 9, he lashed out six hits in as many times at bat, including three two-baggers and a triple.

The 1924 club got off to a slow start and didn't reach fourth place until June 23. The team remained there until July 12, when the Buccos muscled their way to the third perch. The Pirates then scrambled to second, August 3, and diligently chased the Giants all through the late summer. Then a 15-game winning streak lifted the Dodgers into the thick of the race and hoisted them into second place, September 6. The Pirates regained the position for a day in their final visit to Flatbush, when Yde won, 4 to 2, on September 19, and Cooper, 5 to 4 in 11 innings, on September 20. Kremer dropped the third one to Burleigh Grimes, 7 to 1.

When the Pirates next moved over to the Polo Grounds, they seemed to be the hottest thing in the league. The Giants, on the other hand, were badly crippled, as the two infield stars, Frisch and Groh, were out with September injuries. The New York lead had fallen to practically nothing, and all three contenders were so close they almost touched each other. The Pirates apparently also had overcome their New York complex, for up to the final series they enjoyed a 13-to-6 margin on the McGraw men. "This time we ought to lick McGraw and make him like it," Barney told McKechnie.

But again Ballinger, Doyle, and the rest of the Pittsburgh press gang had to send back gloomy tidings from the Polo Grounds. Hugh McQuillan was an easy winner over Meadows in the first game, 5 to 1, played before 35,000, on September 23. Yde lost the second on September 24, to Zeke Barnes, 4 to 3, despite Earl Smith hitting two homers for the Pirates. The old jinx man, Artie Nehf, tossed the third harpoon, 5 to 4, as Wilbur Cooper was the loser. The Buccaneers made a desperate attempt to pull out the game in the ninth, when Carey homered with Schmidt and Eddie Moore on base.

A few days later, September 27, the notorious attempt was made to bribe Heinie Sand, Philadelphia shortstop, at the Polo Grounds. The bribe was offered by Jimmy O'Connell, a prize $75,000 Coast League rookie, who said Cozy Dolan, the New York coach, had put him up to it.

All baseball was in an uproar, and the scandal rocked the game to its foundation. Judge Landis promptly put O'Connell and Dolan on his permanent blacklist, but gave clean bills of health to three other outstanding Giants whose names had been mentioned. Ban Johnson wanted the New York team disqualified from the World Series, and the second-place Dodgers substituted as the National League representative. Dreyfuss went further and wired Judge Landis to call off the Series, whereupon Landis admonished Barney "to keep his shirt on."

Barney continued to shout his indignation to the high heaven. The race was so close that he claimed if there was anything wrong with the final Giant-Phillie series, it could have affected Pittsburgh's chance for the pennant. He also intimated he didn't like all he saw in the final Giant-Pirate series and would welcome an investigation. When the Pirates were running second there were rumors other teams had been offered bonuses for bearing down extra heavy on Pittsburgh.

Dreyfuss didn't attend the subsequent Giant-Washington World Series, but he went to Washington to call on Landis, with the intent of giving him some evidence he thought he had on the Dolan-O'Connell case. McKechnie accompanied him. But when Barney called on Landis, the Judge, still smarting under Dreyfuss' earlier criticism, declined to see him. Barney waited for him in the hotel corridor and asked Landis: "When will you be in? I came all the way from Pittsburgh to talk to you."

"I *will not* be in," said the Judge moving away.

McKechnie tossed in an oar and asked: "Why won't you be in?"

Landis turned on Bill, and fairly shouted: "Who are you? I have nothing to do with you."

XX. IN THE PENNANT SWIM AGAIN

D REYFUSS STEWED over the loss of the 1924 pennant, and its after-math for the next two months, and shortly before he left for the National League's annual meeting in New York, he sprang another of his sensational deals. And this really was a whopper! Charley Grimm, Rabbit Maranville, and Wilbur Cooper to the Cubs for George Grantham, who could play either first base or second, Pitcher Vic Aldridge and Al Niehaus, a rookie first baseman who had had a big season with Chattanooga in 1924.

The author talked to the Pirate boss in New York shortly after the deal, and his comment was: "I got rid of my banjo players."

The remark fitted Charley Grimm, who still likes to strum on his banjo, and the impish Rabbit, but not the serious-minded Wilbur Cooper, who never had been one of the club's playboys. "Where do I fit into that picture?" Wilbur asked.

As for the Pittsburgh fans, they generally gave three cheers for the trade—that is, three Bronx cheers. The happy-go-lucky Grimm and Maranville had both built up legions of followers, and Cooper had contributed 20 victories in 1924. In fact, the left-hander had won 20 or more games in four of his last five years.

Aldridge was a pretty good right-hander, a younger man than Cooper, but hadn't been as consistent a winner. Grantham was a fairly formidable hitter but an erratic fielder. And Pittsburgh fans asked: "Who the dickens is Niehaus?" They were quite proper in asking the question, for after 15 games with the Pirates, Niehaus was sold down the river to the Reds.

Yet Dreyfuss had the last laugh. For the first time in 16 years his club won the pennant in 1925, while the Cubs, with whom he had made the swap, finished last—the only time in the club's 72-year-old history. And when a pennant returned to Forbes Field after the long wait, it came with almost ridiculous ease. Early in the season McGraw had threatened again to be tough, as he went after his fifth straight. Up to late June, the Giants usually were the leaders, with the Pirates only a jump behind, but from June 29 Pittsburgh led in all but three days, and from July 23, the Buccos were never headed. From mid-August on, it was a breeze, with the Pirates galloping home eight and a half games in front of the second-place Giants. The Pirates defeated the Giants, 12 to 10, but oddly enough, lost the year's series to the last-place Cubs by the same margin. Banjo Charley, the Rabbit, and Cooper played their heads off against their old shipmates.

McKechnie had to share the credit for winning his first championship with his coach and first lieutenant—none other than Fred Clarke, the winner of the early 'Pirate pennants. Clarke had been coaxed back from his Kansas ranch, and he had a multitude of titles—vice-president, assistant manager, coach, and stockholder. There is no doubt the old campaigner had an inspiring effect on the players.

The 1925 pennant winner actually was a magnificent team, one that rates well with the great Pittsburgh clubs of 1902 and 1909. The club batted .307 and scored 912 runs, 84 more than the second-best club. It had a devastating punch all the way down the line. Stuffy McInnis, the former crack American League first baseman, was obtained on interleague waivers from the Red Sox and hit .368 for 59 games. He was topped only by Hornsby's magic .403.

From Stuffy down, almost everyone took a hand. Young Cuyler fairly sizzled, and became the talk of the league. He was third among the 100-game players, with .357, scored 144 runs, collected 220 hits for 366 total bases, which included 43 doubles, 26 triples, and 17 home runs. He also stole 41 bases. On September 18, 19, and 21, he bashed out ten consecutive hits, tying an ancient National League mark by Ed Delahanty and Jake Gettman.

Today Kiki is manager of the Atlanta club, and he still looks back to those 366 total bases of 1925 with a proud gleam in his eyes. "It still stands high for total bases on the Pittsburgh club," he said. "That means something, when you consider the club had hitters like Wagner, Clarke, and Traynor. I thought when they got Greenberg in 1947, and moved in the left field-fence that year the record would go. Ralph Kiner threatened it, but my 1925 figures still stand."

Max Carey, though 35, selected 1925 for his biggest season, soaring to .343, while he was still good for 46 steals. Grantham, the former Cub, was well up there with .326; Barnhart was just below him with .324, followed by Traynor, .320, Smith, .313, Wright, .307, and Gooch, .298.

"There were four men who both scored and batted in 100 runs," recalled Cuyler. "And don't forget we had speed to burn. Barnhart and Earl Smith were the only players who weren't fast; yes, we really carried the mail."

The fine work extended to the pitchers, with Meadows winning 19 games and losing 10. Three hurlers, Kremer, Yde, and Morrison, each brought home 17 scalps, and Aldridge, the newcomer from Chicago, won 15 and lost 7, and had one winning streak of 8 straight. Two former American Leaguers, Red Oldham and Tom Sheehan, and old Babe Adams wound up the staff.

The left side of the infield was the toast of the nation, and never in baseball history have fans in any city seen any better defensive ball than Traynor and Wright flashed that season. The right side wasn't so certain. Grantham participated in 102 games at first, McInnis in 45, and young Niehaus in 15. Rawlings started at second, but eventually Eddie Moore, a former shortstop from Atlanta purchased the season before, settled in the position and led off the batting order.

The season of 1925 saw the first unassisted triple play ever made in Pittsburgh. But it came at the end of a game that had McKechnie sorer than a boil, and that left the Pirate fans with a taste in their mouths like stale beer. Leading the Cardinals by a score of 9 to 4, May 7, the Pirates seemed to have the game safely tucked away, when St. Louis unloosened a six-run rally in the eighth. Goodness knows how many more they would have scored in the ninth if Wright hadn't grabbed Jim Bottomley's line drive with runners on first and second and none out. Glenn touched second, retiring Jimmy Cooney for the second out, and then ran after Hornsby and tagged him for the third out. Pittsburgh eventually lost the game, 10 to 9.

2

The opponents of the Pirates in the 1925 World Series were the Washington Senators, the Capital City team that had worn down the Giants in a hard-fought seven-game Series the year before. Bucky Harris, the boy manager of the Senators, had a solid, hard-hitting club, and though his ace pitcher, Walter Johnson, was in his nineteenth year in the majors, the Big Train experienced a magnificent season, winning 20 games and losing 7. Most of the critics and baseball men picked the Senators. Oddly enough, the professional gamblers strung along with Pittsburgh.

On the eve of the first Series game, the American League announced that Roger Peckinpaugh, veteran Washington shortstop, had been voted the loop's most-valuable-player award. Rogers Hornsby, the Cardinals' batting star, won it in the National League.

The Pirates discussed Peckinpaugh with Stuffy McInnis, the old American Leaguer, in the clubhouse. "Is Peck that good?" they asked.

"Roger's had a grand year," said Stuffy. "He's death on ground balls, a tough man on double plays, and has a whale of an arm."

"I guess we better keep the ball away from him," was the comment.

McKechnie overheard it and remarked: "I don't care where you hit the ball, so long as you get on base. Washington only beat the Giants last October because they had all the luck in the world. No club can be that lucky two years in succession. They've got some hitters, but so have we. The Giants slapped Johnson last fall, and there's no reason why we can't hit him. All we have to do is play our game and we'll win."

No one gave too much thought to Washington's right fielder, Joe Harris, a part-time performer from Coulters, Pennsylvania, who played either first base or the outfield—neither too well. He was an injured war veteran, and Washington picked him up from the Red Sox in a midseason trade. Moonfaced Joe almost wrecked the Pirates in the Series.

The first game was played in Pittsburgh on Wednesday, October 7, before a crowd of 41,723. Requests for Series tickets at

Forbes Field came from all over the country, but especially western Pennsylvania, West Virginia, and eastern Ohio. Dreyfuss' offices were swamped with applications, and thousands of dollars had to be returned. However, by erecting extra seats in front of the regular stands, cramming fans into the aisles, and permitting standees in back of the grandstand, the club managed to squeeze in over 43,000 for both the second and sixth games.

Barney was pleased with the turnstile count. "I'm in bad with many of our good customers for sending back their money," he said, "but I am happy that we're able to take care of so many."

In order not to use more of the valuable space in the grandstand, a special press reservation was built in the big foul area, the old "catcher's outfield" between the stands and the home plate. It greatly limited the scope of the catchers' operations.

Prior to the first game, there was a Yuletide spirit at the plate, as the Pirates were showered with gifts by well-meaning hero-worshipers. A delegation from Indiana wished a big clock on Vic Aldridge, while some of Kiki Cuyler's Pittsburgh admirers presented him with a gold bat and baseball. There were posies for Bill McKechnie, and Hans Wagner and Ty Cobb, bitter opponents in the 1909 Series, were greeted with thunderous applause when they took their bows at the plate. Pennsylvania's Governor Gifford Pinchot tossed out the first ball; it wasn't a mean effort, either, his excellency hurling it smack into Earl Smith's big mitt.

Though the aging Walter Johnson had been credited with winning the seventh and deciding game of the 1924 Washington-Giant Series, he had been soundly thrashed in his two earlier efforts. McGraw's New Yorkers had bumped him for 14 and 13 hits, respectively, in his two complete games. As a consequence, neither the Pirates nor the Pittsburgh fans were unduly alarmed when Walter stepped out to warm up for Washington. McKechnie's mound nomination went to Specs Meadows.

However, it wasn't long before all Pittsburgh realized it was seeing Sir Walter at his very best. His blazing fast ball was still smoking, and most of the Pirates looked puny when they tried to connect with it. At times the park was silent as a tomb as Walter blew down ten of McKechnie's boys on strikes. In scoring a rather easy 4-to-1 victory, Johnson never seemed to exert himself; he fairly coasted, as he gave up only five hits. Walter walked only one, but hit Max Carey twice with pitched balls. That surprised the Pirates, especially Scoops.

"I thought in the American League you could stand in the batter's box all season without that big guy ever hitting any one," he said to McInnis. "I'm up there four times and he hits me twice. Don't you think he likes me?"

"Just loosening you up, I guess," laughed Stuffy. "Maybe he thinks you are crowding him."

Meadows pitched well enough to win the ordinary game, giving up six hits in eight innings. That was good pitching, but it didn't suffice. After McInnis batted for Specs in the eighth, the Senators bit into Johnny Morrison's jug-handle curve for two more hits in the ninth.

Joe Harris, the boy from Coulters, served notice early that he intended to be tough, hitting the ball over a low fence in right-center field, in the second inning, for a home run. Harris stopped at second, but Umpire Barry McCormick waved him around, claiming a spectator had interfered with the ball. McKechnie and Clarke argued loudly against the home-run ruling, but it was so much wasted lung power.

The Senators put the game in their locker with two runs in the fifth, but Specs Meadows gave the crowd quite a thrill before he was socked for the runs. Washington filled the bases with none out, when the pesky Joe Harris beat out an infield hit, and Bluege and Peck rifled singles to left.

Specs bore down and struck out the Washington battery, Muddy Ruel and Walter Johnson. The crowd roared its appreciation. Meadows buzzed two quick strikes over on Sam Rice, the Washington lead-off man, and the fans nearly raised the roof. But the yells of joy died in their throats when Rice picked a pitch he liked and shot a single over second base, which sent Joe Harris and Bluege scurrying over the plate.

Pittsburgh scored its only run in the second half of this inning, when Pie Traynor, first up for the Buccos, connected solidly with one of Johnson's fast balls and sent a screeching line drive to right field. It landed in the temporary bleachers, for a home run.

The Senators tallied a final run on Morrison in the ninth. Goose Goslin dropped a single just inside the right-field foul line, and was sacrificed to second by Judge. Morrison fanned the

dangerous Joe Harris, but Bluege clipped Johnny for a single
to center, on which the Goose flew home.

3

Pittsburgh fans left Forbes Field in a happier frame of mind
after the second game, played October 8, which the Buccaneers
won by a score of 3 to 2, to tie up the Series. It was the first World
Series game won by the Pirates on their home grounds since
October 13, 1909, when Babe Adams won the fifth game of the
Series of that year from the Tigers.

Yet there was an air of sadness at the ball park, which the
Pirate victory did not entirely erase. The day before, the famous
former Giant, Christy Mathewson, who had appeared so often
in pitching duels at old Exposition Park and Forbes Field, died
at Saranac Lake, after a long and unsuccessful battle with
tuberculosis. He was president of the Boston Braves at the time
of his death, and a year before he had seemed in reasonably
good health at the Giant-Washington Series. McKechnie had
been one of Matty's teammates in New York and Cincinnati,
while the Dreyfusses long had regarded him as their favorite
ball player, next to members of the Pirates.

Impressive ceremonies were held before the game for the
great pitcher who had pitched the National League to three
shutout World Series victories against the Athletics in 1905. The
players of both teams wore mourning bands around their arms,
and five minutes before game time, Brick Owens, the chief
umpire, lined them up at the home plate. Led by the two teams,
Judge Landis, Barney Dreyfuss, John Heydler, John McGraw,
and other baseball men, the mourners slowly marched to deep
center field. A solemn hush fell over the crowd as the band
played "Nearer, My God, to Thee." It was followed by the national anthem, after which the colors were raised and then
brought down to half-mast. That ended baseball's tribute to the
great Mathewson, but McGraw and Heydler left for Matty's
funeral at Lewiston, Pennsylvania, immediately after the game.

The second-game pitchers were Vic Aldridge for the Pirates
and Stanley Coveleskie for Washington. Coveleskie was the fellow who won three victories for the Indians in the Cleveland-
Brooklyn Series five years before, giving up only fifteen in the
three games. Stan had put on a great comeback with Washing-

ton in 1925, was the American League's earned-run leader, and was credited with twenty victories against five defeats. He was one of the special group of pitchers still licensed to pitch the spitball.

Ossie Bluege, the crack Washington third baseman and later Senator manager, was felled by an Aldridge fast ball in the sixth inning, when an inside pitch struck him on the side of the head. It forced Bucky Harris to play a raw rookie from New Orleans, Buddy Myer, at third base.

Homers played a big factor in the game, as Wright and Cuyler reached the stands for Pittsburgh, and Judge for the Americans. The hits were eight for Washington against seven for the Pirates, but Aldridge had the benefit of perfect support, whereas Peckinpaugh, who had made the only error in the first game, again bobbled twice for the Senators. "We're glad they gave that guy the medal," laughed Pirate fans. "They put a jinx on him." In contrast to the erring Peck, Wright came up with one great play after another, while both of Pie Traynor's assists were on difficult plays.

As in the first game, Washington scored in the first inning. With two strikes on him, Joe Judge slammed a homer into the right-field stands, and Pittsburgh tied the score in the fourth, when Glenn Wright sent a home-run ball whistling into the left-field stands.

Most of the action of the game was crowded into the last two innings, and Buccaneer fans got a good run for their money. Pittsburgh broke the 1-to-1 deadlock with two big runs in the eighth. Peckinpaugh gave them their opening wedge when he fumbled Moore's bounder. Carey sacrificed Eddie to second, and Cuyler delivered the kayo punch on Coveleskie when he lined a home run into the right-field stands.

But the Senators had a big rally left, and almost pulled the fat out of the fire in the ninth. Vic Aldridge had a spell of wildness but showed a lot of intestinal fortitude when the game hinged on every pitch. Vic gave four balls to Joe Harris; Buddy Meyer clipped him for a single, and then he walked Roger Peckinpaugh. All with none out! An ugly kettle of fish, and the boys in the stands didn't dare to breathe.

Bucky Harris sent Bobbie Veach, the former Detroit slugger, to bat for Muddy Ruel, and he drove in McNeely, Moon Harris' pinch runner, with what was then labeled a sacrifice fly to

Carey. Dutch Ruether, the former Cincinnati pitcher—and a pretty good hitter—batted for Coveleskie, but Aldridge cut him down on strikes. There was still the dangerous Rice to be subdued, but Vic retired Sam on a roller to Eddie Moore.

4

The Series was all squared at one victory each, when the two teams moved on to Washington for the third game on October 9. A hard rain was beating down on the Capital City when the baseball specials arrived, and Landis promptly called off the game. McKechnie didn't like the postponement; it meant another day of rest for Walter Johnson.

The rain had stopped, but a young gale was blowing when play was resumed on Saturday, October 10. The wind almost blew off Clark Griffith's roof, but Barney Dreyfuss, Bill Mc-Kechnie, Earl Smith, and lesser Pirates blew a few gusts of their own. After the game they almost blew the roof off their hostelry with their cries of wrath and high dudgeon. Umpire Charley "Cy" Rigler, a National Leaguer, was the object of their wrath, as the game, won by Washington by a score of 4 to 3, hinged on a decision by Cy on a ball that the Pirate catcher, Earl Smith, apparently had belted into a little temporary bleacher that Griffith had built in center field. Few World Series decisions have ever resulted in such verbiage. One still hears the moot play discussed today.

With Washington enjoying a scant one-run margin in the eighth, Smith lashed a clout to the sun seats, and Sam Rice rode out with the fly. Just as Earl's drive was about to drop into the overflow crowd, Sam leaped into the air and made a grab for the ball. But immediately Rice disappeared from the view of all but a few bleacherites. He tumbled head over heels into the bleacher.

After several seconds Rice emerged with the ball in his hand, and Rigler, who had run out to the bleacher, jerked up his thumb to indicate that Smith was out. In a few moments Cy was surrounded by McKechnie and a wild band of jawing Pirates, who wanted to know: "Why is Earl out? Did you see Rice catch the ball?"

The Pirates claimed that when Sam disappeared from sight he had plucked the ball from the hand of one of the spectators, and that this was the ball he exhibited. Sam partly admitted that, and had his story for his tardy return to the ball field. He said he made the catch, but that as he fell a fan grabbed the leather pill out of his hand, and then subsequently returned it. Rigler apparently took that view. McKechnie protested the catch to Landis after the game, but the Judge gave him little satisfaction. The decision rested with Rigler's judgment, and "the umpire is supreme," said the Judge.

Some years later I was in a golfing foursome with Sam Rice at Hot Springs, Arkansas. I asked: "Did you really catch Smith's fly, Sam?" He laughed as he replied: "Well, Cy Rigler said I did; you wouldn't want me to make a liar out of him at this late date."

Bucky Harris stole this game anyway, as he got away with one of his lesser pitchers, Aleck Ferguson, a screwball artist and a discard from the Yankees and Red Sox. Fred Marberry, the talented Washington relief man, finished, after Ferguson went out for a pinch hitter. Fergy's victim was Remy Kremer, who eventually emerged as the Pirate pitching hero of the Series.

The Pirates scored a wind-swept run in the second inning, when Moon Harris fell on his face in going after Traynor's long drive. Pie pulled up at third with a triple, and dashed home after Goose Goslin caught Wright's fly.

Washington quickly got this run back when Rice opened the third inning with a single, scampered to second on Bucky Harris' sacrifice, to third on Goslin's fly, and scored when Judge rammed a double down the right-field foul line.

Ferguson worked himself out of a bad hole at the expense of only one Pirate run in the fourth. It looked like a big inning for the Bucs when Kiki Cuyler opened with a double between Rice and the Goose and crossed the plate when Barnhart bored a single to left. There were passes to Traynor and Earl Smith, filling the bases, but Ferguson got rid of Grantham and Wright on easy chances and blotted out the unhappy Kremer on strikes.

Peck's daily boot gave the Pirates a third run and a 3-to-1 lead in the sixth. Wright was safe at first base when Roger pegged wildly to Judge; Grantham fanned, but Smith's solid drive to right sent Glenn speeding to third. Kremer refused to be the fall guy a second time and punched a single just out of Stan Harris' reach, scoring Wright. After Moore walked, filling the bases, Carey had a chance to sew up the game, but Scoops fanned.

Goslin got one run back for the Senators in their half of the sixth, when he bounced a line drive into the center-field bleachers for a home run. The American League champions then won with two runs in the eighth, when everything went badly for Kremer. The mite, Nemo Leibold, batted for Ferguson and worked Remy for a pass; McNeely ran for him. After Rice flied out, Bucky Harris selected this moment for his first hit of the Series, an infield scratch. The Pirates expected Goslin, the slugger, to swing from the hips, but Goose caught the entire Pittsburgh infield flat-footed when he beat out a bunt, filling the bases. McNeely then crossed the plate with the tying run on Judge's fly to Barnhart, and Stan Harris carried home the winning tally on dangerous Joe Harris' solid thump to left.

The Pirates felt pretty sick when the Sunday game of October 11 was over. Even though President Coolidge and his fan lady passed this one up, it was a Roman holiday for the partisan crowd of 38,301 spectators. The Washington pitching prince, Walter Johnson, once more was supreme, and the Pirates again looked like meek landlubbers, trying to connect with the veteran's fast ball. Johnson yielded only six hits—all singles—walked two, and the Pirates didn't have a real scoring chance all through the pleasant fall afternoon. The score was almost the same as in Walter's earlier effort, but this time the Big Train pitched a 4-to-0 shutout. Sharing honors with Johnson were his little catcher, Muddy Ruel, who rapped out a double and two singles, and the Senator manager, Bucky Harris, who handled thirteen chances at second base. That tied a record set by Claude Ritchey of the Pirates in 1903.

Bill McKechnie started Emil Yde, his left-hander, against the Washington ace. The southpaw went safely through two innings, but the third was a fat Senatorial frame. The District of Columbia ball boys did all their scoring in this lusty inning.

It started well enough for the Pirates, when Johnson opened with an apparent double to left but lost it when he sprang a Charley horse while running from first to second. The limping Walter never reached the bag and was an easy out, Barnhart to Wright. But after that a black squall burst over the Pirate craft. Rice was awarded an infield hit when Wright fell on the ball and couldn't extricate it. Stan Harris hit sharply to Grantham,

ARKY VAUGHAN   BOB ELLIOTT

FRANK FRISCH WITH HANS WAGNER

who tried to start a double play by way of second, but Wright
gummed things up by spilling the ball, both runners being safe.
Barnhart slightly misjudged Goslin's line drive and played it
none too well. He might have held it to a double, but it eluded
his leap and landed in the left-field bleachers for a home run,
Rice and Harris scoring ahead of him. While the fans were still
cheering the Goose, Moon Harris gave them something else to
shout about, when he hit the next pitch high up into the same
stands for another four-bagger.

McKechnie still stuck to Yde but when Emil walked Joe
Judge, even Bill had had enough. Johnny Morrison relieved him
and stopped further scoring. Babe Adams, making his last, fleeting
World Series appearance, pitched the eighth, and got by without
a score, even though he was stung for two hits.

Washington was smug and cocky. This was going to be easier
than beating McGraw in 1924. By another nightfall the Capital
City felt it would be all over, and there was even some premature
celebrating. Baseball men, even hidebound National Leaguers,
saw little hope for the McKechnie entry. Few could see the
Pirates winning three straight games from Griffith's maulers, especially if a long Series brought back Walter Johnson for a third
outing. No club in a seven-game Series had ever overcome such
a deficit.

Yet Barney, the Deacon, Clarke, and the Pirate players clung
desperately to what looked to be a lost cause. That doughty
American League hater, John McGraw—still feeling the sting of
his defeat the year before—also did his best to keep up the fighting spirit of the Pirates. "Keep after them; never give up," he
advised, and he said to McKechnie: "Why don't you get that
Grantham out of there? He's not doing you any good. Why not
play Stuffy McInnis on first? He's been in a lot of World Series,
and knows what this is all about."

McKechnie took the advice, and when the clubs lined up for
the Monday, Columbus Day, game of October 12, the former
Athletic and Red Sox veteran was on first base for Pittsburgh.
There is no doubt Stuffy steadied the Pirates, and when the day's
proceedings were over, Washington had little chance to rejoice.
Their boys had to make another trip to Pittsburgh after all, as
the Pirates, thumping out 13 hits, kept the Series alive by winning, 6 to 3.

The second-game pitchers, Vic Aldridge and the spitballer

Coveleskie, tangled up again, and for the second time the Hoosier triumphed. Though the game was close for six innings, the Bucs enjoyed a comfortable margin at the finish. Everybody but Aldridge took a hand in the thirteen-hit barrage. Ossie Bluege, beaned by Aldridge in Vic's first game, was still groggy but was back in the Washington line-up.

Washington fans had a few brief moments of joy in the first, when the Senators got away to a one-run lead. Rice opened with a single, took second on Stan Harris' sacrifice, and scored on Goslin's Texas League double to left. Coveleskie's wildness and Pirate speed helped the Bucs take the lead with two in the third. Carey walked and stole second, and then Cuyler also drew four balls. Scoops flew home and Kiki to third when Barnhart rapped a sharp single to left. As Barnhart stole second, Ruel pegged down to third to catch Cuyler off base, but Kiki slid safely into Bluege's bag. The speedy Wolverine then scurried home on Traynor's sacrifice fly. The Senators tied it up in the next inning, when Moon Harris again reached his left-field, home-run range.

There was a wild time on the Pittsburgh bench in the seventh as the Pirates jumped ahead again with two runs, knocking out Coveleskie. With one out, Eddie Moore walked, and Carey stabbed a single to left. Kiki kept it up with a single that bounced out of Bluege's glove, Eddie scoring and Scoops tearing around to third. Max scored on Barnhart's second single. Win Ballou was called to Covey's relief and for a moment halted the Buc attack. Washington kept the game close by getting one run back in its half on Pinch Hitter Leibold's ground-rule double and Rice's single.

However, the Pirates kept pecking away and picked up additional welcome runs off Left-hander Tom Zachary in each of the last two innings. In the eighth, Wright's double and Stuffy's single cooked up a run, and Barnhart's walk and singles by Traynor and Wright produced a sixth tally in the ninth.

6

The odds still ran heavily against the Pirates as they returned to Pittsburgh after their fifth-game victory. McKechnie's boys still trailed, three games to two, and one defeat would knock them out. And Johnson's shadow loomed in the background. Yet the spirits of the Pirates were surprisingly good on the train back to their home bailiwick. "That 6 to 3 was the turning point" and "We've just started to hit!" were the rallying cries, as McGraw joined McKechnie and Clarke in singing a new Pirate victory song.

"I'm depending on you, Ray," the Deacon told Kremer, on the train. "Pitch as well as you did in the third game, and you can win."

"I'll win for you," said Ray.

Remy came through as he had promised, and all Pittsburgh went berserk as the Californian pitched the Pirates back to even terms with the American Leaguers at three victories each, winning a hard-fought 3-to-2 victory, October 13, before 43,810 frenzied Forbes Field fans. Kremer's win was especially sweet, as this time he vanquished Aleck Ferguson, who had decisioned him in the third game. Ray started a little nervously, yielding runs in each of the first two frames, but starting with the last two men who faced him in the second, he retired thirteen successive batsmen. However, even Remy had to laugh at his own futile batting. He struck out three times on nine pitched balls. Hits were scarce on both sides, but oddly enough six Washington hits and seven that bounced off the Pittsburgh bats each added up to eleven total bases.

Goslin started the day's scoring by cracking a first-inning homer, his third of the Series, into the right-field stands, and the Senators made it 2 to 0 in the second, when Judge singled to right, was forced by Bluege, and the latter ran home when Peck doubled on a hit-and-run play. After that only three Senators reached base.

Washington's bad boy, Peck, then did the Pirates his almost daily good turn when he helped Pittsburgh tie in the third. Moore walked, and Carey rolled a sharp grounder down to the Senator shortstop. Roger fumbled, made a hasty recovery, but got nobody. The Bucs took full advantage of the break: Cuyler advanced the pair with a sacrifice, Barnhart's infield out enabled Moore to score, and Carey tallied the tying run on Traynor's single.

Eddie Moore, the little second baseman, blossomed out as the game's hero, along with Kremer, when in the fifth inning he shot a home run into the center-field seats. The Senators fought to the finish. Bucky Harris again sent Bobbie Veach, the old clouting ex-Tiger, to hit for him in the eighth, but Moore's home run held up as Pittsburgh's margin of victory.

In the greatest uphill victory scored in World Series competition, the Pirates then became World Champions in a never-to-be-forgotten seventh game, October 15, in which the Corsairs finally battered down the great Johnson, 9 to 7, with Walter blowing early 4-to-0 and 6-to-3 leads. It was the kind of day that was particularly favorable for Pirates, and one in which the Bucs had to give the rain god a great assist for their magnificent victory.

There had been a heavy rainstorm on Wednesday, the fourteenth, the date on which the seventh game originally was scheduled. There also was a fog and intermittent rains on the morning of Thursday, the fifteenth, but the Series had already gone well over a week, and Commissioner Judge Landis wanted to get it finished, if it was at all possible. Eventually the game was started, before 42,856 brave fans, in a cold drizzle that turned into a steady downpour in the third inning and continued without letup for the remainder of the afternoon.

Forbes Field was already heavy and water-soaked from the hard rain of the previous day, and puddles formed in the pitcher's box, on the base lines, and in the outfield. A parade of ground attendants carried buckets of sawdust to the field, which was spread along the base lines and tamped into the pitcher's box to prevent Johnson and a gang of Pittsburgh pitchers—Aldridge, Morrison, Kremer, and Oldham—from slipping off the rubber. The pitchers also were furnished with towels to dry the balls. By the fifth inning a dark mist hung over the field, and the outfielders looked like ghoulish figures in the general gloom.

Pirate spirits sank low when the Senators opened with four runs on Vic Aldridge in the first inning. With Johnson having yielded only one run in his previous eighteen innings, it looked as though the game had been decided before Pittsburgh even went to bat. Who ever heard of Johnson blowing such a lead?

Vic slipped and slid on the wet rubber and was wild and ineffective. Rice greeted him with a single to left, and after Stan Harris flied out, a wild pitch sent Sammy to second. Then Goslin walked, and Rice and the Goose advanced on a wild pitch. A pass to Moon Harris filled the bases, and Pirate fans groaned when Joe Judge also walked, forcing over Rice. Johnny Morrison was called to the relief of the battered Aldridge. Peck hit to Wright, who threw to Moore for an apparent force play, but

Roger argued that Catcher Earl Smith had interfered with his bat as he swung, and Barry McCormick, the National League umpire, allowed the claim.

McKechnie and Smith bellowed, but the umpires permitted Moon Harris to score and called everybody safe on the bases. Eddie Moore fumbled Ruel's grounder on the wet grass, and Judge carried in the fourth run of the inning. With the bases still full and only one out, the inning happily came to an end without further damage, when Morrison fanned Johnson and Barnhart collared Rice's fly.

Pirate fans roused themselves in the third inning, when their favorites suddenly teed off on Johnson as though he were a green rookie. Walter slipped and slithered on the wet mound, called repeatedly for towels, but the Corsairs socked everything he was tossing up. In a jiffy they cut Washington's lead to one run. Morrison started it with a single and scored on Moore's long double to left. Carey's single past Stan Harris drove in Eddie; Scoops took second on an out and then got such a lead in stealing third that Ruel didn't even make a throw. Barnhart's single fetched in Carey.

There was another sinking spell in the stands in the fourth as the Senators scored twice on singles by Rice and Goslin and Joe Harris' double. Again Sir Walter was propped up with a three-run lead.

George Grantham batted for Morrison in the Pirate half of the fourth, which brought Kremer into the game as McKechnie's third pitcher, and Ray's superb performance in the mud, after only one day's rest, was an outstanding factor in Pittsburgh's eventual victory. With Remy nobly holding the fort, the Pirates had the score tied at 6 to 6 by the end of the sixth. A run came across in the fifth when Carey and Cuyler bunched doubles, and two more precious tallies followed in the seventh. The entering wedge again was the erring Peckinpaugh's two-base muff on Eddie Moore's fly. Carey banged Eddie home with his third rainy-day double, and Traynor's triple to deep right tallied Max. Pie tried desperately to put Pittsburgh ahead and exerted every nerve and muscle to stretch his hit into a homer, but he was tagged out by Ruel as he slid into the thick mud at the plate.

Poor Peckinpaugh! The goat of the Series, he tried to make amends for his many blunders by putting Washington ahead again, 7 to 6, when in Washington's eighth he homered into the temporary left-field bleachers. It was the only hit off Kremer in four innings. But Peck's four-bagger was quickly wiped out and he became an even worse culprit in Washington's eyes, as the Pirates put on a terrific three-run rally in the rain, muck, and mist in their half, which gave them the ball game and the Series. At no time in the Series were the Pirates in front until the eighth inning of the last game, and then it meant Pittsburgh won the marbles.

The inning started modestly enough for the Bucs, as Wright fouled to Judge and McInnis lifted to Rice. Earl Smith started the rally with a double to right, and Carson Bigbee kept it up with another two-bagger to left, which scored Yde, Smith's pinch runner, with the tying run. More gold-plated tallies quickly were to follow. Moore was passed, and the rally seemed over as Carey grounded to Peck. But as Roger stumbled in the mud to tag second for a force play, he dropped the ball for his eighth error of the Series. It filled the bases with growling Pirates.

With Johnson weakening fast, Cuyler belted out several vicious fouls and then sent a terrific liner down the right-field foul line. It was difficult to follow the ball in the evening dusk. It looked like a homer, and all three runners on the bases preceded the joyous Cuyler over the plate, while the rain-soaked crowd became a bedlam and the Pirate bench a madhouse. Bats, masks, breast protectors, shin guards, and everything else flew out on the field.

There was considerable confusion when the umpires went into a huddle and decided it was a ground-rule double. They allowed only Bigbee and Moore to score, returned Carey to third and Cuyler to second. The Pirates yelled bloody murder. "It was a homer! It was a homer!" McKechnie's shrill voice could be heard above the patter of the raindrops. But the umpires ruled the ball had bounded among battery men of both teams who were warming up in the distant bull pen—in foul territory—when they last saw the ball.

However, the two runs driven in by Kiki were plenty. It was almost dark by this time, and Red Oldham, the former American League Tiger, squelched the Senators in order in the ninth, fanning Rice and Goslin and getting Bucky Harris on an easy hoist to Moore.

Dreyfuss almost wept with joy as he crowded into the clubhouse. "You did it, Bill! You did it! It was wonderful!" he cried.

The Deacon kissed Clarke and was kissed by Fred in turn. Judge Landis elbowed his way in, followed by Heydler and John McGraw, both with beaming faces. It was a notable, never-to-be-forgotten National League triumph.

In that epic, final struggle, the Pirates whanged Johnson for 15 hits, totaling 25 bases. Cuyler, Carey, and Kremer were the big Pirate heroes; Cuyler for his winning clout, and Max for hitting three doubles and a single in the seventh game and a hefty .458 for the Series. Kremer was acclaimed for his magnificent pitching, after only one day's rest; Remy received credit for winning the last two games and was almost as big a shot as was Babe Adams in 1909.

If there was unabated joy in the Pirate clubhouse, it was all gall and wormwood in the American League quarters. Ban Johnson, American League president, wasn't at the Series but he added to Bucky Harris' grief by sending the young manager a telegram: "You sacrificed a World Championship for our league to mawkish sentiment."

He referred to Harris' refusal to lift Johnson when the Washington lead was melting away. "I would have done it all over again," said Bucky. "Even though they were hitting Barney, I still had more confidence in him on such a day than in any other pitcher on my staff."

And poor Peckinpaugh wound up with eight of his team's nine errors, a World Series record for butter on the fingers that still stands.

It was a happy winter for the Pirates. Not only were the brash Buccaneers World Champions, but each member of the winning team was rewarded with a tidy check for $5,332. That was quite an increase over 1903, when the players received $1,182 (with Dreyfuss tossing in his share) and the $1,825 winning share in 1909.

The players also voted full shares to Coach Jack Onslow and road secretary Sam Watters. Even so, there was a sour note in the divvy. At the players' meeting the question came up as to how Assistant Manager Clarke should be treated. Some felt that as Fred was an officer and stockholder of the Pirates he would share in the club's prosperous season, but as a gesture they voted him a sum of $1,000, the same as was given Scouts Bill Hinchman and Chick Frazer.

Fred, feeling hurt and aggrieved—and that he was entitled to a full share—returned the check.

Barney didn't fare so poorly, either, getting a fat check for $166,445 from the Commissioner's office, as his end. Yes, baseball was doing quite well by the immigrant boy from Freiberg!

XXI. MUTINY ON THE HIGH SEAS

FOLLOWING THE sensational World Series victory of 1925, everyone expected the Pirates to repeat in 1926. Persons who went back to the turn of the century freely predicted McKechnie's club would dominate the National League for a span of years, as did Clarke's three-time champions of 1901-02-03. But despite the fact that the club was strengthened by the acquisition of Pittsburgh's greatest hitter since Honus Wagner, Paul Waner, the club limped home in third place, four and a half games behind the year's dark horse, Rogers Hornsby's Cardinals, and two and a half games in back of the second-place Reds.

Despite their new title of World Champions, the club started the season in a hesitant manner, but the Deacon seemingly got his craft righted in June, and from the seventh to the twenty-fourth, the Pirates made the spirited climb from seventh place to first. For most of the next two months the rest of the league was taking the wake of the Jolly Roger. Jack Hendricks' Reds appeared to be "the team to beat," but the Cardinals were closing in fast, and in a historic six-game series in St. Louis in late August the Pirates won only one game, lost four, and Vic Aldridge battled Grover Alexander to a spirited, ten-inning 2-to-2 tie on a rainy Sunday, August 29. The Deacon's only winning pitcher in the series was Kremer, who won a 3-to-0 shutout from Flint Rhem in the first game of a double-header on June 30, but the Pirates blew the second game and also lost a disappointing double-header, 6 to 1 and 2 to 1, the following day. The pasting

221

that was especially painful was the second one on the thirty-first, in which Allan Sothoron, whose status was that of a semi-coach, tossed a three-hitter to nose out Johnny Morrison. That defeat dropped Pittsburgh out of the lead, and as the Redbirds soared to the top perch, all St. Louis went delirious. The Pirates regained the lead for a few days in early September, but from September 6 on, it was all St. Louis. On their last eastern trip the Buccos slipped behind Cincinnati into third place, their eventual resting place.

There is no doubt that dissension within the Pirate ranks upset the Pittsburgh morale and had much to do with the craft hitting that late August snag on the Mississippi. The trouble started over Fred Clarke, the old skipper, sitting on the bench and offering advice in the salty language of a Pirate sea captain of the old school.

There was an early incident with George Grantham. The infielder was in a batting slump, and Fred gave George a few hints that he thought would be helpful. But it didn't work out so well.

"Hey, Fred," said Grantham, "I wish you'd quit telling me things."

"O.K., George, if that's how you want it," replied Clarke.

"No hard feelings, Fred, but I was just trying to think of too many things at the same time."

However, the explosive rhubarb that started the real mutiny revolved around Max Carey, Carson Bigbee, and Babe Adams, and was called the ABC flare-up. The blowup came in a game in Boston, August 7. Dave Bancroft, the Brave manager, sent in his shortstop, Bob Smith, to pitch, and Bob won by a 1-to-0 score. Smith later developed into a pretty good pitcher, but being shut out by an infielder was enough to fray the nerves of any team battling for a pennant. By this time Max Carey, captain, center fielder, and lead-off man, also was in the blue funk of a slump.

"Why the devil don't you get Carey out of there?" Clarke said to the Deacon. "He isn't hitting a lick."

"Well, who can I play in Max's place?" asked Wilkinsburg Bill.

"Anybody," responded Fred. "Put in the bat boy; he can't do any worse than the fellow you are playing."

Carey didn't hear the remark, but Bigbee did, and Carson was

Max's pal. He repeated the words to Scoops, and the crack, especially the part about the bat boy, hurt the great center fielder's pride. Carey waxed resentful; he and Carson talked it over with several players, including Adams, and asked the latter: "What do you think, Babe?"

"Well, I think the manager should manage, and no one else should interfere," said Babe, with still the friendliest feelings for Clarke, his 1909 mentor.

There was some wild talk of a strike unless Clarke left the bench. Jack Onslow, the other coach, supposedly also was in Carey's camp. The upshot of the matter was that when the club arrived in Brooklyn a meeting was held in Carey's room as to whether Clarke should be asked to get off the bench. In a secret ballot the players cast an overwhelming 18-to-6 vote in favor of the old skipper. Fred had withdrawn from the bench temporarily but returned after the vote and demanded that the mutineers be punished.

Barney Dreyfuss was in Europe as the feud split the team, and his only son, Sammy, was in active charge. But it generally was believed that the father cabled the son as to what action he should take. On August 13 Bigbee and Adams were released unconditionally, and Carey, who was drawing a $16,500 salary, was sold to the Dodgers for $4,000, after Brooklyn had declined to waive on the veteran star.

Babe Adams' remark was typical: "I am eighteen years in baseball without ever opening my mouth, and then when I answer a question, I find myself chucked off the club."

The released players appealed to the National League president, John A. Heydler, against the charge of "insubordination," and Heydler called a hearing, August 17, at the Hotel William Penn in Pittsburgh. After listening to both sides, Heydler exonerated the players of the insubordination charges but upheld the right of the club to fire them. Carey later did well in Brooklyn and managed that club for two seasons. Scoops is now president of the All-American Girls Baseball League.

There were more reverberations of the mutiny. After the elder Dreyfuss returned, Stuffy McInnis was released September 26; he supposedly talked for both sides. A month later Stuffy signed as manager of the Phillies. McKechnie was let go after the close of the season, and signed as a coach of the Cardinals under Bob O'Farrell. And on October 26 Fred Clarke resigned all of his offices and disposed of his stock. Yes, the housecleaning was complete.

Almost as fatal to the Pirates' 1926 chances as their recent mutiny was a serious injury to Glenn Wright, the great shortstop, who was seriously injured when accidentally hit on the head by Pitcher Vic Keen of the Cardinals. Glenn went down like a felled steer, and in terror McKechnie yelled: "He looks as though he is dead!" Wright didn't die but missed many games. As for Keen, he was so shaken by Wright's injury that he never was the same pitcher thereafter.

2

If the 1926 season had its unpleasantness it also had its bright side. Remy Kremer followed up his sensational 1925 World Series with a grand performance; he led the National League pitchers in both earned runs, 2.61, and in winning percentage, .769, with 18 victories against 7 defeats. The nominal batting leader was a young Pirate outfielder, Roy Spencer, with .395 for 28 games. Earl Smith was third among the 100-game players, with .346, and the brilliant Oklahoma youngster, Paul Waner, flashed across the National League sky with a freshman average of .336. On August 26 he joined Beaumont, Cuyler, and the six-hits-in-one-game boys with a triple, two doubles, and three singles in six times up.

Paul was procured in a big cash transaction with San Francisco, Dreyfuss giving $100,000 for Waner and Shortstop Hal Rhyne. Despite the fact that Waner hit .401 for the 1925 Seals, Rhyne, the infielder, represented $60,000 of the purchase money. The Pirates had been scouting him for several years. But it was Paul who was quickly to develop into the real jewel.

His full name was John Paul Waner, but the John was dropped somewhere along the way. Though Paul and his brother Lloyd, who came up a year later, were farm kids born in Harrah, Oklahoma, they were of Pennsylvania Dutch stock. Paul started as a left-handed catcher at Dewey Grade School in Harrah, and walked three miles barefooted to play ball.

Even though he wore glasses in his latter years, Paul had the sharpest eyes of any player then in the National League. He rarely hit a bad pitch and was almost free of slumps. Though only five feet, eight and a half inches tall, he had strong, sinewy wrists, forearms, and shoulders, intuitive timing, and split-second reaction. After 19 years of big-league baseball, Paul Waner left with almost as many records as Wagner. He led the National League three times, compiled a lifetime average of .332, and bashed out 3,152 hits, a total topped only by the Hall of Fame immortals, Cobb, Speaker, Wagner, Eddie Collins, and Lajoie. Waner was anything but a teetotaler; in fact, he was a chap who liked to set 'em up for the boys. There is a story that Barney Dreyfuss once repeated Lincoln's famous remark about General Grant when gossips brought reports of Paul's imbibing. "Find out what brand he drinks," said Barney. "I want to send some of it to some of my other players," said the former Louisville distiller.

Rhyne never lived up to his price tag. Early in the 1926 season Eddie Moore was sold to Boston and Hal installed at second base. After Wright was injured, Rhyne was put in at shortstop, his Coast League position. He played in 109 games and hit a mediocre .251. He lasted only a few seasons in Pittsburgh, returned to the Coast League, but came back later with the Athletics and Red Sox.

The Pirates had another young California infielder in 1926 who also was to write considerable baseball history; a good-looking, lantern-jawed kid named Joe Cronin. Originally picked off the Golden Gate Park sand lots of his native San Francisco by a Pirate scout, Joe was developed in Johnstown and New Haven. The lad, not quite 20, showed much promise and hit .265 in 38 games, most of them at second base.

XXII. BUSH SAILS INTO PENNANT HARBOR

WHEN BARNEY. DREYFUSS replaced Fred Clarke as manager in 1916, he reached into the American League and plucked Jimmy Collins, Comiskey's old manager. When he chose a successor for McKechnie a decade later, he again went into the American League and named Donie Bush, the former Tiger shortstop who had played such spirited ball against the Pirates in the 1909 World Series. Donie had picked up considerable managerial experience with Washington and Indianapolis. He now is president of the latter club.

Under Bush's leadership the Pirates snapped back strongly and re-entered Pennant Harbor in 1927, beating out the Cardinals, the 1926 victor, led by O'Farrell and McKechnie, by a whisker—a mere game and a half. And right behind St. Louis was Dreyfuss' old enemy, McGraw, whose Giants trailed the Cardinals by only a half game. The finish found the three top clubs sailing over the finish line with the Pirates (94-60) .610; St. Louis (92-61) .601; New York (92-62) .597. A total attendance of 869,720, Pittsburgh's record until 1947, enjoyed the pennant frolic.

While the Pirates' eventual lead was slim, they set the pace in 104 days of the race. The Buccos led from May 22 to July 6, when they were jolted out of the lead by the Cubs. Chicago led through most of August, when Joe McCarthy's pitchers faded, and Bush's boys forged out in front again September 1, when they defeated the Cubs, 4 to 3, and thereafter never were headed. But both the Giants, the early-season pacemakers, and the Cardinals closed strongly and breathed hot on the Pirate boot heels all through September. The Corsairs didn't clinch the flag until October 1, next to the last day of the season, when they defeated the Reds 9 to 6. Miljus' relief-pitching job and Pie's three timely hits turned the trick.

The Pirates really won their sixth flag in a fine May campaign, in which they won 18 games and lost 6, and a hot September, in which the skull and crossbones was hoisted triumphant in 22 games out of 31. Yet the Freebooters again almost blew the flag over dissension in the ranks. Again the storm center was an ace outfielder; this time Kiki Cuyler.

Cuyler had had three brilliant seasons with the club and was one of Pittsburgh's most popular players when he got into Donie Bush's hair by unwillingness to swing his cudgel in the second spot in the batting order.

The Pirates had fallen off in their midseason play, and Cuyler also was experiencing a bit of a slump. In an effort to change things around, Bush reshuffled his line-up, and Cuyler came up in the second position. Now Kiki had an almost superstitious aversion to batting second. He felt he wasn't a good hit-and-run man, that he was a straight-away hitter, and that his strongest forte was as third hitter. He also liked to belt in runs.

He gave Bush several reasons why he didn't want to bat second, but Donie replied: "Well, Ki, you just try it. You'll find you will do all right up there."

However, after Cuyler had gone five times without a hit in the second notch, he fumed and swore. Again Bush counseled patience and perseverence. "Don't worry about it; you'll be all right when you get used to it."

Shortly afterward, in a poor game in Cincinnati, Cuyler slammed his bat into the ground and called to Bush: "Take me out of that second slot before I become the worst flop on your team."

Bush's rejoinder was: "You'll stay there until I am ready to change you."

Earl Smith, the catcher, who had learned to needle players from McGraw in New York, added fuel to the flames by kidding Cuyler in front of Bush, saying: "Doesn't Kiki like where the manager wants him to bat? Too bad!"

In a play against the Giants a few days later, Cuyler failed to slide, in going into second base on a double-play ball. Kiki claimed he went into the bag standing up so as to be in a better position to break up the double play. Donie didn't think so and fined Cuyler twenty-five dollars, and there were subsequent hot words in the clubhouse.

Several of the Pittsburgh newspapers defended Cuyler, and one of them quoted Bill Terry, the Giant first baseman, as saying Kiki was right, and that the play called for Kiki to go into the bag the way he did. That peeved Bush, and he benched the brilliant Michigan boy and put the slower man, Clyde Barnhart, in left field. This in turn annoyed Pittsburgh writers and Pirate fans. Columns were written in the sports pages, asking for the return of Cuyler to his regular position, while fans marched into Forbes Field carrying placards, "We want Kiki." They also chanted the same refrain from the grandstand and bleachers.

It is possible that this strong defense of Cuyler by the press and fans merely stiffened the attitude of the Pirate management. Bush might have relented, but Dreyfuss was an obdurate man and hated to yield to pressure. Cuyler never did get back, not even for the World Series. "We're not going to let the fans, or even those fellows up in the pressbox, pick our line-up," he said.

Today Cuyler modestly says: "You know, Barnhart was a real good hitter, but not too good in the field. It was really a case of one player getting hurt and another getting in there and going so good that he stayed." Yet it is only fair to say that for those who speak baseball parlance, when both players were at their peak, "Barnhart couldn't have carried Kiki's glove." Before the row Cuyler hit .309 and stole 20 bases in 85 games.

Yet Kiki looks back with pride and pleasure on that season saying: "While I was in the line-up I played between the two Waners, the greatest fielding outfield I ever had the good fortune to be with. We weren't together long, but I believe if I hadn't been released to Chicago there is no telling what records this trio could have compiled had we held together for a span of years."

Yes, little Lloyd Waner, Paul's younger brother, who was three years "Big Poison's" junior, joined the Pirates in 1927 and broke in with 223 hits and a batting average of .355. He was one of the few players to collect 200 hits in his freshman year and established a modern record for singles with 198. In all major-league baseball, only Willie Keeler, who had 199 in 1897, exceeded Lloyd's mark. Paul, in the meantime, regained Hans

Wagner's old batting crown for Pittsburgh with a .380 average, while his 237 hits established an all-time high for a Pirate ball player. The two Waners carried in 244 runs, 133 for Lloyd and 113 for Paul.

In the first half of the season, Lloyd was in left field, Cuyler in center, and Paul in right. After Kiki was benched Barnhart went to left, and Lloyd moved to center. He was to remain there until the end of his long career. Lloyd was the same height as Paul, five feet, eight and a half inches, and while his weight was given as 150, it usually was well under that, once dipping as low as 135. Hence, the elder was "Big Poison" and the younger "Little Poison." There are two versions as to how they acquired these lethal nicknames. The one generally accepted is that the pair were poison to pitchers. Another is that a fan wanted to see the big and little persons, and pronounced it "poisons," as uttered in the Bronx.

Where Paul both batted and threw left-handed, Lloyd batted from the portside of the plate but threw in orthodox fashion. The younger was Dreyfuss' greatest bargain, costing Barney only a little over train fare. Lloyd played a few games with San Francisco in 1925 and 1926, but the Seals let him go rather than pay him a modest bonus. Paul tipped off the Pirate management to Lloyd's possibilities, saying: "That kid can hit, run, and field as well as I can." He didn't exaggerate. Dreyfuss signed the boy as a free agent and sent him to Columbia, S. C., for development in 1926. There a batting average of .345 showed Lloyd needed little more minor-league education.

There would have been no 1927 pennant without the Waners, but there were other heavy contributors. Traynor hit .342 and played third base as it seldom had been played before. With a distinct recollection of Joe Harris' stick work in the 1925 World Series, Dreyfuss purchased "Moon" from the Senators; the slugger hit .326 and played most of the season at first base. Barnhart hit .319 in 108 games, and Grantham, returned to second base, batted .305.

Dreyfuss made another master move when he regained Carmen Hill, the spectacled pitching Pirate of 1918 and 1919, from the Indianapolis club late in the 1926 season. Carmen was the club's biggest winner, with 22 victories and 11 defeats. Kremer again was the league's earned-run leader and had a 19-8 record. Meadows was right behind him with 19-10; Aldridge followed with 15-10. A Pittsburgh Serb, John Miljus, did a fine job as relief pitcher, winning 8 games and losing 3. Joe Dawson, a bear cat in the minors, had difficulty in getting into the winning brackets and could show only 3 successes against 7 defeats. A pony left-hander, Mike Cvengros, formerly with the White Sox, rounded out a formidable staff.

Pittsburgh fans saw their second unassisted triple play in three years in that hectic 1927 season. It came in the morning game on Decoration Day, and oddly enough, Jimmy Cooney, one of the players retired in Wright's 1925 "triple killing," was the guy who snuffed out a big Pirate rally. By this time Jimmy had moved from St. Louis to the Cubs. The Pirates were on an eleven-game winning streak and trying hard to make it number twelve. They ran into a snag in the fourth inning when Cooney reached out and caught Paul Waner's line drive, stepped on second before Lloyd Waner could get back, and then tagged out Clyde Barnhart, who was trying to retrace his steps from second base to first. The Pirates finally blew the game, 7 to 6, in the tenth, snapping their victory chain, but emerged victorious, 6 to 5, in ten frames in the afternoon session.

2

The 1927 World Series gave Barney four bitter afternoons. The Yankees, 110-game winners in the American League, rolled back the Pirates in four straight games. It was only the second time a blue-ribbon competitor swept a Series in four successive games, the other being 1914, when the miracle Braves crushed the supposedly invincible Athletics. The 1907 Cubs and 1922 Giants both scored four victories without a defeat but were held to one tie game.

The author encountered Dreyfuss shortly after the last game in New York. He was heartbroken and not too laudatory of the victors. "No team that is good enough to win the championship of a major league should lose four straight games to the pennant winner of the rival league," he said with bitter scorn. To make it even more painful for Dreyfuss, the American League manager was little Miller Huggins, who as Cardinal boss had taken Barney to the cleaners in that big "Five for Three" swap of 1913.

Barney was fully aware that the previous year the Cardinals had beaten that same Yankee team, four games to three, but he couldn't know that since 1927 those Yankees generally have been recognized as the super team of all time. It was the year Ruth established his home-run record of 60 and Gehrig a former American League record of 175 runs batted in. The dreadful pair, batting third and fourth, hit for 854 total bases, Lou for 447 and Babe for 417.

Pittsburgh staged the first two games, and the Series got under way at Forbes Field, October 5, before 41,567. Many writers have said that the Yankees defeated the Pirates, before a ball was pitched, in batting practice before the first game. That right field at Forbes Field was considered pretty far away in National League competition, but Ruth, Gehrig, and lesser Yankee lights slapped balls into the stand and to the roof as though it were a soft-ball park. The Pirates couldn't help but look on in awe. Yet Bush, who had seen plenty of American League ball, said: "The heck with that demonstration. We'll show 'em we have a few hitters ourselves."

The Pirates showed they had some hitters, outhitting the Bronx Bombers in the opener, nine to six. They even knocked out Waite Hoyt, Huggins' right-handed ace, but were stopped by Wilcy Moore, New York's great relief artist of that year. The Buccos made it close, but yielded 5 to 4. In his World Series baptism, Paul Waner hit a double and two singles; brother Lloyd rammed out a two-bagger. Ruth collected half of the New York hits—all singles.

Bush opened with Kremer, the Deacon's ace in the glorious victory two years before. But this was another Series, and Remy lasted only five innings. Both teams picked up single runs in the first. The crowd yelled its pleasure when Kremer retired lead-off man Earle Combs on a fly and shot three strikes over on Mark Koenig, who became the batting star of the Series, with a .500 average. Ruth then thumped a single to right. Paul Waner, playing deep for Gehrig, tried to make a shoestring catch of Larrupin' Lou's fly. He missed and the ball rolled through Paul for a triple, Ruth pounding around the bases to score the first run.

The Pirates quickly got the run back, with Paul atoning for his lapse of the first half. Lloyd Waner was hit by a pitched ball; Barnhart flied to Ruth, but "Big Poison" rapped Hoyt's first pitch to right for a double, Lloyd skipping around to third, from where he scored on Wright's fly to Combs.

The third was a bad inning for the Pirates and their well-wishers, the Yanks garnering three cheap runs. Those tallies practically decided the issue. With one down, Grantham dug Remy's pit by fumbling Koenig's grounder. Ruth tagged the first pitch for a single, and then Kremer made things worse by walking Gehrig and Meusel, forcing home Koenig. Lazzeri forced Bob at second, Ruth crossing the plate, and Lou advancing to third. As Earl Smith made a feint to throw to second, Gehrig left third and tore for the plate. Earl then threw down to Traynor, and Lou was caged between third and home, but scored when Pie's return throw skipped out of Smith's outstretched hands.

The Yanks did a bit of bobbling in their half, when Kremer hit a double, and Bob Meusel was guilty of a rank muff on Barnhart's fly. Ray held second, but scored on Paul Waner's second hit. Hoyt then pulled himself together, as Wright and Traynor hit into successive force plays.

Each team scored a run in the fifth, with the Yankee marker representing New York's winning run. It came over on Koenig's two-bagger, Ruth's infield out, and Gehrig's long fly. The Pirates scored theirs on the smaller Waner's double and Barnhart's single.

The Pirates sprang their last rally in the eighth, but despite the screeching and beseeching of the Pittsburgh fans, it flickered out with one run, leaving the tying and winning runs on base. With one out, Wright and Traynor poled clothesline singles and knocked out Hoyt. Huggins rushed in Wilcy Moore.

"Keep after that old geezer!" implored Bush. The best Grantham could do was to force Traynor, Glenn taking third. Harris came through nobly, his single scoring Wright, but the rally faded when Smith rolled harmlessly to Gehrig.

3

Huggins pulled a surprise out of his hat when he pitched George Pipgras, later a crack American League umpire, in the second game, played in Pittsburgh, October 6. Pipgras was still young and inexperienced, and it wasn't until the latter part of the season that he was used as a starter. "George's got a lot of stuff when he gets it over," advised Bush, "but he's hotheaded and when he gets sore, he loses control." But Pipgras walked only one batter, while Vic Aldridge, Donie's pitcher, encountered two three-run innings and retired underfire in the eighth. The Yankees won this one easily, 6 to 2.

After Aldridge blotted out the Yanks in order in the first inning, Pirate fans had brief visions of Victory when in the home half Lloyd Waner greeted Pipgras with a booming triple to right center and made pay dirt on Barnhart's fly to Ruth. It gave Pittsburgh a brief 1-to-0 lead, which vanished in the third, when the American League champs exploded their first three-run barrage. Quite involuntarily, Lloyd Waner gave them a helping hand.

Combs opened on Vic with a single, and Koenig shot another hot single to center. The ball went through little Lloyd like a greased pig, rolled to the fence, and by the time the Pirates ran it down, Combs had sprinted home and Koenig rested on third. Ruth sent Mark home with a long fly, and the Yanks put together a third run on Gehrig's double and Meusel's single.

The game remained reasonably close until the eighth, when Aldridge wilted, and the Bronx Bombers posted a second "3" on the scoreboard. Meusel poked a single past Grantham and sped to third on Lazzeri's single to right. Lanky Bob scampered home on Vic's wild pitch. There was a lull as Gooch grabbed Dugan's attempted sacrifice bunt and threw out Lazzeri at third. Then Vic took a complete balloon ascension, walking the two Yankee batterymen Bengough and Pipgras, to fill the bases.

Bush yanked Aldridge and sent an SOS to the bull pen for the little left-hander, Mike Cvengros. Mike's first act was to plunk Earl Combs in the ribs, forcing in Dugan, while Koenig's single to left drove in Bengough. With the bases still full and the power of the Yankee batting order up, it looked like an avalanche of runs, but Pirate fans were saved this further humiliation. Ruth forced Pipgras at the plate and Gehrig grounded to Traynor for a force play on Koenig at second. The Pirates got back a consolation run in their half, when Lloyd Waner walked, dusted to third on Barnhart's single, and scored his second tally of the day on brother Paul's long fly.

4

The scene shifted to Yankee Stadium, where the third game was played October 7, before a crowd of 60,695. The Yankees took this one, 8 to 1, and it was a distressful afternoon for the faithful Pirate rooters who followed the Series by radio or news ticker. It was the day of Herb Pennock's World Series master-piece, as he pitched seven and a third innings of perfect baseball, retiring the first 22 Pirates to face him.

Radio still was new then, and a West Virginia mountaineer rigged up a primitive set to tune in on the Series. He became thoroughly disgusted as inning after inning the late Graham McNamee graphically reported Pennock's pitching wizardry and Pirate batting futility.

"Something is wrong with this durned thing," said the West Virginian. "Not a Pirate hit comes out of it."

There was good reason, as there were only three hits, and they didn't come until Pie Traynor broke Pennock's left-handed magic in the eighth. After Koenig threw out Wright, first batter in that inning, amid wild whoops of delight from the New York stands, Pie dashed Pennock's dream of a perfect World Series game by rifling a single to left. What's more, Barnhart followed with a long double on which Pie scored, while Lloyd Waner collected a third Pittsburgh hit in the ninth.

The game really was closer than the final score indicates, a six-run Yankee broadside in the seventh eventually blowing the legs from under the Buccaneers. Meadows was Bush's starter, and after giving up two runs in the first, Specs hurled shutout ball for the next five innings. Combs opened New York's first with a single through the box, and Koenig beat out an infield scratch to Rhyne. Big Gehrig pounded in the two runs with a terrific clout to deep right center but lost the decision at the plate when he tried for a homer.

In the seventh the Yankees blew out Meadows with one of their typical explosions, six big Bronx runs crushing the Pirates beyond any hope of succor. Lazzeri started it with a single, and on Dugan's sacrifice bunt Meadows pegged too late to second to get "Push 'em up Tony," and everybody was safe. Cedric Durst batted for Grabowski and shoved along both runners with an infield out. Pennock poked a grounder to Rhyne at second, and this time it was Hal who threw too late to shoot down the elusive Lazzeri at the plate.

"Blast it! Now we are in trouble!" muttered Donie.

Bush said it, for the avalanche quickly followed. Combs stung a single past second, scoring Dugan, and Pennock crossed the plate on Koenig's double to right.

At this juncture Bush dismissed Meadows and again called on

the left-handed Cvengros to face Ruth, who swung from the portside of the plate. But Babe in his heyday didn't care a whoop whether victims pitched with their right paw or their left. He hit a Gargantuan home-run wallop, the first of the Series, deep into the right-field stands. It had so much power that after clearing the screen it traveled almost all of the way up the stand. Combs and Koenig, of course, were Babe's vanguards as the grinning Ruth trudged around the bases, acknowledging the plaudits of the partisan New York crowd. Just to lock the stable door after the cause was lost, Cvengros next fanned the danger-ous Gehrig and Meusel.

5

The fourth game, won by the Yankees, 4 to 3, on Saturday, October 8, giving the New Yorkers their clean sweep, has always remained one of the Pittsburgh club's most painful defeats. In New York 23 years before, on the last day of the season, the Yankees lost an American League championship on a wild pitch by Jack Chesbro, the former Pirate. This time they won the World Series on John Miljus' wild pitch, on the last day of the World Series.

Bush did his best to rally his team, as he said to his players: "McKechnie's club pulled it out two years ago, and we can pull this one out. Those Yankees aren't as good as all that."

He called on Carmen Hill, his twenty-two-game winner, to make the final Pirate stand. Carmen moved out for a pinch hitter after six fair innings, and John Miljus, the native Pittsburgher, wound it up. Huggins used Wilcy Moore, who had relieved Hoyt in the first game. The contest was a hard-hitting affair, with a goose-flesh ending, in which the Pirates poked out ten hits and the Yankees twelve. Lloyd Waner wound up with three.

Each team scored a run in the first inning, with Hill doing a heroic job in limiting the biffing New Yorkers to a single tally. For the Pirates Lloyd Waner opened with a single to center, got around to third on the outs of Barnhart and brother Paul, and trotted home on Wright's single.

The Yankees started off with a quick rush on Hill and put over a run in a jiffy on successive singles by Combs, Koenig, and Ruth. Then Carmen buzzed three strikes over on Gehrig, and after the Bambino stole second, Hill also set down Bob Meusel

and Push 'em up Tony on strikes. Even the New York crowd
gave Hill a generous hand.

Hits then were skimpy for the next three innings, but Ruth
broke the 1-to-1 deadlock in the fifth when he followed Combs'
single with his second homer in two days, another powerful clout
into the right-field stands.

Wilcy Moore's sharp down-breaking delivery wasn't too difficult for the Pirates, and a courageous seventh-inning rally tied
the score. A pair of Yankee errors opened the door of opportunity
for the Bucs. Moore gave Earl Smith a life when he dropped
Gehrig's toss while covering first base on the catcher's grounder.
Yde ran for Smith, and Fred Brickell, batting for Hill, was safe
when Lazzeri was all thumbs trying to pick up Fred's roller.
Lloyd Waner advanced the pair with a sacrifice bunt, after
which Yde scored on Barnhart's single and Brickell tallied the
tying run on Paul Waner's lift to Combs.

Miljus took over for the Pirates in the seventh, and after Koenig
greeted the Pittsburgh Serb with a single, John won the acclaim
of his mates by inducing Ruth to ground into a double play.
Both teams failed to cash on scoring chances in the eighth, and
then came Miljus' historic ninth.

The big right-hander started his own downfall by walking
lead-off man Combs, after which Koenig beat out a bunt for his
ninth hit in eighteen times at bat. While John was pitching to
Ruth the second time, he uncorked his first wild pitch of the
inning. It advanced the two runners and induced Bush to change
his strategy. As one run would beat him anyway, he ordered
Miljus to walk Ruth, filling the bases with none out.

John almost worked out of the nasty situation, and the stadium
rocked with applause as he shot over third strikes on the two
toughies Gehrig and Bob Meusel. Miljus then started concen-
trating on Lazzeri but tried too hard. He threw a sailor that,
instead of coming down, continued to rise and sailed over
Johnny Gooch's shoulder. For years many persons who attended
the 1927 Series have argued that the play should have gone into
the box score as a passed ball for Catcher Johnny Gooch, but
whether it was a Miljus wild pitch or a Gooch passed ball, it
permitted the fleet-footed Earl Combs to dart home with the
run that sent the Pirates down to the ignominy of their fourth
straight defeat.

Unless one has business in a clubhouse in which a team has

lost four straight World Series games, it is a good place from which to stay away. If the men weren't cursing and snapping in the Pirate dressing room, they were glum and sullenly silent. "I didn't think it could happen to us," repeated Donie over and over again, while Barney was sad and sarcastic. Losing the Sunday stadium crowd on October 9, and the necessity of returning the receipts for a sixth game at Forbes Field on the tenth, didn't make the veteran owner feel any more kindly toward his beaten team. Each of the Series of 1924, 1925, and 1926 had gone the seven-game limit; now with the players and the Commissioner getting most of the money for the first four games, Dreyfuss barely made expenses. But deep down he felt so bad because he regarded the four-straight wallop as a humiliation for his beloved National League.

There were also repercussions in Pittsburgh. Even though Barnhart, playing left field, hit .313 in the Series, Pirate fans resented Cuyler's absence from the line-up. Bush even passed him up when there were occasions to use pinch hitters. "If they'd played Kiki, we still might have lost, but we wouldn't have been licked four straight," said more than one disgruntled rooter.

What little honor there was in the Series for the Pirates went to the Waners. They hadn't been completely eclipsed by the American Leaguers. "Little Poison," on top of the batting order, hit .400 and scored 5 of his team's 10 runs; Paul hit .333 and after the Series was voted the National League's most valuable player, getting 72 out of a possible 80 votes. And when the individual players cashed Judge Landis' losers' checks for $3,728, the boys didn't feel so bad.

XXIII. BARNEY'S SPAN RUNS OUT

WHENEVER BARNEY DREYFUSS won a pennant he always expected to repeat. And 1928 was no exception. "Forget about last year's World Series; that's water over the dam," he told Bush in the spring. "You've still got the best club in the league and you should win again."

"I think we have another winner," said Donie.

"Well, that's what I want to hear," snapped Barney.

But Bush's 1928 club flopped even worse than did McKechnie's team of 1926. The Bucs tumbled down the standing to fourth, while Bill McKechnie, the Wilkinsburg Deacon, led the Cardinals to his second National League pennant. Yet the pennant victory brought little joy to Bill. Sam Breadon demoted him to the Rochester farm club after the Yankee Juggernaut crushed the 1928 Redbirds in four straight games, just as it had flattened the Pirates the previous fall.

Following the 1927 trouble with Cuyler, it was a certainty the obstreperous Kiki would be traded. And Barney put on white whiskers and his Santa Claus coat when he made his Cuyler deal with Bill Veeck, the Cub president, the Pirate boss giving away his crack outfielder for Earl "Sparky" Adams, a pint-sized infielder, and Outfielder Floyd "Pete" Scott. Sparky was just a mediocre player in Pittsburgh and soon passed to the Cardinals. Scott almost dashed out his brains in a collision with the concrete right-field wall at New York's Polo Grounds. As for Kiki, he rose to new heights under Joe McCarthy in Chicago.

If Dreyfuss played Santa to Bill Wrigley and Bill Veeck of the

Cubs, it wasn't such a bad trading winter for Pittsburgh. Barney's old Broadway foe, John McGraw, decidedly played Mr. Claus to Dreyfuss. The Pirates regained the services of Burleigh Grimes in a straight swap for Vic Aldridge. This deal made McGraw look bad and unquestionably cost him the 1928 pennant. Burleigh was a veritable bear cat for the 1928 Pirates, winning 25 games and losing 14. He hurled 331 innings and appeared in 48 games, 28 of them complete. In contrast, Aldridge was a holdout for half of the season, won only 4 games, and lost 7 for McGraw.

Dreyfuss would cackle his well-known little laugh whenever he looked over the pitching averages. Grimes' showing in contrast to that of Aldridge almost made up for the disappointing fourth-place finish.

The 1928 Pirates led the league in team batting with .309 and unquestionably would have fared better if it hadn't been for Glenn Wright's lame arm. The great shortstop developed a misery in his once powerful throwing wing, which defied the treatment of trainers, bonesetters, and medicos. Glenn took part in only 108 games, in many of them playing only a few innings. And as he fretted over his ailing arm, there were reports of Wright's failure to keep in condition.

If the 1928 Bucs finished fourth, they were only eight and a half games off the pace. The club got off to a stumbling start, and strangely enough, had a percentage of .429 for both April and May. It went up to .542 in June and .586 in July, followed by a terrific .719 gait in August, when the Pirates won 23 games out of 32, which put them in the thick of the fight. But they subsided to 14 victories and 11 defeats and .560 for September. However, there was one September game that pleased Barney. Fred Fussell, a Pirate pitching rookie, stopped a nine-game Giant winning streak with a 1-to-0 Sunday win at the Polo Grounds. It had much to do with the Giants subsequently losing the pennant to St. Louis by only two games.

Paul Waner had another glorious season, finishing second to Hornsby with .370. "Big Poison" drove out 223 hits and scored 142 runs. Traynor did heavy damage with a .337 average. Adam Comoroskey, a speed boy from Swoyerville, Pa., who had played a little with the Pirates in 1926 and 1927 became an outfield regular in place of Cuyler, while a truculent, high-spirited kid from Chicago, Dickie Bartell, made his presence felt in the infield and helped out at second and shortstop. Bartell had the cockiness of a bantam rooster, and stars as well as fledglings felt the sting of his barb-wire tongue. He had only a semipro reputation when the Pirates picked him off the Chicago sand lots in 1927, and one season in Bridgeport readied him for the big leagues. Dickie showed he could hit as well as talk, compiling a .307 average for his freshman season in the majors.

There were considerable changes in the club's catching personnel. Earl Smith got into Barney's bad graces and was sold to the Cardinals just in time to get into another World Series. To take Smith's place, Barney purchased Charley Hargreaves from Brooklyn, only to have his new catcher suffer a bashed nose almost as soon as he joined the club. A young catcher, Ralston "Rollie" Hemsley, was acquired from Frederick, Maryland. He quickly showed the ability that put him into three All-Star games, also the carefree ways that won him the sobriquet of "Rollicking Rollie" before he became one of Alcoholics Anonymous' outstanding members.

2

At the National League meetings of December, 1928, Dreyfuss traded his erratic-throwing shortstop to Wilbert Robinson, then president-manager of the Dodgers, for Jesse Petty, a playful left-hander, and Harry Riconda, an infielder.

"I won't guarantee Wright's arm, and you know just what you're getting," said Dreyfuss.

"I'll take the chance," said Robbie. "If his arm comes back, he can win the pennant for me."

Pirate fans didn't like the deal and thought Barney gave up too quickly on the popular Wright. The deal looked better for Pittsburgh when Glenn played only 24 games for the 1929 Dodgers, though the shortstop made a partial comeback in 1930 and almost helped Brooklyn to that year's flag.

The 1929 Pirates were the league's runner-up, but the second-place Bucs actually finished a game further out of first place than did the 1928 fourth placers. They failed to satisfy Barney. McCarthy's Cubs, who had been threatening ever since Marse Joe took over in Chicago in 1926, finally made it in 1929, coming home with 98 victories and 54 defeats against an 88 to 65 finish by the Pirates. Yet Pittsburgh fans had the thrill of being in the race for two thirds of the season. Pittsburgh led for 37 days, and as late as July 23. The Bucs then ran second from July 24 to the end.

The team floundered through a bad August, winning only 13 games and losing 16, which enabled the Cubs to draw far away. And poor Donie Bush lost his job during the slump.

He lasted until August 29, when after a mediocre trip he was called to Forbes Field for a conference with the boss. After it was over Dreyfuss announced: "Owen Bush has tendered his resignation as manager of the Pirate club, and I accepted it. There is nothing further to say, except that Jewel Ens has been named to succeed Bush for the remainder of the season."

Ralph Davis couldn't help but call attention that a month before when Dreyfuss had been asked whether there would be any change in the pilot cabin, he dismissed the thought almost hostilely. "Why should I make a change?" he had demanded. "I don't know where I could find a better man than Donie."

"All told, it was a tough season for Donie Bush," wrote Davis. "Injuries held back his team, and the fans never gave him a break after benching Kiki Cuyler in 1927." Cuyler hit .360 for the 1929 championship Cubs, collected a flock of extra-base hits, and stole 43 bases.

As for the deposed manager, he had no beef. "I never came in contact with a finer bunch of fellows than these 1929 Pirates," Bush remarked in his farewell interview. "They all did their best for me, but we simply couldn't get going this season."

The new skipper Jewel Ens was a manager on the same order as McKechnie, a fellow who was only a big-league utility player but had plenty behind the ears. He had been head coach under Bush, and many still think "Jewel" is his nickname. But that's how he came into the world—Jewel Willoughby Ens, though his middle name of Willoughby is one of his secrets. He is a St. Louis Dutchman, one of the many who moved into the big leagues from the Mound City's sand lots. For years he has been manager of the Reds' Syracuse farm.

Infield troubles on the 1929 Pirates plagued both Bush and Ens. In that perennial hunt for a first baseman, Earl Sheely, a former White Sox, was drafted from the Sacramento club. One of Earl's legs was a little shorter than the other, and he stayed only two seasons. Bartell, Grantham, and Adams played second base at various times, and Bartell, Adams, Stew Clarke, and Coburn Jones all tried their hands at the old Wagner-Maranville-Wright shortstop stronghold.

Grimes wasn't quite as active as in 1928, winning 17 games and losing 7, while he worked in 233 innings, 108 less than the year before. There was a good reason. He had an 11-game winning streak, and while trying for the twelfth at the Polo Grounds, he suffered a broken thumb while trying to knock down Bill Terry's line drive. Erv Brame, a right-hander from Jersey City, did a lot of smart pitching and won 16 games against 11 setbacks, while big Steve Swetonic and Heinie Meine, now a St. Louis thirst-quencher, were other useful pitching acquisitions.

However, the pitching newcomer who was to write the most interesting Pirate history was a hefty left-hander from Visalia, California—Larry French, a handsome 200-pounder who had attended the University of California. Something of a hothead, he really could pour in his southpaw missiles and became one of Pittsburgh's better pitchers until trade winds blew him to Chicago six years later.

3

The general feeling in Pittsburgh was that Jewel Ens was on trial in the final five weeks of the 1929 season. If he was, he apparently won Barney's approval, as he was engaged to run the team for the next two full seasons. They were uneventful fifth-place seasons for the Pirates on the field, and years of tragedy for the family.

For years Barney's only son, Samuel "Sammy" Dreyfuss, was the apple of his father's eye. He had been a studious boy—keenly intelligent like his father—and had been graduated with honors from Princeton. Much of the father's joy in the operation of his ball club was that he was building it up for Sammy. Since the youngster's high-school days he had been taught the office end of the baseball business, and by 1931, Sammy, in his thirty-sixth year, held the office of vice-president-treasurer-business manager. And then suddenly the hand of death struck down the young executive. Sam Dreyfuss was a victim of pneumonia, and passed from this life, February 19, 1931, four days before his father's sixty-fifth birthday.

The father was grief-stricken, and for weeks was like a man in a daze. His famous Pirates, which he had hoped Sammy would inherit, had become just a ball park, a paper franchise, and a collection of ball players. League president John Heydler and club owners who sought to comfort him said the sight of his suffering tugged at their heartstrings.

Shortly after Sammy's death, Dreyfuss called up his son-in-law, William Edward "Bill" Benswanger, who was married to Barney's daughter, Eleanor Florence. Bill was partner in an insurance business started by his father, and though he had been a Pirate fan since he was knee-high, his main side interest was music. Both Bill and Eleanor were talented pianists; Benswanger was prominent in all of Pittsburgh's better musical activities; he was on the board of the Pittsburgh Symphony Orchestra, and for years had written its program notes.

"Will you come out here and help me?" asked the saddened Dreyfuss.

"If you want me, I'll come," replied Bill.

"If I want you!" shouted back Dreyfuss, his nerves strung by his grief. "What in the dickens do you think I called for, if I didn't want you and need you?"

"All right. When do you want me?"

"Not longer away than two weeks."

By an odd prank of fate, Benswanger was born in New York on Washington's Birthday, a day before Dreyfuss's natal day, and on the twenty-third—Barney's birthday—he assumed his duties with the ball club. Dreyfuss quickly convinced Benswanger his new association with the Pirates would be a full-time undertaking, even though it meant giving up an insurance business into which he had put 18 years of hard work.

But the elder Dreyfuss never really recovered from the shock of his son's death. The following February—always an eventful month in Dreyfuss's life span—he joined Sammy in the great unseen world. Following an operation for a glandular difficulty, in Mt. Sinai Hospital, New York, January 5, a month later, he also died of pneumonia, February 5, 1932.

Not only baseball men but big business executives and other citizens high in the nation's life expressed their regret over the passing of the doughty little baseball warrior.

"I cannot tell how deeply I feel the loss of Barney Dreyfuss," said league president John Heydler. "My friendship with him dates back to the time we first met in Louisville thirty-five years ago. He was the esteemed senior baseball man of the country at the time of his death. Dreyfuss discovered more great players than any other man in the game. He built the first steel plant in the National League, and his abiding faith in the future of the game continued to the end."

The American League chief, William Harridge, said: "Mr. Dreyfuss was one owner who refused to allow commercialism to interfere with his ideas of how to operate a club."

George Gibson (by this time again Pirate manager) said: "After serving practically my entire baseball career under Barney Dreyfuss, I long learned to look upon him as a father. It is my resolve to carry on along the line he mapped out, just as though he still were alive."

And good old Honus Wagner commented: "I have lost a great friend. I played for Mr. Dreyfuss three years in Louisville and eighteen in Pittsburgh. Our friendship warmed through these years, and I feel a great loss at his passing. His generosity was only one of the fine things I remember about Barney Dreyfuss."

After the veteran club owner's death, the bereaved widow, Mrs. Barney Dreyfuss, became chairman of the board. Her first move was to call in Eleanor's husband, Bill Benswanger, and through tear-filled eyes she said: "Bill, you are the only one who is left. I want you to be president of the Pirates."

So with less than a year's experience in baseball, William Edward Benswanger took over the presidency and direction of the valuable Pittsburgh baseball property at the pit of the depression. An incessant pipe smoker, Bill was known as the man of the pipes, Pirates, and pianos. In his fifteen years in charge, the Pirates won no championships, though they had several near pennants, but Benswanger ran the business ably and soundly. He strove to maintain Dreyfuss' standard of first-division ball and has a justifiable pride that only three teams fell out of the first four during his interesting regime. And the Dreyfuss family regularly received their dividend checks.

Bill liked to play baseball as a kid, but his mother, an accomplished pianist, recognized rare talent in her son and made him practice by the hour. Bill tired at the stool and escaped when he could—to play baseball. Later in life music became more than a hobby, a real passion.

"When I was a youngster my mother and dad, both music lovers, wanted me to take up the piano," the former club owner recalled. "I did, but sports, especially baseball, often interfered. Then one night I attended a concert and after that I needed no

PIRATE OFFICIALS

JOHN W. GALBREATH, BING CROSBY, PRESIDENT
FRANK E. McKINNEY, THOMAS P. JOHNSON,
and BILLY HERMAN, 1947 MANAGER

Pittsburgh Pirates Publicity Department

HANK GREENBERG

further urging. To me, music is the highest form of expression—
a universal language. You may not understand Italian, Hun-
garian, or Russian, but attend a concert where the music of
those countries is played and you feel kinship with the composer,
the grief of the country he knew, also its joy, hopes, and
aspirations."

But "Bensy," as his music friends call him, also had an early
love for the Pirates. "When I was a kid of ten my mother used
to give my brother and me seventy-five cents each to see the
Pirates play at old Exposition Park," he recalled. "For that
seventy-five cents we didn't sit in the grandstand but sat in the
bleachers and saw three games.

"And what a club we young Benswangers, and the other Pittsburgh kids, had to root for! They were all stars—Fred Clarke,
Tommy Leach, Kitty Bransfield, Claude Ritchey, Ginger Beaumont, Deacon Phillippe, Jack O'Connor, Jimmy Sebring, Ed
Doheny, and the others. But there was one who was head and
shoulders above all the rest—the mighty shortstop, Honus Wagner. In those days kids didn't go on an autograph hunt as they
do today, and I used to think: 'If only I could shake hands with
that big fellow.' Little did I suspect that some day I would be
in a position to do the grand player a good turn, be his boss, as
well as president of that great club."

XXIV.   GIBSON BACK AT THE HELM

JEWEL ENS' two fifth-place seasons in 1930 and 1931 were not without their moments. Several times the little St. Louisan felt he had the Pirate craft headed in the right direction only to encounter fresh squalls. The 1930 team wasn't a bad ball club, and with 80 victories and 74 defeats the Pirates finished only 12 games behind the leading Cardinals. What vexed Pittsburgh fans was that they could whale the tar out of the top and bottom teams and couldn't do too much with the clubs in between. The Bucs rolled back both the championship Redbirds and the tail-end Phillies by the same margin—13 games to 9.

It was the season of the big sock in the National League. With six clubs hitting better than .300, the Pirates were sixth with .303. As usual, Paul Waner led the Steel City crew with .368. Others well up in this hitting season were: Grantham, .324; Bartell, .320, and Comoroskey, .313. Lloyd Waner was ill much of the season, playing in only 65 games. He became a real lightweight, and there were reports his lungs had become affected.

A newcomer from San Francisco, Gus Suhr, took over at first base and got away to a good start, hitting .286 for 151 games. He was to set a National League consecutive game record—822 games, from September 11, 1931, to June 4, 1937.

On the mound Larry French worked like a plow horse, winning 17 games and losing 18. Kremer won 20 and lost 12, but the boys scored runs for him in droves, as Remy's earned-run figure was 5.02, fifth from the bottom. Erv Brame again was a consistent winner with a 17-8 rating.

In one of his last moves, Barney had done Ens a bad pitching turn on the very eve of the 1930 season. After Burleigh Grimes had dropped from 25 victories in 1928 to 17 in 1929, Barney attempted to cut the big spitballer's substantial pay, and Burleigh became a determined holdout. Dreyfuss became sorely vexed, and on April 9, traded Grimes to Boston for Percy Lee Jones, a left-hander, and a wad of bills that Judge Fuchs, the Boston man, could ill afford. Jones was of little use to Ens and by August was released to Columbus, Ohio. Fuchs soon traded Grimes to the Cardinals in another deal, and Grimes promptly won the 1930 pennant for Gabby Street.

Following the 1930 season, Barney made another rather sour deal with the Phillies; giving up Dickie Bartell, soon to become all-star material, for Shortstop Tommy Thevenow and Pitcher Claude Willoughby. Tommy had been the crack shortstop of the 1926 Cardinal World Champions; he broke a leg in 1927 and made a partial comeback in Philadelphia.

By an odd twist of scouting fate, the 1930 Pirates came up with a coming shortstop and future batting champion, Floyd "Arky" Vaughan. Art Griggs, the Pirates scout, who wintered in Los Angeles, was tipped off to a young catcher in the Fullerton, California, High School, Willard Hershberger. Vinegar Bill Essick, scouting for the Yankees, had his tip on Arky Vaughan, the Fullerton team's hard-hitting young shortstop. He was called Arky because he was born at Clifty, Arkansas.

Both scouts headed for Fullerton, but Vinegar Bill decided first to look at another young player at Long Beach who played only on Sundays. In the meantime Griggs went to Fullerton to scout his catcher but soon was captivated by the play of Vaughan. He signed the young shortstop and became so enthusiastic with his prize that he forgot all about the catcher. When Essick bobbed up at Fullerton the following Sunday, he learned to his dismay that the young shortstop was "Pirate property," so he signed the catcher, Hershberger, who later developed fast in the Yankees' Newark farm and then committed suicide as a member of the Reds in 1940.

The Yankees didn't give up on Vaughan. While the Pirates had the young infielder out to pasture at Wichita, in the Western

League, Ed Barrow, Ruppert's business manager, offered $40,000 for the young player.

"Are you going to take it, Barney?" Chilly Doyle asked the Pittsburgh president, who was then still alive.

"If he's worth $40,000 to Barrow, he must be worth as much to us. No, I'll keep Vaughan," he replied. It was a wise decision.

The season of 1931 was known as the Pirates' screwy year; the boys were either very good or terrible. In June the club won only 8 games and lost 18, for a monthly percentage of .308. In July the Bucs won 19 and lost 10, for .655. In August they sagged again to 15-20, only to enjoy a hot September in which they won 16 and lost 9. But it all added up to a fifth-place club that won 75 and lost 79 and cooked Jewel's goose as manager.

Ens had the usual first- and second-base troubles of his managerial predecessors. The new first baseman from the Coast, Gus Suhr, was benched after hitting only .211 for 86 games, while Grantham and Paul Waner helped out at the jinxed bag. An array appeared at second: Howard Groskloss; Bill Regan, a former Red Sox; Tony Piet, whose full name was Pietruszka; and Grantham. Groskloss was a medical student at Yale and is now a Pittsburgh physician.

Larry French, the husky southpaw, accompanied a team of big-league stars that the author conducted to Japan after the 1931 season. There was an amusing scene at the San Francisco dock just as the Japanese N.Y.K. liner, *Tatsuta Maru*, was preparing to sail. There was a lot of commotion, excitement, and waving of the hands at the pier. The gangplank was again lowered, and an insurance man, Benswanger's San Francisco representative, rushed on board waving a paper. It was a new $100,000 policy on Larry French. The Pirates already had insured their prize left-hander for $50,000 but at the last moment decided to double it.

Before Dreyfuss' death in February, 1932, he had decided that Jewel's number was up as Pirate manager, and he brought back the former hefty Canadian catcher George Gibson, who had resigned in midseason of 1922. Benswanger, a kid fan when Gibby caught those 151 games for the World Champions of 1909, was pleased to have Gibby in charge when he took over. "We'll get along fine," he told George. "I have every confidence in you."

The confidence was merited, as Gibson immediately jacked up the club from fifth place to second. In fact, for quite some time Benswanger, the young insurance man, felt he would celebrate his first year in the Pirates' presidential cabin with a winner. The 1932 Corsairs led for 44 days, were first on both June first and July first, and it wasn't until August 10 that the Cubs took first place to stay. It was the season that Charley Grimm, Barney's old banjo-playing first baseman, succeeded Rogers Hornsby as Cub manager on August 4, and went on to win the pennant. The Pirates remained in the race until the last week of the season and lost by four games.

"Well, you tried, George, and gave them a good fight," said Bensy, "and in this depression period the boys can use the second-place checks."

Gibson's most radical move was to place Arky Vaughan, with only one year's professional experience, at shortstop, and station Piet at second. It worked out well, as from the start Vaughan showed himself to be a natural hitter. He broke in with a .318 batting average and never fell below .300 in his ten seasons in Forbes Field. Lloyd Waner again regained his health and hit .333 in 132 games. Gibson helped Suhr regain his confidence; Gus showed vast improvement at bat and became the National League's "Iron Horse." In fact, the entire team hit well, considering much of the TNT had been taken out of the ball. Only the Phillies topped the Pirates' team-batting average of .285.

The loss of the pennant was largely blamed on an arm injury, suffered by Steve Swetonic, which kept the big fellow on the shelf for weeks. Even so, Steve won 11 games and lost 6. French was the same old work horse; he took part in the most games and gave up the most hits but couldn't get far away from .500, winning 18 and losing 16. Bill Swift and Heinie Meine had good years, while Kremer dropped to four wins and three losses.

3

Gibby had another second placer in 1933. The pattern was almost the same as in 1932, only this time the Giants, a sixth-place club the season before, were the champions, defeating the Buccaneers by five games. Actually the 1933 team had one more victory and one less defeat than the '32 runner-up.

They took more of the dynamite out of the ball, and batting averages melted all down the line. Compared to the 1930 Jack rabbit, the ball behaved like one of Connie Mack's icebox-treated pills of the nineties. Even so, the Pirates stroked it well, and easily led in club batting with .285. The champion Giants were sixth with .263. However, Bill Terry, putting in his first full season in charge of the New Yorkers, had air-tight pitching. The Giants won 23 shutout games and lost 11; the Pirates were victorious in 16 goose-egg games and lost 8.

Terry's elevation to the management of the Giants as John McGraw's successor, in 1932, paved the way for the acquisition of Freddy Lindstrom, hardhitting third baseman–outfielder, by the Pirates. Terry and Freddy were pals when both were high-salaried privates on the Giants, and just before McGraw stepped down he told Lindstrom he would be Mac's successor. Charles A. Stoneham, Giant president, had other ideas and appointed Terry. It created an awkward situation on the Giants, and Freddy was put on the trading block the following winter.

Bensy was an immediate bidder. A rather involved three-cornered deal was cooked up, with the Pirates, Giants, and Phillies the participants. Pittsburgh came up with Lindstrom, the Giants with Outfielder George Davis and Infielder Glenn Spencer, and the Phillies with Outfielder Chick Fullis and Infielder Gus Dugas. Benswanger gave up Spencer and a sizable check.

And Benswanger brought good old Honus Wagner back to the fold. Things hadn't gone so well with the great Dutchman after he severed connections with the Pirates in 1917. For a while he owned a garage in Carnegie and then tried his hand in politics. He ran for the office of Sheriff of Allegheny County, but there were just too many Democrats, and Honus ran second. He landed in Harrisburg as Sergeant at Arms of the Pennsylvania State Legislature, but decided it was a lazy man's job. He went into a sporting-goods venture in Pittsburgh, later with Pie Traynor as a partner, but his store ran smack into the nation's worst depression.

Early in 1933 Honus appeared in Benswanger's office, along with Mrs. Wagner. Honus' lady did most of the talking and wanted to know whether there wasn't a job for the old favorite in the Pirate organization. Times were awfully tough; banks were closing all over, and President Franklin Roosevelt soon closed the others after he took over. The Pirates already had engaged two coaches for 1933, the old Giant battery—Otey Crandall and Grover Hartley.

"What kind of a job have you been thinking of?" asked Benswanger.

"A job with a uniform," replied Honus.

Pictures of Wagner's great performances flashed through Benswanger's mind. Bensy couldn't have said no if he wanted to. "I never sign a man as coach without the manager's approval, but if it's all right with Gibby, it's all right with me," he said.

Gibson was away at the time on a hunting trip, and it was some time before Bill's telegram caught up with him. Wagner and his lady spent several anxious days telephoning to the Pirate office. Finally the reply came from Gibson. Of course, he would be only too happy to have Wagner associated with him as a coach and assistant.

Honus' re-engagement was warmly received not only in Pittsburgh, but all around the circuit. In Brooklyn they paraded him around the downtown streets and presented him with a shotgun on the steps of Borough Hall. Wagner has remained with the Pirates ever since, and his job was never considered as a pension post.

"Honus has been invaluable to the Pirates for his instructions and good counsel to young players," said Benswanger. "Just re-engaging him built up good will for the Pittsburgh club that you can't even measure in dollars and cents."

Bensy also picked up Waite Hoyt, the former Yankee pitching great, who after being released by the New York Americans in 1930, drifted to the Tigers, Athletics, Dodgers, and Giants. At the time, any slight lurch of the Pirate craft could have jolted Waite overboard, according to Benswanger. "Hoyt came to us to spend only a short time. We picked him up as a free agent, but he lasted five years and did some great work."

And quite a friendship developed between the club owner and the still somewhat errant pitcher. "Waite was one of the most interesting and intelligent players I ever knew," added his former boss. "He used to come to my office or to my hotel room when the team was on the road, and we often talked by the hour. Hoyt used to say he always felt better after one of these talks, and I know they had the same effect on me.

"Waite was with us nearly five seasons, and he called them his happiest years. He used to tell me that barring only Miller Huggins, his old manager on the Yankees, I was the best friend he ever had in baseball. He had lost his famous fast ball when he came to us, and we used him largely in relief, but win or lose, it was a pleasure to see him work. It always made me think of an architect and his design. Every pitch had a meaning and a purpose, whether or not it succeeded."

During the minor-league meeting in Galveston in December, 1933, Benswanger made a trade with the Reds of which he is still proud. It was Larry MacPhail's first major-league deal. "The deal was made at the Buccaneer Hotel, which was a good omen for us," said Bensy. "Larry had just gone to Cincinnati, and Donie Bush was still the Red manager, though he soon was replaced by Chuck Dressen. Gibson was there with me as our manager.

"Larry was lounging on a bed as we made the deal. We gave up Adam Comoroskey and Tony Piet for Fred 'Red' Lucas, a pitcher, and Outfielder Wally Roettger. The reason the deal brought me so much pleasure is that Lucas started 13 games for us against Cincinnati and won them all. Larry still remembers it well; I used to josh him about it when I was still in baseball. Lucas not only was a smart pitcher, but quite a hitter, and won many games for us as a pinch hitter."

And Bill Benswanger had the sad duty of telling Ray Kremer, former faithful pitching servant, that he was through. He sent for Remy and gave him the bad news. The pitcher smiled and said: "I am surprised you didn't do this to me a year ago." Though Benswanger made Kremer a free agent, he was so touched that he called up Devincenzi, the Oakland owner, and asked him to give Remy a job. Kremer pitched for his home-town team another few seasons, before giving up baseball for a job as mail carrier in Oakland.

4

No favorable Ontario stars shone on George Gibson, the husky ex-catcher, when he was born. He was released in midseason, 1922, after a second-place finish in 1921; he again went out in midseason, 1934, after two successive runners-up. But somehow they always expected more of George. Benswanger was sure he had a winner, and when the club slumped in June, the young president made a sudden managerial shift and put Pie Traynor in the driver's seat. At the time, the Pirates were in fourth place with 27 victories and 24 defeats, for a .529 percentage, and seven and a half games off the pace. Bensy always had been a Traynor admirer and felt the personable Pie was natural managerial material.

Ralph Davis wrote: "When Jewel Ens was relieved as manager after the 1932 season, the first reports were that Traynor would get the post, but it is understood that Mrs. Dreyfuss prevailed on Benswanger to give Gibson another chance. Now Traynor gets his opportunity."

Poor Pie had a difficult year. That famous throwing arm, which could whip the ball across the diamond like a machine gun, had lost its speed and sense of direction. It pained like a toothache, gave Pie torture all year, and limited his play to 119 games, though he still could hit .309. And his managerial appointment failed to give the club the expected shot in the arm, with July being the team's worst month, when the Bucs won only 11 and lost 19. During the time Traynor was in charge the club won 47 games and lost 52 for .475, 84 points under Gibby's spring record. Eventually the 1934 club staggered home in fifth place, with two more defeats than victories. To add to the humiliation, Bill McKechnie nosed out the Pirates for fourth place with his former, chronic second-division Braves.

The 1934 campaign was a cockeyed Pirate season, with neither rhyme nor reason. It was the year Frankie Frisch's Gas House Cardinals won a spectacular World Championship and were the talk of the nation. But did the Freebooters knuckle down to the brash Gas Housers? Most emphatically not! They smacked back the two Deans, Pepper Martin, Lippy Durocher, Ducky Medwick, and the rest of that notable cast as though they were tailenders, beating them on the year's series, 13 games to 9. But Casey Stengel's sixth-place Dodgers laughed the Pirates right out of the park. Pittsburgh won just six games from Brooklyn all season, only one at Ebbets Field.

The club was handicapped by injuries and weak pitching. In addition to Traynor's lame arm, Lindstrom suffered a broken finger and played in only 97 games. The newly acquired Roettger and Woody Jensen helped the Waners in the outfield. Harry "Cookie" Lavagetto, a Coast League star, was purchased from Oakland and played 87 games at second base. Paul Waner had a glorious season and won his second batting crown—his first since 1927—by whaling the ball for .362. Vaughan was up there with .333, and Tommy Padden, a Holy Cross catcher—passed up by the Yankees—hit .331. The Freebooters were still toughies at the plate, hitting .287, only one point under the Gas House leaders.

The pitching dug Gibby's grave in the spring and hung like an anchor on the club all season. French fell to 12 victories and 18 defeats and for weeks couldn't finish a game. Swift slumped to 11-13, and though Lucas won 10 and lost 9, he was last in earned runs among the regular pitchers, with 4.37 earned runs. Hoyt saved something from the wreckage, winning 15 and losing 8, though he was in only 8 complete games.

The Pirates had Sunday ball for the first time in 1934, and won their first home Sabbath tilt from the Reds, April 29, by a score of 9 to 5 before 20,000 shivering fans. Oddly enough, Barney Dreyfuss never had plugged for Sunday ball in Pennsylvania. "It'll kill our Saturday afternoon business. It has ruined Saturday as a baseball day every other place," he used to say. That was true, to a degree, but Pittsburgh quickly became one of the best Sunday towns in both leagues.

XXV. ARKY VAUGHAN WEARS HONUS'
OLD CROWN

PIE TRAYNOR had the league's batting champion and most valuable player, and the loop's number one and two low earned-run pitchers in 1935, but it only added up to a fourth-place aggregation. The new swat champion was the talented kid from the Coast, Arky Vaughan, who led the league with .385, a tidy 32 points above Ducky Medwick, the second hitter, and 5 points above Honus' best average, .380 in 1900. For a good part of the season Arky boomed along at a .400 pace, and though injuries limited his play to 137 games, he whacked out 34 doubles, 10 triples, and 19 homers. He batted in 99 runs and walked 97 times, being well ahead in the latter department. As a result of this grand year, a plaque for the most valuable National League player of 1935 hangs in the den of Vaughan's ranch home at Potter Valley, California.

The pitching leaders were Darrell Elijah "Cy" Blanton, of Waurika, Oklahoma, and Bill Swift, with earned-run lows of 2.59 and 2.69, respectively. In games won, they weren't such standouts, with Cy winding up with 18 victories and 13 defeats and Bill with 15 wins and 8 setbacks.

A strange twist of luck figured in the Pirates' acquisition of Blanton. In early 1934 Benswanger disposed of the Tulsa club, which the Pirates had operated as a farm, to Art Griggs, the former scout, now deceased. In the course of the conversation, Bill asked about a pitcher, Cy Blanton, who had won 21 out of 28 games for St. Joseph and struck out 284 men. "Was that fellow really that good, or was there some misprint in that strike-out figure?" asked Bensy.

"No, that record's right," said Griggs. "What's more, the Tulsa club owns him; we optioned him to St. Joe."

"Well, if that's the case, Blanton goes into the deal and comes to Pittsburgh," said Benswanger. Griggs assented; the strike-out ace was farmed to Albany, a new Pirate farm, in 1934, and brought up in 1935. Cy had everything except control of himself. After several good years in which he made the National League All-Star squad, Cy eventually was released to the Phillies in 1940 and died in the Oklahoma state hospital for the mentally ill five years later.

Mace Brown, destined to be the game's best relief pitcher for several seasons, also started to make his presence felt on the 1935 Pirates. Like Blanton he had been former Tulsa property and was farmed to Kansas City in 1933 and 1934.

Following French's poor 1934 season, a trade involving Larry seemed logical, and the big left-hander, along with Freddy Lindstrom, was swapped to the Cubs for two pitchers, Guy Bush, the Mississippi Mudcat of the high sideboards, and Jim Weaver, six-foot, six-inch Kentuckian formerly with the Yankees, and the fabulous Babe Herman, once a .393 hitter and 35-home-run man in Brooklyn. No one in the Pirate organization ever pinned a medal on himself for his part in that transaction. Bush, who had been a top-ranking pitcher in Chicago, proved a hard man to sign, and after a seven-hour conference, Bill Benswanger shoved a contract under his nose and said: "Fill out the amount for what you think you're worth." Guy wasn't worth too much to Pittsburgh. In 1935 he broke even in 22 games, and in midseason of 1936 Bensy released him unconditionally. Bush later caught on with the Braves. The huge Weaver had two fair seasons in Forbes Field before being sold to the Browns in 1938. As for Herman, his outfield gyrations in 26 games convinced Pie and Bensy he didn't belong in spacious Forbes Field, and Babe was passed along to the Reds.

In another trade the Pirates gave up Claude Passeau, a rookie pitcher who soon reached stardom, and Catcher Bob Grace to the Phillies for Catcher Al Todd, who used to feud and swap punches with Dizzy Dean in the Texas League.

A pretty good outfielder, Forrest Jensen, became a 1935 regular, working with the two Waners. The Pirates purchased

Forrest from Wichita in 1930, and developed him in Newark. In his first season on regular left-field patrol, he cracked out 203 hits and batted .324. Floyd Young also became an infield regular, shifting between second, shortstop, and third, as Traynor, the old third-base king, played in only 57 games.

During the greater part of the 1935 season, it was a two-team race between the World Champions of 1933 and 1934—the Giants and Cardinals—with Chicago and Pittsburgh never far behind. Grimm, the former Pirate, helped by French and Lindstrom eventually piloted the Cubs first over the line on the momentum of a 21-game September winning streak. Pittsburgh finished a respectable fourth with 86 victories, 67 defeats, and a percentage of .562. Just to make sure McKechnie's Braves wouldn't beat them out again, the Pirates were really tough on the Deacon's boys, blowing them down 20 times in 22 attempts.

And just before Babe Ruth sang his swan song, the old fellow had a real Ruthian home-run spree at Forbes Field. Back in the early twenties, Ruth, then in his prime, hit a historic exhibition homer in Pittsburgh, but early in 1935 he visited Pittsburgh in his ill fated triple role of Brave vice-president, assistant manager to Bill McKechnie, and outfielder. Babe's brief National League career is not one of his pleasant memories, as he hit only .181 for 28 games, but in one stupendous day at Forbes Field, May 25, Ruth again was king for a day. He drove out three homers in successive times at bat, the third being the only ball ever driven over the roof of the right-field stands. A few days later Babe hung up his spikes and called it a career.

2

So often Pirate teams in successive years have followed the same pattern, and Traynor's 1936 club again came home in that fourth-place slot. The race involved the same four teams as in 1935, only this time the Giants, helped by Carl Hubbell's late-season, 16-game winning streak, came out on top. This one was closer, as the Pirates remained in the race until mid-September; they finished only eight and a half games out of the lead, and three behind the Cubs and Cardinals, tied for second place. The Bucs started off well and had an especially big June, but from there on Pie couldn't move the Pirate ship any faster than a .500 pace. If Barney's ghost followed the old crew around the circuit, it had an especially unhappy time at the Polo Grounds, where the Bucs lost nine games and won only two.

The Pirates again had the league's batting champion; while Arky Vaughan dropped back to fifth with .335, Paul Waner again ascended to the top, winning his third title with an average of .373. An odd record was made by Forrest Jensen, shoved up to the top of the batting order as Lloyd Waner dropped to second. Jensen had 696 official times at bat for a major-league record that still stands. While Vaughan lost batting honors, he was the league's prize walker for the third successive season.

And if the 1935 Pirates had Babe Ruth pull a three-home-run trick on them, Chuck Klein of the Phillies went the Bambino one better and jolted four homers into the right-field stands at Forbes Field, July 10, 1936. Klein was only the fourth big leaguer to perform this feat, Bobbie Lowe and Ed Delahanty in the nineties, and Lou Gehrig four years before. Klein delivered his fourth in the tenth inning, after the Pirates knocked out their former rookie, Passeau, to tie the score in the ninth. Chuck's clouting carnival gave the Philadelphia tailenders the game, 9 to 6. Rain fell late in the contest and for a while threatened to wash out Chuck's fourth homer before the Pirates could complete their tenth inning.

The Pirates were in the thick of the fighting when Klein had his day of days. "Now why should Chuck do that to us, when the Phillies are going nowhere and we need games so bad?" asked Traynor sadly.

Pie didn't play at all that season. Wilbur Lee "Bill" Brubaker, a collegian, appeared at third, and Young settled at second base. A graduate of the University of California, Brubaker had been in the Pirate organization for several years and was given post-graduate courses at Toronto and Albany. Harry Lavagetto did general utility work in 1936, and at the end of the season the colorful California Cookie and Pitcher Ralph Birkhofer were traded to Brooklyn for Ed Brandt, a big left-handed pitcher.

Larry MacPhail, then the hotheaded directing head of the Reds, got into Commissioner Landis' doghouse following the 1936 season, over two young players, Lee "Jeep" Handley, a St. Louis infielder, and Johnny Peacock, a University of North Carolina catcher. The old Judge suspected shenanigans as Larry manipulated the minor-league contracts of Jeep and Johnny, and made both of them free agents. Handley had played 26 games for the 1936 Reds, hitting .308, and 109 with Toronto, where he batted .297. Lee had several good offers, but Bensy and Pie sat down with Jeep and convinced him his future would be best assured if he signed a Pittsburgh contract. A $20,000 bonus was an especially convincing argument. Handley grabbed it and quickly became one of Pittsburgh's most popular players.

With a new infield of Brubaker, Vaughan, Handley, and Suhr, the 1937 Pirates moved up a peg to third place. But again Pie remained in that same groove. In three seasons his clubs varied only two games: 1935, .558 (86-68); 1936, .545 (84-70); 1937, .562 (86-67). Yet the Bucs had an interesting time in winning third place from the Cardinals. In late September they dropped three straight to the Redbirds, only to clinch the show position by wiping up the Reds in the next four. The Reds were cousins all year, the Pirates smearing them 21 times in 22 games. That offset to some measure the dismal showing against the champion Giants, the Corsairs winning only six from New York.

Weak pitching weighed down Traynor's club, but Pie came up with a promising freshman from Knoxville, Russ Bauers, who won 13 games and lost 6. For the first time in three years, the Pirates didn't have the batting champion, as Joe Medwick, the clouting Cardinal, went to the head of the class. Paul Waner was a good fourth with .353; brother Lloyd poked an effective .330, and Arky Vaughan was good for .322.

One of the Pirate outfielders that season was Johnny Dickshot, a Lithuanian from Waukegan, whose ancestral name was Dicksus. He played left field one day, and Benswanger says he'll never forget it. "Dickshot came in for a short fly, and as he did so, his cap flew off," related Bensy. "Instead of chasing the ball, Johnny chased his cap, as two runners circled the bases."

XXVI. HARTNETT'S HOMER EXPLODES PENNANT DREAM

THE PIRATES' season of 1938 always has been one of that "Why bring that up?" sort of thing for Pirate fans. Also for Bill Benswanger. A seventh Pirate flag at one time looked like a virtual certainty, so much so that Bill had a World Series press stand built on the roof of Forbes Field, and acquired 1,000 Series press buttons, which are still among the game's quaint souvenirs.

This finally looked like Pie Traynor's year, the year pennant dreams come true. The club got off to a strong start, winning its first seven games. The Giants, champions of 1936 and 1937, did a lot of front-running in the early part of the season, but the Pirates never were far from the top, and a strong June and July in which the Pittsburgh club won 40 out of 54 games definitely was a pennant pace. The Bucs swept into first place June 12, on the momentum of a 13-game winning streak, and soon were well in front of the pack.

While August wasn't as good as June and July, the Pirates enjoyed a 7-game lead on September 1, over Chicago and Cincinnati, tied for second place. On August 2, the Chicago club shifted managers, Gabby Hartnett, the big tomato-faced catcher, succeeding the old Pirate favorite, Charley Grimm. Then something happened much as when Charley succeeded Hornsby in 1932. It gave the Cubs a shot in the arm, and they started to climb. But the Pirate lead looked to be foolproof; even if the club played .500 ball in September, it was reasonably safe.

The Pirates were stalled by a hurricane on their last eastern

260

trip, and they stumbled through games that were played and gradually saw their big lead melt away. However, it wasn't until the last week of the season that the Pirates became panic-stricken. On September 26 the Cubs defeated the Cardinals, while Pittsburgh was idle. That reduced the Pirate lead to a game and a half, as Traynor's forces invaded the Cub lair for a three-game series, September 27, 28, and 29. "If we win one out of the three, we're still all right," Traynor told his battered forces. But that was the tough rub. They didn't win one.

Dizzy Dean, who won only 7 games for the Cubs that season with his $200,000 dead arm, hung up number 7 before 42,238 shouting fans, defeating Jim Tobin and Bill Swift, 2 to 1. It was Dizz's first start since August 20; he wasn't scored on until the ninth, and then Bill Lee relieved him with two out, to blot out Pittsburgh's brief rally. The Pirates closed the day still a half game to the good.

It was the game of September 28, that really sent the Pirates to the cleaners, as a partisan 34,465 Chicago crowd went home delirious and slap-happy. The Cubs thundered home winners on a mighty ninth inning home run by Manager Gabby Hartnett, coming with the score tied at 5 to 5, two out and two strikes on the batsman. It was then so dark that the umpires and fans could just about follow the flight of the ball. Had Mace Brown retired Hartnett on that pitch, the game would have ended in a tie.

It was one of the titanic struggles of baseball, with Traynor using three pitchers and Hartnett six. The Pirates muddled things for their gunners with four errors. After the Cubs scored an early run in the second, the Pirates assumed a 3-to-1 lead in the sixth, routing Clay Bryant with a three-run rally built around Johnny Rizzo's twenty-first homer. The Cubs tied it in their half on doubles by Hartnett and Rip Collins and Billy Jurges' safe bunt.

There was a big rhubarb in the seventh inning, when the Pirates claimed Vance Page was guilty of a balk on a pitch which Rizzo slammed into a double play. The score was 3-all, with one out, when Lloyd and Paul Waner singled in succession to put runners on third and first. Then Rizzo blazed into the double killing, Stan Hack to Billy Herman to Rip Collins, but the Pirates quickly raised the point that it wasn't on a legal pitch. Four umpires were on the job—Barry behind the plate and Stark, Goetz, and Campbell on the bases—but after a lot of jabbering, the Pirate claim was disallowed. Members of the 1938 Pirates still insist that it was a balk and that Dolly Stark actually had started to run onto the diamond to call it so, but suddenly changed his mind and put down his arm.

The Pirates then again pushed forward with two runs in the first half of the eighth. After Vaughan walked and Suhr singled, Gabby rushed in the former Pirate, Larry French, to relieve Page. But Heinie Manush, batting for Young, singled home Vaughan. Then Bill Lee went in for his third straight game. Jeep Handley's single scored Suhr and sent Manush to third. There still was none out, but the rally quickly blew up in thin smoke. On Todd's jab to Jurgess, Heinie was nailed at the plate and Klinger hit into a double play.

Pie might just as well have sent in a pinch hitter for Klinger, as he pulled Bob after Collins' single opened the Cubs' half of the eighth. Swift was summoned from the bull pen, but Bill had little luck. He walked Jurges, and pinch hitter Tony Lazzeri, the former Yankee, cracked out a double, scoring Collins. Herman's single tallied Jurges with the tying run, but Joe Marty, Push 'em up Tony's pinch runner, was thrown out at the plate. Mace Brown came in and retired Demaree.

Mace also got rid of Cavarretta and Reynolds, first Cubs to face him in the ninth; he also buzzed two strikes over on Hartnett, and then the big blow fell. Gabby swung with his full heft at a curve, and it was curtains. Through the shades of night a small white streak described an arc from the plate until it disappeared behind the left-field barrier. While the joyous Cub rooters did all but tear up Phil Wrigley's park, Bill Benswanger crumpled in his box seat, so exhausted he could scarcely pick up the pieces.

The victory now gave the Cubs a slim, half-game lead. Poor Pie—he did his best to restore the shattered morale of his retreating forces. But the retreat became a shambles next day, when the Cubs, with Lee working in his fourth successive game, won a 10-to-1 breeze.

Only three days of the season remained. The retreat was still on when the Pirates moved to Cincinnati. While the Cubs idled, Derringer defeated Pittsburgh in the first game of a doubleheader, 7 to 1, but Russ Bauers kept a faint glow of hope alive by winning the second game, 4 to 2. The Reds again sandbagged the Corsairs, 9 to 6, on Saturday. The Cubs lost their first game to the Cardinals, 4 to 3, but a 10-to-3 victory in the nightcap was

Chicago's pennant-clinching game. As each contender lost its final Sunday contest, the Cubs' final margin was two and a half games. The Cubs won 89 and lost 63 for a percentage of .586; the Pirates closed with 86 victories and 64 defeats.

2

While Benswanger admits that Hartnett's homer was a damaging poke, he doesn't think it did as much to kill his former club's 1938 pennant chances as the freak hurricane that ripped through the north Atlantic coast in September. "In my mind, the pennant was lost *before* that Cub series started," said Bill. "It is my firm belief that the hurricane that swept through the East prevented us from winning. We went East on the final trip, good and hot. Everybody knows that when a club is hot, it can make wrong plays and win; when it is cold, nothing turns out right. Well, we were winning game after game, close ones and easy ones. For example in Boston we defeated Tom Zachary, the left-hander who always had been a nemesis to us. And how did we do it? Hits by Gus Suhr and Lloyd Waner, both left-handed hitters against a southpaw, which gave us a 2-to-1 victory in the ninth. That's the way things were going when the hurricane struck.

"We were unable to play in Brooklyn and Philadelphia just when we needed every game, even with the odds all in our favor. I wanted to play. Ford Frick, John Kieran, and other newspapermen told me not to worry, as we had the pennant sewed up. To my way of thinking, pennants are won only by winning ball games, and ball games can be won only if you play them. To lose by losing ball games is one thing; to lose by idleness is another.

"If we had played all those games in the East we would have gone to Chicago with such a lead that we could have lost all three games and still have won the flag. But as we sat around hotel lobbies during the storm, a hot team cooled off and never regained its winning momentum. The Hartnett home run was an anticlimax, not the cause of our defeat."

The final standing of the clubs showed Benswanger has something to his contention. The 1938 Pirates had four unplayed games at the finish, two each with the tail-end Phillies and seventh-place Dodgers. Had the Pirates played and won these games, the entire race would have been different.

Another reason the Pirates blew on the stretch was that Traynor had no outstanding pitcher other than his superb relief man, Mace Brown. He took part in 51 games, only 2 complete, but was credited with 15 victories against 9 defeats. Mace was such a ball of fire that season that he had the distinction of pitching the final three innings for the National League in the old loop's 1938 All-Star victory in Cincinnati.

Brown's 15 victories were high for the Pirate staff, as the others turned in ordinary performances: Klinger, 12-5; Bauers, 13-14; Tobin, 14-12; Blanton, 11-7; Swift, 7-5. Even old Burleigh Grimes was signed as a free agent late in the season for his third Pirate engagement.

However, the season had its pleasant features. Johnny Rizzo, the outfielder, bought from the Cardinals' Columbus farm, hit .301 and smacked 23 home runs, a record for a Pirate at that time. Johnny had the distinction of hitting at least one in each of the nine National League parks. The reason there were nine is that the Phillies shifted from their old Baker Bowl to Shibe Park in midseason. Arky Vaughan topped the Pirate hitters with .321, and 1938 was one of the few seasons in which Lloyd Waner was far ahead of Paul, .313 to .280. Had Paul repeated his .354 of 1937, the 1938 pennant story also might have been concluded on a happier note.

3

When a club suffers a collapse such as the Pirates did in September, 1938, it takes something out of it that is almost impossible to restore. The Pirates were still groggy from the blow when Pie assembled the gang at San Bernardino the following spring, and Traynor never did bring order out of the chaos. The 1939 Pirates had only brief sojourns in the first division and spent most of the season in sixth place, their eventual resting place. The club experienced one disastrous losing streak of twelve straight, the longest in the National League that year, and as the defeats piled up in the standing of the clubs, it sounded the death knell of Pie Traynor as manager. He was one of Bensy's favorites, but few managers can survive a one-year plunge from a close second to sixth.

Paul Waner bounced back from his .280 of 1938 to .328, and while Big Poison and Vaughan were the club's only .300 hitters, the Pirates had enough of a punch to rate third in club batting.

As had happened before, the club was a victim of its soft pitching. Pie's staff was so weak that he had only one pitcher listed among the league's regular pitchers, men who appear in ten complete games or more. And Klinger just barely made it with the minimum of ten "completes." Mace Brown wasn't nearly as effective in relief, dropping from 15-9 to 9-13. A sandy-haired Alabaman, Truett "Rip" Sewell, a third-stringer in 1938, was given more work, winning ten games and losing nine. He had been up before with Detroit, and was a distant cousin of Joe and Luke Sewell, former American League stars.

The club made several changes, most of them advantageous. Despite the fact that Catcher Al Todd took part in 138 games in 1938, there was considerable dissatisfaction with his work during the September collapse. At the December, 1938, National League meeting, Benswanger traded Todd, Johnny Dickshot, and cash to the Braves for Catcher Ray Mueller, a latter-day iron man. Gus Suhr, the iron-man first baseman, showed signs of slowing in his position, and Benswanger made another swap with the Braves in June, 1939, whereby he landed Elbie Fletcher, the skillful-fielding first baseman, for Infielder Bill Schuster and more Pirate gold. Suhr then was passed along to the Phillies on waivers.

Realizing the Waners were getting along, and in an effort to insert more batting power into the line-up, Benswanger brought up two young outfielders from the Toronto club, Bob Elliott and Maurice Van Robays. Both joined the club in the late season and produced immediately, Bob hitting .333 in 32 games and Van .314 in 27.

"I signed Bob Elliott in the lobby of our training hotel at San Bernardino," recalled Benswanger. "He had been brought up at our expense, being recommended by our old player, George Cutshaw. Bob played two years for Savannah and one with Toronto; then he moved up to the Pirates and quickly made the grade. Bob's father is a real friend and helped considerably in his boy's development. I still value his friendship and fine influence, as his son was just a sandlotter when I signed him. I still regard Bob as 'one of my boys.'"

And Traynor's last season at the helm saw handsome Frankie Gustine, then only nineteen, join the club in the late season. While Frankie could play anywhere on the infield, his favorite position was third base, Pie's position. A lad from Hoopestown, Illinois, in the Chicago outskirts, Gustine was a Pie Traynor worshiper from the time he was knee-high.

At fourteen he awaited Pie Traynor's arrival in the lobby of a Chicago hotel, right after the Pirates had absorbed a crushing defeat. Frankie was recommended by his neighbor, Sam Roberts, a Pittsburgh scout. Somehow Pie saw in Frankie the Somerville, Massachusetts lad of some twenty years before, and an immediate friendship kindled between the man and boy. Traynor kept in touch with Gustine, and three years later Frankie was signed to a contract with Hutchinson, Kansas, a Pittsburgh farm club. Injuries held back Gustine's career and prevented him from getting into the armed services during the war—much to his own chagrin—but he developed into a fine fielder, dangerous hitter, and great competitor. Pie may well be proud of him.

When Traynor passed out at the end of the 1939 season, it was with the many friends and well-wishers he had had when he started his managerial career six years before. He remained in the Pirate organization as scout and farm director, and later went into radio as a sportscaster.

If Barney Dreyfuss had Marty O'Toole, his expensive pitching mistake, in 1911, his son-in-law, Bill Benswanger, had his Johnny Gee in 1939. While pitching for Michigan, John Alexander Gee, a huge left-hander, grew to six feet, nine inches and 225 pounds. They said big Johnny was Michigan's top baseball prize since George Sisler, the big fish that got away from Barney Dreyfuss.

Pitching for his home-town team, Syracuse, New York, Gee was the International League's 1939 pitching standout, with 20 victories against 10 defeats, top shutout honors, and 133 strikeouts. Naturally Johnny was much in demand, and Bensy baited his line with $75,000 to yank the "whopper" into Forbes Field. In the fall of 1939 Gee was introduced to Pittsburgh with great fanfare, and won one game and lost two.

But almost as soon as Gee got into big-league waters, he developed a long pain in his long left arm. It was such a misery that it kept Johnny out of action all of the 1940 season, as Benswanger sent him to specialists all over the country. In 1941 and 1942 the pitching giraffe was farmed at various times to Portland, Oregon, and Toronto, with the hope he could work out the kinks against minor-league batsmen. Eventually the

Pirates gave up on him and released him to the Giants in 1944. By that time he had won five games and lost eight for Pittsburgh. Considering Johnny's purchase price, salaries, and other carrying charges, it is estimated each of Johnny's five victories stood Benswanger around $25,000.

XXVII. FORDHAM FLASH TAKES THE TILLER

IN LOOKING over the field for a successor to Traynor, the man who appealed most to Bensy was Frankie Frisch, the old Fordham Flash, famous as a hard-playing, high-powered second baseman on the Giants and Cardinals and later as directing head of the unforgettable Gas House Cardinal World Champions of 1934. After managing the Cardinals from 1933 to 1938, the Flash was let out after the Redbirds dropped to sixth in the latter year and Sam Breadon felt an urge for a new manager. Frisch was out of organized baseball in 1939, broadcasting games in Boston, and according to his own story, "sleeping better than any time in fifteen years." But when Benswanger gave him another opportunity to run a club, he willingly returned to sleepless nights for the fun and excitement of again directing a big-league team.

As a player and manager, "the Dutchman from the Bronx"—as John McGraw used to call him—always was good copy. He worried and fretted the umpires—and often his own players. No man in the game could brood more over a defeat. The author once chatted with Frisch after a particularly successful three weeks' play, in which the Pirates won 17 games out of 20. Frankie made little mention of the 17 games he had won but cried plenty over the three he had lost. "We really should have won the entire 20," he insisted.

Frisch had much of John McGraw, his New York mentor, in his make-up. As a Giant player, he was one of the few New York athletes who dared talk back to the famous leader. But he never lost his respect and admiration for the former "little round man of the Polo Grounds," and when the Flash graduated to the managerial ranks, he became a driving autocrat much like McGraw. Some of his players resented it, and when Dizzy Dean pitched for him on the Cardinals, he once remarked: "I enjoy driving that Dutchman nuts."

Frisch's first season in Pittsburgh was highly satisfactory. In 1940 he moved the Pirates up from sixth to fourth, with a one-year percentage gain from .444 to .506. Frankie won two more games than he lost. Benswanger had the same pride in the first division as his deceased father-in-law. If a club finished among the first four, the season couldn't be called a failure. "Frankie Frisch has us back in the first division," said Bensy. "I think we are definitely on our way up again and can expect further improvement."

Frankie's worries were real, not imaginary, early in his first season. After winning the first five games, his team dropped eleven of the next twelve, nine of them in succession. But the Flash started to get results in June and July, won twenty out of thirty-two in August, climbed into third place with a six-straight streak in early September, only to fall back to fourth when his team lost five games to Leo Durocher's Dodgers in as many days. Those defeats really made Frankie suffer.

Debs Garms, who came to the Pirates from the Red Sox, had the distinction of wearing the National League batting crown formerly worn by Wagner, Beaumont, Paul Waner, and Vaughan. But it was a slightly dented crown. Debs made his .355 average in 103 games, which he played at third base, the outfield, and as pinch hitter. But Ford Frick ruled his 103 games and 358 times at bat were sufficient to give him the title. Catcher Spud Davis, one of Frisch's former St. Louis players, was purchased from the Phillies and hit a stout .326 in 99 games.

Frisch really had quite a run-making machine, as his club led in team batting and in scoring with 809 runs, 102 more than were scored by Cincinnati, the 1940 World Champions. Garbs was Frisch's only official .300 batter, but Vaughan missed by the width of a gnat's ear with .2996, while young Elliott showed a lot of promise with .292, with a liberal sprinkling of extra base hits, 34 doubles, 11 triples, and 5 homers. The two Waners began to peter out, Paul playing in 89 games and Lloyd in 72. Paul was given his release the following winter, and he signed with Brooklyn. In May, 1940, the Pirates traded Rizzo to the Reds for Vince DiMaggio, oldest member of baseball's "royal family." Vince took a hefty swing, and he either hit or missed. He had the doubtful honor of leading the league four times in strike-outs, once with a record crop of 134 with the 1938 Braves.

Rip Sewell came fast this year, winning 16 games and losing 5, while he ranked third in earned runs, with 2.79. Pittsburgh's only other representative in the "ten-or-more-complete-games" class, Joe Bowman, stood at the very bottom of the class with 4.45 earned runs. In December, 1939, Benswanger procured the spectacled New Englander, Danny MacFayden, from Boston for Bill Swift, but Danny was used mostly in relief.

On June 14, just before the dead line on big deals, Frisch obtained one of the foremost catchers in the two majors, Al Lopez, in a deal with the Braves. Bensy sent Catcher Ray Berres to Boston, and pinned on Ray's knickers was a sizable check made out to Bob Quinn, then the Brave president. It was a good deal for Pittsburgh, as the personable Alfonso Ramon, a Tampan of Spanish ancestry, played some of his greatest ball and wrote new records into the book during his stay at Forbes Field. Though 1940 was Al's eleventh season in the league, the sturdy Latin was still good enough to catch over 100 games for the next four seasons.

And Pittsburgh played its first night game at Forbes Field, June 4, 1940, with the Pirates defeating the Braves, 14 to 2, before a crowd of 20,319.

In 1941 the Pirates scored 119 less runs than in 1940, but tacked 20 points to their percentage, as Frisch's boys again finished fourth. That year the Buccos held their own pretty well with the champion Dodgers, losing the year's series to Durocher's Dandies by only 10 to 12, but Frankie's old charges, the second-place Cardinals, by this time directed by the old ex-Pirate, Billy Southworth, smacked down the Bucs 16 to 6. "Why do you guys always have to look your lousiest against my old team?" wailed Frank.

Frankie weakened on Arky Vaughan and for some time had him on the bench, even though the Californian led the team at bat with .316 for 106 games. Though chosen for the National League All-Star squad, Arky, after an injury, was sitting out Pirate contests just before the big game in Detroit. Vaughan came near being the game's big hero, hitting two homers, each with a runner on base, only to have Ted Williams steal the thunder with a dramatic three-run homer in the ninth, giving the American Leaguers the ball game.

Frisch brought in Stu Martin, once slated to be Frankie's second-base successor on the Cardinals, and got some pretty good ball out of him. Stu was the team's second .300 man, but he made his average of .304 in only 88 games. And Frisch enlisted the services of the old Ripper, Jim Collins, former first baseman of Frankie's Gas House Gang. Rip hit only .211 but subsequently served the Pirates well as manager of the Albany farm club. Lloyd Waner lasted only a few months longer than his brother Paul, for after playing three games in the spring, Little Poison was traded, May 7, to the Braves for Pitcher Nick Strincevich, formerly a Yankee farm hand. Pirate fans were still arguing who would be the better, Van Robays or Elliott. This season, Van outhit Bob .280 to .273. Vince DiMaggio hit .267 while collecting 21 homers, but Frisch suffered through an even hundred of "DiMag's" gustful strike-outs.

Frisch was proving more and more of a card around the league, and Ford Frick and his umpires were constantly combing Frankie out of their hair. Once when he thought the umpires didn't call the game soon enough because of a heavy drizzle, the Flash appeared on the coaching lines with gum boots and carrying an umbrella.

Frankie was also having a lot of fun with other managers who were having their own troubles with the umpires. Though he played alongside of Leo Durocher on the old Cardinal infield, he and Leo never could be called pals. As Dodger manager, the Lip had had several squabbles with the umpires in a game at Forbes Field, and when Durocher bolted out of his dugout to protest a third strike, Frisch knew exactly what was coming. "Quick! The towels!" he said to Pirate trainer Jorgensen.

Jorgensen brought the towels, and Frank had some of his players lay them out making a carpet in front of the Pirate dugout, where Leo would have to pass in leaving the field. Durocher didn't relish all this attention in his exit march. He kicked each of the towels, and reaching the Pirate ball bag near the bench, he kicked that too, raining baseballs all over the dugout.

"What a man! What a man!" said Frank on the bench, convulsed with laughter. The Pirates could then hear Leo going up the ramp to the clubhouse. Every time he came to an electric light he smashed the bulb. Frisch thought the latter much funnier than did Bill Benswanger.

After Vaughan sat out some 50 games of the 1941 season, a trade involving the Californian became a winter order of business. Arky hadn't hit it off too well with Frisch. At the December, 1941 annual meeting, held right after Pearl Harbor, Benswanger returned to Pittsburgh with a lot of quantity for quality. He swapped Arky to the Dodgers for a raft of players: Pitcher Luke "Hot Potato" Hamlin, Catcher Babe Phelps, Infielder Pete Coscarart, and Outfielder–First Baseman Jim Wasdell. Many of the faithful shook their heads; they didn't want to see Arky get away.

3

The Pirates slumped to fifth place in 1942. Bill Benswanger didn't like that. It wasn't progress, but slipping back into baseball's badlands. It was the first season that the nation was in the war, and the Pirates suffered fewer losses of key players than most clubs. One of the first Bucs called up was Billy Cox, an acrobatic little shortstop bought from Harrisburg the previous fall for $20,000, one of the biggest sums ever paid for a Class B player. But Pie Traynor, then a scout, went all out for Billy and said the Newport, Pennsylvania, boy couldn't miss. Another early loss to the services was a promising rookie catcher, Vincent Smith, who became Bob Feller's catcher in the Navy.

The spring of 1942 saw the Pirates in San Bernardino for the last time, and infield worries wrinkled Frankie's brow. Lee Handley, who had played most of the team's third base for the past five years, came up with a dead arm, the result of a winter automobile collision near Peoria, which almost took the Jeeper's life. Handley was released to Toronto with the hope he could work the arm back into condition.

Frank then got the idea of making a third baseman out of Bob Elliott. When he first broached the suggestion to Bob, the San Franciscan was offended. "Am I really that bad an outfielder?" he asked.

"No, it's not that," Frank replied. "You'll really like to play third base; it's a nice position. I played it a lot myself. Why, you can stay in the game eighteen years playing that old hot corner."

Not long afterward Elliott came in fast for a slow-hit ball and collided sharply with Al Lopez, the chunky little catcher, who also tried to field the ball. Bob was knocked out and at first appeared to be badly hurt. Frisch naturally ran over to where his transplanted outfielder lay to ascertain the extent of his injury.

As Frisch leaned over him, Elliott opened an eye and said: "There goes five years off that eighteen, Frank."

Even so, Elliott played third base most of the season; Coscarart and Alf Anderson took turns at shortstop, and Stu Martin and Frankie Gustine at second. The club got off to a good enough start and ran second in early May, with seven wins and five defeats. In middle May, they still were a respectable third, but by the end of the month they sagged to seventh. The club eventually limped home with 66 victories, 81 defeats, and a .449 percentage.

The 1942 pitching staff told the story of the Pirates' relapse into the second division. There was only one Buccaneer in the ten-complete-game group, Rip Sewell, and he ranked sixth from the bottom. The Pirates had 46 more runs scored against them than they scored, as Frankie wore out his arm waving to the bull pen sending hurry-up calls for Hank Gornicki, Max Butcher, Bob Klinger, Johnny Lanning, Luke Hamlin, Aldon Wilkie, Ken Hentzelman, and Lloyd Dietz.

"Everybody pitches but Frisch," a fan yelled at Frankie.

"Yes, and I can pitch better than most of those humpty dumpties," snapped back the Flash.

Two outfield rookies who had started in American League farm organizations joined the Pirates that year and quickly made good. Johnny Barrett, a fleet-footed Massachusetts boy, who was raised to be a Red Sox, came in the spring from Hollywood. Once one of "Hughie Duffy's boys," Johnny could really pick 'em up and lay 'em down. Jim Russell, a refugee from the Brown chain gang, was acquired from Toronto and brought up in the fall. A Fayette City, Pennsylvania, product, big Jim carried a lethal punch in his wagon tongue.

4

It was back to fourth again in 1943, as Frisch coaxed 14 more victories out of the club than he did the year before. The 1943 Pirates lost only two of their year's series, to the champion

Cardinals and sixth-place Braves. But Benswanger was getting a little tired of fourth place finishes. "Can't we do any better than wind up fourth all the time?" he asked Frank Frisch.

The Pirate pitching perked up noticeably. More players were going to war, and the league was getting weaker. In place of one pitcher in the first group in 1942, Frisch now had four: Sewell, Butcher, Klinger, and Wally Hebert. The latter was a left-hander, formerly with the St. Louis Browns, who was drafted from the San Diego club. Sewell had an excellent season, winning 21 games and losing 9, and won a berth in the year's All-Star game.

Vince DiMaggio also crowded his way into the 1943 All-Star game in Philadelphia, and though the American League again won top honors, Vince almost stole the show. In three times at bat he hit a homer, triple, and single. His illustrious brother, Joe, made only three hits in twenty-one times at bat in his first five All-Star games.

But Vince again led the league with 126 strike-outs and got into a rumpus with Sam Watters over one of his dinner checks. After a night game in Philadelphia, Vince claimed the regular dining room at the Hotel Ben Franklin was closed. So he ate in the hotel's swank night club and signed a check well above the Pirate allowance. Barney Dreyfuss had been dead eleven years, but they couldn't do that to Sam Watters, vice-president, treasurer, and road secretary. The matter was given considerable newspaper publicity, as Vince and Sam aired their views, and the following winter Vince—and his expensive appetite—was traded to the Phillies for Lefty Al Gerheauser.

Bob Elliott really broke loose that season, hitting .315, fourth among the 100-game players. He missed only one of Pittsburgh's 157 games. Frankie Gustine had a fine season and worked his hitting up to .290. The National League batting leader that year was a likable Polish lad from the Pittsburgh outskirts—Donora, Pennsylvania. Pittsburgh fans pulled for Stan Musial, but with a feeling of "if we'd only seen him first." In 1938 Musial came to Forbes Field for a trial, only to have Pie Traynor and the Buc scouting staff learn that Stanislaus already had signed a contract with Williamson, West Virginia, of the Cardinal chain.

5

Frankie Frisch reached the high tide of his Pittsburgh managerial career in 1944, when his Pirates came home second. It wasn't a very good second, as the Bucs trailed the Cardinals, 105-game winners, by fourteen and one half games, but there was plenty of honor for the boys from the Steel City. Not only was the team's .588 percentage the best since that of Bush's 1927 champions, but the Bucs had the good fun of beating the pants off the proud Redbirds, eventual 1944 World Champions, in the second half of the season. After the Cardinals won 10 of their first 13 games from Pittsburgh, they didn't win another game from the Bucs, the Pirates gaining 9 victories and one tie in the last 10 games. Twice Frisch had the pleasant satisfaction of sweeping four-game series with Southworth's formidable aggregation.

After a slow start in April, the Flash drove his team from last to second in the first three weeks of May, and then with the exception of a few weeks in midsummer ran in the runner-up spot all season. Valiantly the Pirates tried to cut in St. Louis' big early-season lead, but it was a heartrending task. In August the Pirates ran off an 11-game winning streak yet picked up only half a game on the leaders, as the Cardinals won 11 out of 12 games at the same time.

Featuring the club's play was big Jim Elliott, who got a lot of distance out of a .298 season, hitting 28 doubles, 16 triples, and 10 homers, and ranking second to Bill Nicholson of the Cubs in driving in runs with 108. Jim Russell also did heavy damage with a .315 rating, and while Johnny Barrett wasn't high in the averages, he led in triples with 19 and stolen bases with 28. Elbie Fletcher went into the Navy after the 1943 season, and the Pirates picked up the much-traded first baseman, Babe Dahlgren, in a deal with Philadelphia for Catcher Babe Phelps, and Dahlgren had one of his best seasons, hitting .289 and driving in 101 runs. For weeks Frankie Zak, a pint-sized shortstop from Passaic, New Jersey, was a revelation, and nobody could get him out; eventually he subsided and closed with .300 for 87 games. Eugene Francis "Huck" Geary, the shortstop who was always disappearing, gave Frisch a few additional wrinkles; Jeep Handley was back from Toronto, and Lloyd Waner was regained from Brooklyn in June.

Though Frisch's pitching staff was well below the caliber of the champion Cardinals and third-place Reds, Frisch worked wonders with his mound corps. Frank made a lucky pickup, June first, when he acquired the then thirty-seven-year-old left-hander, Fritz Ostermueller, after Branch Rickey of the Dodgers tried to send Fritzie to the Syracuse club. Including a few early-season games with Brooklyn, the southpaw won thirteen games that season and lost eight.

Truett Sewell repeated his twenty-one victories of 1943, and won international fame with his "blooper" pitch or "ephus ball." It was a freak pitch, and Catcher Al Lopez first named it "the ephus." It was also called the "backbreaker," "balloon ball," and "parachute pitch." It was the slowest of slow balls and very high, about twenty-five feet at its highest point, and it dipped suddenly as it crossed the plate at the batter's knees. Rip took his usual windup, but the ball left his hand with a shot-put motion. The batter had to apply his own hitting power against it, and extra-base hits against the delivery were rare. It took the fancy of the fans, and every time Rip was scheduled to pitch, it was good for another 3,000 to 5,000 fans, at home or on the road.

Nick Strincevich was a lively factor in the second-place finish, winning 14 games and losing 7, while Preacher Roe and Max Butcher each won 13 and lost 11. Roe, a left-hander from Harding College, Arkansas, was an ex-Cardinal farm hand, purchased from Breadon's Columbus, Ohio, club. Xavier Resigno was a steady relief man and appeared in 48 games.

A pleasant midsummer event for Pittsburgh fans at Forbes Field was the 1944 All-Star game, and it saw the National League win its fourth and most impressive victory by a score of 7 to 1. It was the last baseball event attended by baseball's first commissioner, Judge Kenesaw Mountain Landis. The Judge was also present at a little cocktail party given by Mrs. Barney Dreyfuss and Bill Benswanger at the Schenley on the eve of the game. "Mrs. Dreyfuss is a most gracious lady," said the Judge, of the widow of the man he once admonished to keep his shirt on.

And Frankie Frisch had his usual battles with the umpires during the 1944 season. "We'd had something of a rumpus in Pittsburgh; it wasn't very serious, but I was chased with two of my players. The next day the players received wires from Ford Frick advising they had been fined fifty dollars each. But

RALPH KINER

BILL MEYER

nothing apparently happened to me. I was quite pleased that I had escaped, when two days later I received a wire: 'I'm sorry I overlooked you, but you are fined seventy-five dollars.'

"Well, I was pretty peeved, and I quickly grabbed a phone, put in a call for Frick in New York, and told the operator I wanted the charges reversed. I hung on the phone, heard the operator ask Ford whether he would accept the charges, and he said he would. When I got Frick, I asked him why he had fined me; he explained, and I objected. And then I objected some more, and for ten minutes we had a merry time of it. Suddenly Frick yelled: 'Hey, Frisch, I just remembered I am paying for this conversation. The heck with you, Frank,' and he hung up on me."

6

By 1945 the Services had cut deeper and deeper into the major-league rosters. The Pirates alone had thirty-five players on their "armed forces" list, though a good many of them were youngsters who were on the Pittsburgh winter-reserve list. Tucked away in that group was a rookie outfielder, Ralph Kiner, in the Navy Air Force, a name that in the postwar years was to write interesting history at Forbes Field. The Navy even took the grizzled southpaw, Fritz Ostermueller, in May, but returned him to the Pirates in August.

On the whole, however, the Bucs did not lose as many of their top-notch regulars as most of their rivals did. Sam Breadon of the Cardinals also had been quite fortunate in holding star players, but draft boards suddenly bore down heavily on Sam's 1944 World Champions. Pitcher George Munger was called up during the 1944 season, and after its close Uncle Sam sent urgent invitations to Stan Musial, the club's batting star, Walker Cooper, the great catcher, Max Lanier, crack southpaw, and Left Fielder Danny Litwhiler. Then Mort Cooper, the team's ace pitcher, became involved in a salary wrangle with Owner Breadon and was sold to Boston.

It looked like a grand chance for the Pirates, the runner-up team of 1944, and many were brash enough to predict a pennant for Frankie's men. As war teams went, Pittsburgh apparently had a stout aggregation. The Cardinals didn't make it four straight, 'ut to the dismay of Pittsburgh fans it was the Cubs— who in 1944 won 15 games less than the Pirates—who nosed out

St. Louis. Frisch found himself back in his old, fourth-place niche with 82 victories and 72 defeats. "Gosh almighty; are we anchored in that fourth spot?" asked the Flash.

The club led for only a few days in June, dipped down to fifth around the Fourth-of-July holidays, ran fifth during the summer months, and didn't beat out the Giants for a first-division berth until September. The team's key hitters, Bob Elliott, Jim Russell, and Babe Dahlgren, all slumped, while the pitching staff also fell well below expectations. Sewell lost much of his former effectiveness; opposing batsmen hit not only his "rainbow," but everything else he served up. Rip figured in only nine "completes," and was credited with eleven victories against nine defeats. Lefty Gerheauser, of whom much had been expected, proved almost a complete flop, as he won only five games and lost ten. The lanky Preacher Roe was high in earned runs, had his brilliant moments, but could match thirteen defeats with only fourteen wins. Strincevich won the most games, sixteen, and lost ten.

Two likable and deserving newcomers made the team that year, Al Gionfriddo, a pint-sized Italian outfielder from Dysart, Pennsylvania, and Bill Salkeld, a catcher. Al, released from the Army early in 1944, could scamper around the bases like a jack rabbit and in 122 games he hit .284, the same as big Russell. The bobby soxers adopted little Al as their own and greeted him with the same squeals their sisters gave Frankie Sinatra when the crooner broke into song.

Salkeld, one of the few Idaho boys to make the majors, had a real Horatio Alger story. Plucked off a California high-school team when he was 17, in 1934, he caught in 89 games for the Sacramento Coast League club. Bill seemed ready for major-league picking when Moose Clabaugh, a minor-league veteran, caught his spikes in Salkeld's right knee. Bill was out for two and a half seasons, and the operating surgeon said he never again could play league ball. But Bill thought differently, plugged away, got back in the Coast League, and the Pirates bought him as help for the aging Al Lopez after the 1944 season. "Salkeld is slow and has difficulty in stooping, the result of his early injury," Frisch explained. "He's not likely to hit too much, but our scouts tell me he is the most experienced catcher in the minors."

But here was the most interesting thing about Salkeld's 1945 play. With the San Diego Pacific Coast League club in 1944, he hit .241 in 115 games and slapped only 3 homers. With the 1945

Pirates he hit .311 in 95 games and poled 15 homers, most of them of the game-winning variety. The Coast League product was Frisch's only .300 hitter in 1945.

"Salky's" fellow catcher, the hard-working little Latin, Al Lopez, made his own history in 1945. On September 5 he caught his 1,794th game, knocking Gabby Hartnett's record out of the book, and by catching his 1,805th a fortnight later Al established a new record for games caught for both majors.

XXVIII. FRESH BLOOD COMES INTO FRONT OFFICE

THE FAMOUS Dreyfuss baseball dynasty in Pittsburgh came to an end during a turbulent, unhappy 1946 season. There were reports as far back as the previous winter that Mrs. Barney Dreyfuss was getting her fill of baseball, and a story in *The Sporting News* saying that Bing Crosby, the popular crooner of the screen and air waves, would be associated with a syndicate that hoped to buy the club was hotly denied. Perhaps, at the time, Mrs. Dreyfuss and Bill Benswanger intended holding on, but an unhappy series of incidents helped bring on an August sale.

For one thing, neither Bill Benswanger nor Frankie Frisch had to worry about the "old fourth-place notch." The team cracked early, ran last from June 24 to September 9, and just barely limped in ahead of Mel Ott's Giants. That was really a new deal for the National League when a Pirate team escaped the cellar by beating out New York. It was enough to make the old enemies Barney Dreyfuss and John McGraw sit up in their graves. The once slugging Buccaneers were blanked 20 times, 6 times more often than any other team in the league, and a seventh-place finish was the worst position held by a Pittsburgh team since the terrible 1918 tailender of World War I. Even so, the Pirates drew 759,117, one of the club's best attendances.

The Pirates occupied the same lowly spot in team batting as in the standing of the clubs, with Russell hitting only .277, Elliott .263, Fletcher, back from service, .256, and Gustine .259. While

Sam Breadon was unloading prewar stellar talent, Frisch prevailed on Benswanger to purchase Jimmy Brown, former Cardinal second base–captain, for $30,000. But Jimmy was 34, had lost his fine edge in 3 years in service, and helped little; he took part in only 79 games, hitting .241.

The pitching again wabbled badly. Preacher Roe suffered one of the oddest injuries ever to befall a ball man. He was coaching a basketball team back in his native Arkansas when he got into an argument with the referee. No doubt Roe used the unpreacher-like jargon of the forecastle on the official, who smacked down the tall pitcher. "Preach" hit his head hard on the floor and suffered a concussion. He never fully recovered; he had a feeble 1946 season, winning only three games and losing eight, while his earned-run average zoomed to 5.15. "Old Folks" Ostermueller again tried to carry the staff with a record of 13-10, but Sewell skidded to 8-12. Even so, the Alabama redhead wiggled his way into the annual All-Star contest in Boston, where Ted Williams proved Rip's "blooper" wasn't home-run-proof when the swing was timed perfectly.

The bright spots of the 1946 season were two returned servicemen, Outfielder Ralph Kiner, and Shortstop Billy Cox. Probably at the end of the season Cox was considered the more valuable, but Ralph McPherran Kiner was destined to ascend to high places—up in the slugging stratosphere with the Babe Ruths, Lou Gehrigs, Jimmy Foxxes, Hack Wilsons, and Hank Greenbergs.

Though hitting a modest .247 in his freshman year, Kiner lashed out twenty-three homers, which were good enough to win the 1946 postwar homer championship in the National League, and to beat out Johnny Rizzo of the 1938 Pirates for the all-time Pittsburgh home-run leadership.

And Ralph wasn't picking on the cripples, as eight of his homers were made against the famous St. Louis Cardinals, 1946 World Champions. He smacked at least one in every park, getting his four-base lick in Ebbets Field in his final appearance in Brooklyn. What's more, Kiner was talked into the National League leadership in the last few days of the campaign. The husky youngster was suffering from a heavy cold and was inclined to knock off work—perhaps call it a season. At the time, he was the proud possessor of twenty-one home runs, but Chilly Doyle and other Pirate writers pointed out he was right next door to a couple of records. So with eyes and nose running and a high temperature, Kiner continued swinging and knocked out the extra two homers to bring his 1946 total up to twenty-three.

Though born in Santa Rita, New Mexico, of Scotch–Pennsylvania Dutch ancestry, Kiner grew up in Alhambra, California. His fellow Pirates call him Ozark Ike. The Pirates literally snatched him out of the cradle, as he was a gangling kid of only seventeen when Hollis Thurston, the Pittsburgh scout, delivered him personally at the Pirate training camp at San Bernardino, California, in the spring of 1940. Ralph had already shown some of his famous power and had been a standout high-school player. Benswanger paid him an $8,000 bonus to bring him into the Pirate fold.

Kiner started with Albany in 1941, and his prewar showing was only fair—nothing to warrant the belief he might some day be a fellow who would challenge Ruthian records. In two seasons at Albany, the Pirates' Eastern League farm, Kiner hit .279 and .257, respectively, though in the latter year his 14 home runs were good enough to lead the league. He hit only .236 in 43 games for the 1943 Toronto Maple Leafs, before being called into the nation's armed forces. Ralph served for nearly three years with the Navy Air Corps. And during his stay with Uncle Sam he developed the broad back and powerful arms and wrists that since have made him such a menace to National League pitchers.

Shortstop Billy Cox returned in 1946 from four years of service in the Pacific theater. Billy was all that Pie Traynor said about him in 1941. Though the acrobatic kid was down to around 135 pounds when the season ended—the aftermath of tropical fever—Cox, coached by old Honus, played a sprightly shortstop and led the Bucs at bat with .290.

Pirate morale was shaken by dissension and labor-union agitation. The hard-riding Frisch wasn't too popular with some of his men. A Harvard-educated Boston attorney, Robert Murphy, with some experience in labor relations, organized The American Baseball Guild, and as Pittsburgh is an industrial town, he concentrated on the Pirates. At one time he claimed a 95-per-cent membership in the crew of the Jolly Roger. It prompted Bill Benswanger to say: "Since I've been in baseball all I've known is depressions, wars, and now a labor union in the clubhouse."

Murphy early tangled with Benswanger over Bill's refusal to

bargain with the Boston Irishman as a representative of the players. Bensy said he would take up the players' grievances after the season. Vice-President Sam Watters was even more outspoken and was quoted as saying: "What is this, a new racket?"

Later when Watters attended a meeting, Murphy said: "Sam, I understand you're not in favor of these new rackets. I get it, you are in favor of the old ones."

There was a lot of commotion before a night game with Brooklyn at Forbes Field, June 5. Tempers flared as Benswanger and his barrister, Seward H. French, exchanged warm compliments with Murphy and F. X. Doherty, another Guild attorney. Benswanger appeared in the clubhouse for the first time in twelve years and had a heart-to-heart talk with the players. With a 26,026 crowd in the stands, Murphy recommended a strike, but by a show of hands, the athletes voted it down and played the game.

Two days later, June 7, before another night game with the Giants, Murphy called on the players to take a strike vote. Frankie Frisch, the coaches, Spud Davis, Del Bissonette, and Hans Wagner; the newspapermen and photographers; even Murphy, the labor leader, were all barred from the clubhouse, as the players balloted on whether or not to take the field for the scheduled game with New York. Murphy walked back and forth in front of the closed door, and as time went on, his smile became more confident.

Then somebody called to Bob Rice, at that time Pirate farm director, to step inside. Bob quickly brought back the news all were waiting for: "No strike!" Murphy looked disturbed and amazed at the outcome. The players voted 20 to 16 to strike, but as it needed a three-quarter vote, the measure lost.

Rip Sewell and Jimmy Brown were the leaders of the anti-strike faction, but Lee Handley spoke for the fellows who voted down the strike: "We don't strike, because we hold President Bill Benswanger in high regard. His record in dealing with the players is so fine we fellows thought twice before doing anything so drastic.

"I don't think we gave Murphy a square deal. We let him down, and I was one of those who did it. We're not radicals. We didn't want to be affiliated with any labor organization; we want our own group, like the Professional Golfers' or Actors' Guild. We believe thoroughly in some plan for representation."

Apparently the strike agitation didn't hurt the Pittsburgh players, as they had one of their best batting nights of the season immediately after the strike vote. Before 16,884 fans, they flattened 6 Giant pitchers for 15 hits, to win by 10 to 5.

Murphy's influence with the Pirate players waned after he was defeated on the strike issue. The big-league owners granted important concessions to their players in midseason, and Murphy received a stinging rebuke August 20, after the Pennsylvania state relations board ordered an election by the Pirate players to decide whether they wanted the Guild as a bargaining agent. They voted 15 to 3 against Murphy, with 10 players not voting.

Another unpleasant situation developed that vexed the Dreyfuss family and had some bearing on the team's subsequent sale. It was partly the blame of the portly Sam Watters. Sam, a former theater-ticket seller, had been with the club 41 years. Like Bensy he was well up in music; he had an admirable sense of humor, but often was lacking in tact in dealing with the press and public.

The *Pittsburgh Post-Gazette* had a day for its 500 newsboys at Forbes Field, but it rained, and all the kids swarmed to the park next day, only to be tossed out, supposedly at Watters' orders. The repercussions were unpleasant. The Pittsburgh news dealers became very sore at the club, and the *Post-Gazette* put on a blast in the way of a strongly worded editorial. It not only annoyed and riled Mrs. Dreyfuss, but she was deeply hurt.

There had been numerous bids for the Dreyfuss controlling stock. A combination of irritants, the tail-end position, the near-strike, the trouble with the newsboys, all had their effect. Mrs. Dreyfuss told Benswanger: "Bill, I guess we better sell."

So on August 8, Pittsburgh learned the Dreyfusses were out of baseball, and that a new combination, mostly out-of-towners, would run the club. And as was predicted months before, the popular crooner, Harry L. "Bing" Crosby, bobbed up as one of the new owners. The others were: Frank McKinney, an Indianapolis banker; John W. Galbreath, a Columbus, Ohio, realtor, and Tom Johnson, vice-president of the Standard Steel Spring Co. Though born in Newcastle, Pennsylvania, Tom was the only Pittsburgher in the new combine. He was only thirty-four and before the war had played baseball at Rollins College in Florida.

It was announced that "the purchasing price did not exceed $2,500,000." During the negotiations Senator John Bricker of

Ohio was one of the attorneys for the syndicate. McKinney was president of the Indianapolis club, in 1946 a Brave farm, and also had a 10-per-cent interest in the Braves. Commissioner Happy Chandler saw to it that McKinney got rid of his Boston stock before he sanctioned the deal.

Before the McKinney syndicate acquired control, a minority stockholder, Charles J. Margiotti, former attorney general of Pennsylvania, tried to get in a favorable position by rounding up some of the larger minority interests, especially the stock owned by John Harris and the Bernheim family, relatives of Mrs. Dreyfuss. He did not succeed but Margiotti still owns a sizable chunk of stock, 880 shares, third only to McKinney's 1,200 and Galbreath's 1,000.

Under the new setup, McKinney became president; the singing Bing, vice-president; Galbreath, treasurer; and Johnson, secretary. For a while Bill Benswanger remained as assistant to the president. Frankie Frisch was shuffled out of the deck at the end of the season, as was the former treasurer, Sam Watters.

H. Roy Hamey, a former Yankee farm executive, and in 1946 president of the American Association, came in as general manager, and Ray Kennedy, another former Yankee minor-league head, took over as new farm director. Bob Rice, who formerly held the farm post, became road secretary, and the new owners made a popular move with Pittsburgh fans and the press by retaining the popular publicity director, Jimmy Long. The equally popular A. K. "Rosey" Roswell, the Pirates' radio voice, became director of public relations. Spud Davis, coach under Frisch, went on the scouting staff.

XXIX. EVERYTHING HAPPENS TO
THE PIRATES

No ball club ever had a season such as the 1947 Pirates. Barney Dreyfuss, the man who had such an aversion to the second division, would have jumped out of his casket had he known about it. A Pittsburgh team, which finished tied for seventh with the lowly Phillies, drew the unbelievable home attendance of 1,283,611, shattering the 869,720 record of the 1927 Pirate champions, the former high-water mark, by over 400,000, while the Buccos were a sufficient draw on the road to coax an additional 1,162,371 fans through the turnstiles.

It truly was a dizzy season with a great early start, high expectations, a topple with a resounding crash, but a ball club with a home-run punch that often had the fans doing handsprings in the stands.

The new owners made their biggest mistake when they selected the popular Billy Herman, Brave infielder and former brilliant second baseman of the Cubs and Dodgers, as managerial successor to Fordham's unhorsed Flash, Frankie Frisch. Naming Billy as their managerial choice wasn't so bad in itself; for years people were saying that the swarthy Hoosier was a natural as a team leader. The big mistake was the players sacrificed by McKinney, the new president, to obtain Billy.

The Cincinnati Reds, who later engaged the able Johnny Neun, also were in the market for Herman as a managerial successor to Bill McKechnie. As a result, Lou Perini, the Brave president, caught the Pirates in a squeeze play, and Lou squeezed hard.

Yes, he'd agree to let the Pirates have Herman, along with three second stringers, Infielder Whitey Wietelmann, Pitcher Elmer Singleton, and Outfielder Stan Wentzel, but there was a big "If" attached to it. He wanted the hard-hitting Bob Elliott, third baseman–outfielder, and Catcher Hank Camelli. In his first proposition he had asked for Elliott and Kiner.

Even Herman, the new manager, objected to the price Mc-Kinney eventually paid. Of course, the big names involved were Herman, then nearing 38, who had been good enough to hit .298 for 122 games in 1946, and Elliott, aged 29, who had a comparatively mediocre .263 hitting year in his last Pittsburgh season. That's probably what threw off McKinney. But the respective ages made a big difference. Elliott, who hadn't always seen eye to eye with Frisch, became a better player than ever under Billy Southworth in Boston. Bob batted .317 in 1947; he was second among the loop's 100-game players and a big factor in the Braves' strong third-place finish. The deal tasted even worse for Pirate fans when Bob Elliott was voted the National League's most valuable player for 1947. As for poor Billy, his arm went bad at the Miami Beach training camp, and he played only a few league games.

The Pirates didn't stop at getting Herman. Roy Hamey, the former Yankee executive, sitting in the general manager's office carefully scanned the waiver lists and picked up a drove of discards from clubs of both leagues, especially pitchers: Hi Bithorn of the Cubs, Jim Bagby, Jr., of the Red Sox, Hugh Mulcahy of the Phillies, Roger Wolfe of the Senators, and Ernie Bonham, Mel Queen, and Al Lyons of the Yankees. In fact, the Pirates plucked so many players out of the waiver grab bag that Willard Mullin of the *New York World-Telegram* drew the new Pirate president, Frank McKinney, as "the old clothes man."

However, the prize pickup was big Hank Greenberg, for many years one of the top-ranking stars of the American League with the Detroit Tigers, and the highest-salaried player in baseball. Some of the youthful spring had gone out of Hank's 36-year-old legs, and his 1946 Tiger batting average was down to .277, but Greenberg still had been good enough to lead the American League in home runs with 44 and runs batted in with 127.

Hank's leaving the Tigers created something of a stir not only in the American League, which was losing one of its ace players, but in the National, especially in Pittsburgh, where the fans were in the clouds over the happy tidings that the Pirates had corralled the two home-run kings of 1946, Greenberg and Kiner.

Yet after Frank McKinney announced the acquisition of big Hank, there were grave doubts for several weeks whether Greenberg would swing his home-run cudgel while wearing the skull and crossbones of the Buccaneers. In fact, the big Bronxonian indicated he'd had his fill of big-league baseball. An army veteran with four years of service, he felt pretty bad over the way he was shuffled out of the American League. Shortly before the general managership of the Tigers had become vacant when George Trautman took over the czarship of the minor leagues, Greenberg applied for the job, and according to Hank's version, he never even got a reply. His subsequent release to Pittsburgh left him miffed. He had married the comely and well-to-do Caral Gimbel, and reports were Hank would become a merchant prince.

John Galbreath, the new treasurer, appointed himself a personal emissary to enlist Greenberg for the Pirate crew. About the time of the February meetings of the big leaguers in New York, he cornered Hank at the Lexington Hotel, and by piling enough Pirate moneybags on the table he induced Greenberg to sign for a six-months cruise on the Jolly Roger. The official family of the Pirates let the fans and writers guess at the exact figures, but it generally was understood that Greenberg's 1947 stipend was $80,000. As the Pittsburgh club gave another $40,000 to Walter Briggs, multimillionaire owner of the Tigers, the Greenberg investment of the new owners was around an eighth of a million. But the Pirates got it back—with interest—at the gate.

Having acquired Long Hank, the next thing was to change about Forbes Field so as to capitalize on the Greenberg investment to the utmost. Hank, a sturdy right-handed hitter, pulled most of his balls to left field. As a consequence, Greenberg Gardens were laid out in Forbes Field's spacious left field. A double bull pen was built; it extended from the bleachers in left field, across in front of the scoreboard, to a point in left center. The so-called "Gardens" are 200 feet in length, 30 feet in width, and the screen—one yard of boarding topped by wire mesh—is eight feet in height. It shortened the home-run zone at the left-field foul line from 365 to 335 feet.

It can't be said that Greenberg took full advantage of the Gardens. Bone chips in his left elbow and an old back ailment limited his play to 125 games, and he collected 25 homers while hitting a rather lowly .251. At one time Pirate fans quipped: "They call it Greenberg Gardens, because everybody hits home runs there but Greenberg." Eventually, as the new slugger, Ralph Kiner, went on a furious late-season home-run spree, finishing in a tie with Johnny Mize of the Giants with 51, the new sector became known as Kiner Korners.

Greenberg Gardens was only one of the 1947 innovations at Forbes Field. McKinney and his associates renovated the entire park, painted and refurbished it, put in new boxes, new clubhouses and showers for players and umpires, concession stands, and a new press box. The "little outfield" in which the catcher used to roam between the home plate and the stands was cut down from 110 feet to 81, as more front-line boxes were installed. Old Barney would scarcely have recognized his park.

As for Frank McKinney, he said: "I started to spend $250,000, but each succeeding month showed additional things to be done, and our improvements eventually added up to $750,000. They used to speak of Forbes Field as the most beautiful park in the National League; well, if it was possible to improve on that, we did."

2

It was Billy Herman's plan to start the 1947 season with Greenberg in the outfield, where Hank had played in his latter years in Detroit, but Elbie Fletcher suffered a bone separation in his ankle in a late training-trip injury, and Hank was brought into the infield, with a lusty newcomer, Waldon Westlake, filling in the outfield. An early spring injury also incapacitated the veteran catcher, Clyde Kluttz, purchased from the Cardinals, and a catching novice, Leroy Jarvis, had to do Pittsburgh's April backstopping.

Despite these mishaps, the Pirates started the 1947 campaign with a rush, and for a few weeks Pittsburgh was pennant dippy. The club won six of its first seven games, and the Pirates were the last of the National League teams to be defeated. Pirate fans already were saying: "Could this be the year?" As for the boys, they could do nothing wrong. They won their road opening game in Chicago, 1 to 0, April 15, and their home opener at Forbes Field, April 18, by 12 to 11. That was a gala occasion for the new owners, as 38,216 were on hand, and Bing Crosby, one of the new owners, made a big hit broadcasting part of the game. Bing then could poke a lot of fun at Bob Hope, one of Cleveland's stockholders, whose Indians had started in reverse. Later it was Bob's turn to snicker up his sleeve when talking baseball with the irrepressible Bing.

It was fun watching the Pirates ride high, wide, and handsome in those early weeks. After sharing the lead with other clubs for two days, the Pirates took undisputed possession of first place April 17, and held it until April 26, when they were pushed out by Brooklyn. Chilly Doyle, Les Biederman, and Ralph Johnson sent glowing reports back home about the boys, and in mid-May, Friday night and Saturday afternoon games with Brooklyn and a Sunday double-header with the Giants drew over 100,000, with 41,000 turning out for the Sabbath show. "It took the luck of the Irish for McKinney to play these games," beamed Chilly Doyle. "Before each game it looked like rain, and the prediction was rain, but Frank got in his crowds."

And Frank was getting tired of being called the "old clothes man." In what looked like a master stroke on May 3, he purchased five Brooklyn players, including one of the Dodger pitching aces, Kirby Higbe, for a sum "in excess of $200,000." The other players procured were Pitchers Hank Behrman and Cal McLish, Catcher Homer "Dixie" Howell, and Shortstop Gene Mauch. Branch Rickey wouldn't close the deal until McKinney threw in Outfielder Al Gionfriddo, the bobby soxers' friend, and the little Italian from Dysart, Pennsylvania, was destined to star for Brooklyn in the 1947 Dodger-Yankee World Series.

Something was knocked off the original price when Behrman, who was acquired under a conditional agreement, was returned to Brooklyn. The Long Islander, who worked in five of the 1947 World Series games, couldn't win in Pittsburgh, or didn't like the air out there. But the man the Pirates really wanted was Higbe, who had a prewar 22-9 record with the 1941 Brooklyn champions and a 17-8 showing with the 1946 Dodgers. Some of Rickey's Brooklyn constituents were all for frying old Branch in oil for selling the stouthearted "Koiby" down the Monongahela, but Rickey won the pennant without ol' Higgleby, and Kirby was only moderately successful in Pittsburgh. McLish and Mauch were farmed out, but Howell helped the sorely pressed Pirate catching department in the latter half of the season.

A month after Kirby came the bubble really burst. The pitching, which held up fairly well in the early weeks, suddenly collapsed like the one-horse shay. There was a horrendous period in June, in which the club went through nineteen successive games without a starting pitcher going the distance. Higbe went the route as the Pirates lost a 5-to-2 decision to the Cubs in the second game of a Memorial Day double-header, and it again was Higbe who broke the string when he defeated the Giants, 12 to 2, on June 19. During those nineteen wretchedly pitched efforts, the Pirates won only three games and the April front-runners plunged to the bottom.

Yet quite amazingly the crowds kept coming. The fans knew the new owners were trying, and they gave them the most generous support. And even though the Pirates rode seventh or eighth through the late spring and summer months, they had their moments, as when the Buccos gave Brooklyn a stunning setback by crushing them in a midseason Sunday double-header, and later ruined the debut of big Dan Bankhead, Mahatma Rickey's Negro pitching find. The Pirates were down, but there never was any telling when the lightning in their batting order would ignite a keg of powder. One day Billy Herman couldn't find his pencil to write down his batting order. Les Biederman had a pencil, so Billy said: "Go ahead and write my batting order." Les did, and the Bucs exploded all over the place.

Greenberg was the big early-season magnet, but after that it was all Kiner. Despite Ralph's fifty-one home runs at the finish, his early-season play was only average. He wasn't even selected for the National League's All-Star squad on July 8, and goodness knows the N. L. lads needed power, losing to the American League, 2 to 1.

Ralph turned on the heat in midseason; he passed Mize at one stage, and once he even threatened to go after Babe Ruth's magic mark of sixty in 1927. Ralph and Mize were only the fifth and sixth players to pass the fifty-home-run mark, the others being Ruth, Greenberg, Jimmie Foxx, and Hack Wilson, the last the only National League representative in that kind of company. What's more, most of Ralph's Pittsburgh homers didn't land in convenient Greenberg Gardens but sailed majestically over the left-field fence. They would have been homers before the field was changed. And Greenberg refused to take any credit for the young fellow's homer splurge. There were reports Kiner had profited by Greenberg's expert coaching. "Ralph had it all the time," said Hank. "He's just a natural home-run hitter."

Ozark Ike Kiner had two magnificent surges in which records fell like persimmons dropping from a tree. The first, seven homers in four games, ending with three against the Cardinals, August 16, tied an old major-league record by Tony Lazzeri. Other records tied during that spree were six homers in three games, five in two games, and four in four successive official times at bat. In the Friday night game of August 15, Kiner's second home run—off Ted Wilks—came in his last time at bat. On August 16, he walked on his first time up in the first inning; he hit homers in the third and fourth innings; walked again in the sixth, and homered in the eighth. Of the seven circuit clouts hit during Ralph's four-game bombardment, six cleared the outer brick left-field wall, 365 feet from the home plate.

In that August 16 game, Greenberg and Billy Cox also bagged two homers each, and seven home runs in one game for one team tied an old National League record, while ten for the two teams equaled a major-league record. It also was on August 16 that Pittsburgh's turnstile count crossed the million mark for the first time, a Saturday afternoon crowd of 35,927 swelling the attendance to 1,022,829 for 57 games.

More records were toppled a month later, when Kiner created a brand-new one of eight homers in four successive games. That knocked Lazzeri's old one completely out of the book. On September 10, Ralph smacked two off Larry Jensen, freshman pitching star of the Giants, and after that the Braves' staff felt the full fury of his attack. In a double-header on the eleventh, Kiner belted Johnny Sain for one in the first game, and poked two more in the nightcap, with Bill Voiselle and Walter Lanfranconi the victims. Just to keep up the fun he slapped Charley "Red" Barrett for two more on the twelfth. As in the August splurge, all four games were at Forbes Field.

The drives off Barrett were Ralph Kiner's forty-eighth and forty-ninth, and with the season having over a fortnight to go, Ruth's sixty-homer peak seemed in sight, but the young Pirate slugger subsided to two home runs in his remaining fourteen games.

Actually the Pirates hammered out 156 homers, second only to the Giants among the sixteen major-league clubs, but weak pitching hung like a millstone around Billy Herman's neck. Perhaps another early mistake by the new owners was to permit Al Lopez, the veteran catcher, to get away, though Zach Taylor, former coach and manager of the Browns and a specialist on pitching, made his presence felt. And whenever old Fritz Ostermueller or Ernie Bonham, the tall ex-Yankee, was on the hill, the other side knew they were in a ball game.

With it all, the formerly brittle Frankie Gustine had a magnificent season, hitting .297 and playing in each of Pittsburgh's 156 games. He also was the only Pirate to make his team's All-Star squad, starting the midsummer classic at third base for the National League. Little Billy Cox also had another good season, but the weak spot of the infield was Herman's old spot, second base. Early in the campaign, Eddie Basinski, a pickup from Brooklyn, and Wietelmann, the Zanesville gamester who came from Boston with Herman, tried to fill in for Herman. Later the veteran American Leaguer, Jimmy Bloodworth, recalled from Indianapolis, plugged the gap after a fashion.

Herman had been signed to a two-year managerial contract, but as the season neared its close, there were rumors that he wouldn't carry over into 1948. The Pirates seemed assured of at least seventh place, with still a chance to rise as high as fifth, when the Phillies bowled them over three out of four in a mid-September series. It meant the loss of the year's series, thirteen games to nine, to the lowly Quakers, generally accepted as the weakest outfit in the league. That apparently was the last straw, and Herman's managerial days were numbered. Several of his bosses also felt he should have made a greater effort to jump into the game at second base, despite his ailing arm, and on September 25, the club announced that Herman had resigned the management of the Pirates and that the resignation had been accepted. Roy Hamey also announced the club "would not duck its responsibility to Herman"—that is, his $25,000 1948 salary—and that Billy would remain in the organization. Herman subsequently stepped out to go into private business in Louisville.

Coach Bill Burwell handled the club in its last game of the season, September 28. And here was another amazing example of the loyalty of the Pittsburgh fans; a crowd of 33,704 turned out for the final Sunday session with the Reds. On the same Sunday the Yankees—exhibiting the great figures of American League and Yankee history—Babe Ruth, Ty Cobb, Tris Speaker, Cy Young, Frank Baker, Waite Hoyt, Everett Scott, Jimmie Foxx,

Bob Grove, Mickey Cochrane, Herb Pennock, etc., in a pregame spectacle, drew 25,085 at Yankee Stadium for their pre-World Series brush-up with the Athletics.

Perhaps the bait that enticed the final Sunday turnout to Forbes Field was curiosity to see whether Kiner could break his home-run tie with Mize and finish the season as the year's undisputed home-run king. Ralph couldn't make it, but that faithful outpouring saw about the best Pirate-pitched game of the season, as Ernie Bonham held the Reds to two hits and Pittsburgh won easily, 7 to 0. It assured the Pirates of a tie for seventh place and avoided the ignominy of sole possession of the cellar. "Gosh, why couldn't we have had pitching like that all year?" moaned the fans, as they filed regretfully out of McKinney's beautiful park.

While the Yankees and Dodgers were battling for the 1947 World Series, Frank McKinney, John Galbreath, Tom Johnson, and Roy Hamey, who were in attendance, were more interested in finding a Pirate manager than in the result of the big games. They came up with the man they wanted in Billy Meyer, who for many years had been a manager in the Yankee farm system and had done well in both Kansas City and Newark. Meyer had been with Roy Hamey in Kansas City, and elsewhere in the old Ruppert-Barrow-Weiss empire. His outstanding assets were ability to develop young players and ability to get the most out of his pitchers. He was just the type of manager Pittsburgh needed.

At the same time that Meyer's appointment was announced, October 2, the club also sent out word that the man for whom Greenberg Gardens was named, Hank Greenberg, would not be a Pirate in 1948. Hank, who always had remained an American Leaguer at heart, had requested his unconditional release, and it was granted. It marked the end of a noble—and expensive— experiment.

XXX. A FUTURE FILLED WITH HOPE

No ONE in the Pirate organization sat on his haunches after the 1947 club tied for seventh place. President Frank McKinney and General Manager Roy Hamey realized that mistakes had been made in players hurriedly plucked out of the waiver grab bag after the new owners took charge. But they were gambles rather than mistakes. President Frank, Bing, Roy, and the rest did so want to improve the club and be worthy of that remarkable 1,283,611 patronage.

With the naming of Billy Meyer as 1948 manager, many Pirates were asked to walk the plank. Day by day, names were lopped off the roster and new names substituted. There was still gambling with veteran players—working for better things in 1948—but special attention was focused on the long-term approach, building a young club for the future.

Like old Barney, the new owners were willing to give good players to get men they wanted. Such a swap was the one whereby big Jim Russell, the at-times clubbing outfielder from Fayette City, Pennsylvania, was sent to join Bob Elliott on the Braves. Jim, Bill Salkeld, the catcher, and Al Lyons, the former Yankee pitcher, were sent to Billy Southworth's Boston Club for Outfielder–First Baseman Johnny Hopp and Second Baseman Danny Murtaugh, former Phillie second baseman but in 1947 with the Braves' Milwaukee farm.

At almost the very moment that the deal was made public, an announcement was made by National League headquarters that

Bob Elliott, the former Pirate and 1947 Brave headliner, had been named the loop's most valuable player for that season. That brought many pangs of regret in Pittsburgh. "Let's hope that this Jim Russell thing doesn't backfire on us the same way as did that sad Elliott deal," they said morosely. But with the fleet-footed Johnny Hopp patrolling Forbes Field's still expensive center-field acres, there seemed no such danger.

In the 1947 postseason draft, the Pirates won another outfielder, thirty-year-old Max West, a prewar Brave, who in 1940 won the All-Star game for the National League with a first-inning three-run homer off Charley Ruffing. Outfielder Joe Grace was purchased from Griffith's Washington club.

However, the club did its biggest business with Uncle Branch Rickey, the cagey Mahatma of Brooklyn. But Frank McKinney and Roy Hamey were willing to back their respective seventh senses against the Mahatma's inner voices. There was a quick succession of autumn and early winter deals between the 1947 National League clubs that finished at the top and bottom. The start was the purchase of Stan Rojek, utility Dodger shortstop, and Ed Stevens, 1946 Brooklyn first baseman, for a chunk of cash. To clear the way for Stevens and to let him know the jinxed Pirate first-base job was his, Elbie Fletcher was traded to the Cleveland Indians for Les Fleming. The latter was promptly sent to the Pirates' farm in Indianapolis.

At the minor-league meetings in Miami in early December, 1947, the Pirates acquired one of the jewels of the Brooklyn farm system, Romanus "Monte" Basgall, who spent the 1947 season with Rickey's Fort Worth team. To get the Latin Monte, the Pirates gave up another wad of cash, also Jim Bloodworth and Vic Barnhart, Clyde's boy, who were sent to Montreal by Rickey.

The biggest Pirate-Brooklyn deal remained for the December meetings in New York, when the Pittsburgh club obtained Fred "Dixie" Walker, the "People's Churce" of Flatbush, and Pitchers Vic Lombardi, pony southpaw, and Hal Gregg for Shortstop Billy Cox and Pitcher Elwin "Preacher" Roe, the latter a Rickey discovery when the Mahatma was still with the Cardinals. Infielder Gene Mauch, who figured in the Kirby Higbe deal of the previous season, also was returned to Brooklyn in the transaction.

While there was a little grumbling over the passing of the agile Pennsylvanian, Cox, from Forbes Field, the trade looked like a fine swap for Pittsburgh. In obtaining Walker, who in 1944 wore

Honus Wagner's old National League batting crown, the Pirate board of strategy realized it was taking on a thirty-seven-year-old athlete, but Dixie had won the reputation of a player who improved with age; in 1947 he still was good enough to hit .306, win a position on his league's All-Star squad, and star in the World Series. Gregg, an eighteen-game winner in 1945, was expected to improve under Meyer's skillful coaching, while little Lombardi was rated a more consistent winner than the erratic Preacher Roe. Elmer Riddle, a twenty-one-game winner with the 1943 Reds, was purchased from the Cincinnati club for the $10,000 waiver price, in the hope he would regain his earlier stuff and pitching acumen.

The Pirates also did extensive shopping in the minors, obtaining Catcher Eddie Fitzgerald of Sacramento—said to be the best 1947 catcher in the minors—for cash and three young players. Pitcher Bob Chesnes, San Francisco right-hander, came in another big deal for secondary Pirates and cash. Other new pitchers were draftees Forrest Main from Kansas City and Jim Kleckley from Birmingham, while Steve Ferek and Dick Patnek moved up from the Indianapolis farm.

Zack Taylor, Billy Herman's 1947 coach and assistant, was released so that he could return to the Browns as manager, but the Pirates regained the services of good old Pie Traynor, engaged as a good-will ambassador and to scout the Pittsburgh district, and Al Lopez, who was put in charge of the number one farm in Indianapolis. The farm system was vastly increased by the acquisition of New Orleans, Waco, Texas, and smaller teams.

And as he looked ahead, Frank McKinney, the fan president, had only one thought, to put the Pirates back to where he felt "they belonged in baseball," back to the merry days of Wagner, Clarke, Leach, and Carey. And he had this message for Pirate fans, not only those who reside in Pittsburgh but the land over.

We are well aware of the rich background of the Pirates, a team which looks out of place in the second division. But we intend doing something about it, and I feel we can anticipate a future as brilliant as our past; in that I believe I reflect the opinions of my associates, Bing Crosby, John W. Galbreath, and Thomas P. Johnson.

Yet we realize the extent of our task. We believe that we are just looking over the fence, but are on the right footing when it comes to building a real contender. We don't expect miracles and know it may take three to five years to accomplish our purpose. But, while in this stage of development, we intend to give Pittsburgh fans the best teams we can give them, and hope before long to restore the Pirates to their old place in the first division.

However, we feel strongly that the avenue through which we must do our building is a sufficient and efficient farm system in which we can develop our own playing talent. The major-league clubs of today have learned that to become successful, year after year, one needs the "brood" field for development of the youngsters, and others who have potential possibilities for the stiffer action that comes later.

When our group took over the ownership and operation of the Pirates in the latter part of the 1946 season, we inherited only four farm clubs. We immediately set about to build our farm system to the point where today we have seventeen clubs in our organization, and we expect to increase this number by several more in the near future. It is our purpose to have a sufficient number of clubs in each classification so that players may be graduated upward as their development and ability warrant.

A splendid encore to our efforts to give Pittsburgh the same kind of baseball as provided by the late Barney Dreyfuss all through the building-up process of the new management was reflected in our 1947 gate, the first year of our operation. We drew within a few of 1,284,000 cash customers, which is an all-time Pittsburgh record, and surpasses by about 400,000 the previous records established in 1927, when the club won its last pennant, and 1938, the year that Gabby Hartnett beat the Bucs in Chicago with that never-to-be-forgotten ninth-inning home run, in what was practically the deciding tilt.

We are particularly proud of the remodeled and renovated Forbes Field, which was accomplished at a cost of approximately $800,000 within the last year. We believe that Forbes Field ranks high among the most beautiful parks in the country, and we will keep it that way.

The key to our farm system is the Indianapolis club of the American Association in Triple-A classification. This club will be the real clearing house and the final proving ground for young ball players on their way up to the Pirates. At this time—in the early part of 1948—Pittsburgh is not boasting of a pennant winner. However, we are a young and aggressive organization and are building on a sound and solid foundation, and pointing to the time not far off when the Pirates can take their place among the truly powerful baseball organizations of the country.

With that kind of spirit, hustle, and business acumen behind the Pirates, it doesn't take a seventh son of a seventh son to predict that it won't be long before the Pirates again start shooting up the National League and meeting the American in World

Series combat. If they didn't, the wraith of Barney Dreyfuss would surely descend on Forbes Field and squeeze his ectoplasm into the new remodeled clubhouse. Barney was strictly a first-division man, and he'd ha'nt any Pirate teams that didn't live up to the old traditions.

INDEX

Jack Carlson of the Society for American Baseball Research prepared this index. Corrections of spelling errors in the original text are from John Thorn and Pete Palmer, eds., *Total Baseball: The Ultimate Encyclopedia of Baseball*, 3rd ed. (n.p.: Harper Perennial, 1993).

301

304INDEX

Other Books in the Writing Baseball Series

Man on Spikes
ELIOT ASINOF
Foreword by Marvin Miller

Off-Season
ELIOT ASINOF

The American Game: Baseball and Ethnicity
EDITED BY LAWRENCE BALDASSARO AND RICHARD A. JOHNSON
Foreword by Allan H. "Bud" Selig

The Chicago Cubs
WARREN BROWN
Foreword by Jerome Holtzman

My Baseball Diary
JAMES T. FARRELL
Foreword by Joseph Durso

The Brooklyn Dodgers: An Informal History
FRANK GRAHAM
Foreword by Jack Lang

The New York Giants: An Informal History of a Great Baseball Club
FRANK GRAHAM
Foreword by Ray Robinson

The New York Yankees: An Informal History
FRANK GRAHAM
Foreword by Jack Lang

The Best Seat in Baseball, But You Have to Stand!
The Game as Umpires See It
LEE GUTKIND
Foreword by Eric Rolfe Greenberg

Line Drives: 100 Contemporary Baseball Poems
EDITED BY BROOKE HORVATH AND TIM WILES
Foreword by Elinor Nauen

Full Count: Inside Cuban Baseball
MILTON H. JAMAIL
Foreword by Larry Dierker